CW00486122

Catholic
Education

〜〜〜〜〜〜〜

Praise for
Catholic Education: A Lifelong Journey

£3.50
11/6

'This collection of high-quality papers provides a rich variety of approaches to Catholic education with a particular focus on Catholic education as a lifelong journey. This invaluable set of papers makes a major and innovative contribution to contemporary international research into Catholic education. The book is highly recommended and merits a wide readership.'

Professor Stephen McKinney, University of Glasgow

'Byrne and Whittle's carefully curated volume invites the reader into a sustained engagement with the multi-faceted reality of contemporary Catholic education. In bringing together new conceptual, qualitative and quantitative research, the collection offers welcome, and sometimes challenging, insights into the formal and informal spaces where Catholic education occurs. This is an indispensable resource for anyone interested in Catholic education; it will certainly have a place on my bookshelf.'

Doctor Sandra Cullen, Head of School of Human Development, Dublin City University

'It would be difficult to exaggerate the importance of this book. Religious education requires exploration and discussion, shaped by religious values, experiences and theological discourse, and the individual's critical reflection upon these. There is need, therefore, within religious education for both the formal and informal approaches, the encouragement of personal reflection and openness to criticism, and the sowing of seeds which will continue to bear fruit when schooling has been left behind. The book therefore emphasises the wider vision of education as it would be continued through adult education particularly within the parish settings. I feel very excited about this book.'

Professor Richard Pring, Emeritus Professor of Education, Oxford University

'This highly accessible, innovative, and expertly written volume explores the most forgotten dimension of ongoing adult Catholic education. It is a dynamic, comprehensive and scholarly analysis of formal and informal Catholic education that is bound to become essential reading in the field.'

Doctor Patricia Kieran, Director of the Irish Institute for Catholic Studies, Mary Immaculate College, University of Limerick

Catholic
Education

A Lifelong Journey

EDITED BY
GARETH BYRNE AND SEAN WHITTLE

VERITAS

Published 2021 by
Veritas Publications
7–8 Lower Abbey Street
Dublin 1
Ireland
www.veritas.ie

ISBN 978 1 84730 983 9

Copyright © Gareth Byrne and Sean Whittle, 2021

10 9 8 7 6 5 4 3 2 1

A catalogue record for this book is available from the British Library.

Designed by Jeannie Swan, Veritas Publications
Cover image courtesy of Gareth Byrne
Printed in the Republic of Ireland by SPRINT-print Ltd, Dublin

Veritas books are printed on paper made from the wood pulp of
managed forests. For every tree felled, at least one tree is planted,
thereby renewing natural resources.

Dedicated to the memory of
Eoin G. Cassidy,
1949–2021,
priest, philosopher, colleague, friend

Contents

~~~~~~~~~~~~~~~~~~

List of Abbreviations

〜〜〜〜〜〜〜〜

AREFD	Adult Religious Education and Faith Development project
BEC	Basic Ecclesial Communities
CCE	Congregation for Catholic Education
CEIST	Catholic Education, an Irish Schools Trust
CES	Catholic Education Service (England and Wales)
CoP	Communities of Practice
CPSMA	Catholic Primary School Management Association
DCU	Dublin City University
GCSE	General Certificate of Secondary Education (England, Northern Ireland and Wales)
JMB/AMCSS	Joint Managerial Body/Association of Management of Catholic Secondary Schools
MDCCE	Mater Dei Centre for Catholic Education
NCCA	National Council for Curriculum and Assessment (Republic of Ireland)
NfRCE	Network for Researchers in Catholic Education
PRS	Psychology of Religion and Spirituality
RCIA	Rite of Christian Initiation of Adults
RE	Religious Education
RECD	*Curriculum Directory for Religious Education* (England and Wales)
SCC	Small Christian Community
SEC	State Examinations Commission (Republic of Ireland)
SGN	*Share the Good News: National Directory for Catechesis in Ireland*

Foreword

It is clear that a renaissance of scholarship and research in Catholic education in Ireland is in process today, driven by the work of Irish writers and by those of Irish heritage as evidenced since 2009 in the pages of the journal *International Studies in Catholic Education*. There have been significant contributions from John Lydon (2009), Eamonn Conway (2011), Marcellina Cooney CP (2012), John Sullivan (2012), Sean Whittle (2014), Jim Gleeson (2015), Brendan Carmody SJ (2017), Richard Byrne OCarm and Dympna Devine (2017) and Paddy Walsh (2018). This book takes this renaissance to a new stage.

An important source of this rebirth in Irish scholarship and research has been the Mater Dei Centre for Catholic Education (MDCCE) at Dublin City University. Many Dublin City University staff associated with the MDCCE, as well as those who have recently competed doctorates with the team, or are presently on a doctoral programme at Dublin City University, have contributed to this volume. Others from the United Kingdom who attended the Network for Researchers in Catholic Education conference hosted in Dublin by the MDCCE in October 2019, and whose contribution related to the theme of the volume, have been included here, too. The Adult Religious Education and Faith Development research project at MDCCE, which is quickly gaining international attention (see *British Journal of Religious Education*, April 2021), was responsible for stimulating discussion around adult education, religious education and faith development, suggesting it as the theme of the conference.

Thanks to the initiative of the editors, Dr Gareth Byrne and Dr Sean Whittle, this text advances the renaissance in Catholic education I am observing by providing sixteen thoughtful and original chapters on topics related to new thinking, new scholarship and new research in the field of studies. This text is ground-breaking because it addresses themes which the conventional literature largely ignores such as adult learning and adult religious education, primary school pupils talking about the faith in the home, lifelong learning in the Church, the place and role of small groups, and the question of faith development itself.

It breathes a fresh spirit of inquiry and imagination into the whole mission by extending our vision beyond formal institutions to serious engagement with lifelong Catholic education in its various forms.

This volume provides a larger frame of reference by bringing together formal, informal and lifelong education. It challenges us to take a more catholic view of Catholic education. We have become preoccupied by institutional analysis in the formal sector of schools, colleges and universities to the neglect of more community-based educational cultures in homes, in parishes and in informal adult education and small group discussions provided by various agencies. This is what those writing from the perspectives of liberation theology have called in Latin America 'base ecclesial communities', or as they have named it 'new ways of being "school" and "church"'. There are many roads to faith.

Byrne and Whittle are to be congratulated for providing an innovative text of new research, new ideas and new learning which invites us all to embrace a much larger vision and framework for what Catholic education study can be in the future. We need to evaluate and to research the relatively 'invisible pedagogy' of community-based faith learning and its consequences.

Gerald Grace,
Professor of Catholic Education, St Mary's University, London, UK,
Executive Editor, *International Studies in Catholic Education*

Introduction

~~~~~~~~~~~~~~~

Catholic Education:
Learning through All that Life Offers

Gareth Byrne and Sean Whittle

Pinning down the meanings of Catholic education is a surprisingly tricky challenge. In large part this is because for many of us it is an everyday concept that is integrally connected with schools and universities – the formal places of learning and education. When we start talking about Catholic education we almost immediately glide into matters to do with Catholic schools. Whilst the assumptions at play in this tendency are perfectly understandable, there is value in taking stock once more of what is meant by the phrase 'Catholic education' and the reflection it invites participants into on their journey through all that life offers.

Catholic Education in Schools and Beyond

One of the primary goals in putting together this volume of edited and peer-reviewed chapters is to recognise and promote engagement with both formal and informal aspects of Catholic education. The service provided by Catholic schools for young members of the faith community and their families, for all who partner with and participate in their offerings, whatever their worldview, and indeed for society generally, is often commented upon. The relationship between home, school and parish and the contribution of religious education in particular in schools is always of interest. Ever evolving and developing, Catholic schools are encouraged to respond creatively, in a given time and place, to the needs of students, their parents and parish. Our conviction, however, is that the school focus needs to be balanced by a recognition of the ways in which Catholic education also takes place in informal contexts, and often with adults.

Catholic education has its source, support and destination in Jesus Christ, in his life, ministry, passion, death and resurrection. The historical Jesus, as presented in the gospels, spent his time mostly with adults, in their ordinary life and everyday concerns. He helped them think deeply about the meaning of their life and it possibilities. He opened them up to new ways of living and loving, celebrating their growing relationship with God and with each other, in their families, in their community, in the world. The gospel accounts of the risen Christ describe his continuing accompaniment of his expanding community, walking with them along the road, opening their eyes to his unfailing presence, and gifting them with his Spirit to assist them on their journey.

The challenge here is to reach for a rich set of meanings for what can more fully describe Catholic education today, founded on Christ, and the range of settings within which it can play its part imaginatively. This publication expresses and explores the multi-levelled nature of Catholic education, in its formal and informal settings, and in its aspiration to be a lifelong and life-enhancing endeavour.

The Right and Invitation to Ongoing Christian Education

An apt starting point for a richer or more nuanced account of Catholic education is to be found in the broad vision defining the vital importance of education described in Vatican II's declaration, *Gravissimum Educationis* (1965). In this short and frequently overlooked document, the foundations of Christian education are explicitly framed in terms of the rights which flow from being baptised. Having received the gift of baptism there is the need for ongoing and deepening education. The declaration firmly grounds this in the language of rights (see *Gravissimum Educationis*, par. 2), such that the Christian person is helped to 'give witness to the hope that is within them' (see 1 Pt 3:15). In this document the Church also expresses its availability to contribute to the education and care of all peoples, promoting 'the complete perfection of the human person, the good of earthly society and the building of a world that is more human' (*Gravissimum Educationis*, par. 3). Catholic Christian education is, according to Vatican II, far more than what happens in the formal setting of the Catholic school and in the university. It is understood as being, and necessitating, an invitation into a lifelong process of engagement so that the whole life of the Christian, and of others who are interested, may be uplifted and inspired by Christ.

This volume has the ambitious goal, then, of embracing precisely this richer way of understanding Catholic education. Rather than simply equating Catholic education with the formal context of the school, attention will focus on a variety of settings, frequently informal and often adult focused, which together offer a full understanding of Catholic education. In highlighting the essential lifelong nature of Catholic education an important service is rendered, that of reframing the dominant or typical meaning which presumes to define Catholic education in terms, only, of schooling.

Adult Education and Faith Development

In so many respects, then, the forgotten dimension of Catholic education has been adult ongoing education. This important engagement typically happens not so much in formal but in informal settings, that is in unplanned, incidental learning moments such as within the family or around a parish social justice group for instance, or, alternatively, in non-formal, semi-structured and open-ended situations, for example a book club discussion or prayer group sharing. The efforts made by adults, not only in supporting the faith of young people at home and in the faith community, but in coming to reflect on and live their own faith intentionally in the home and beyond it, is fundamental. Yet somehow, we, any of us laity and clergy, give adult action in this regard, and thoughtful deliberation on it, little time and energy, presuming, it seems, that it will develop and flourish of its own accord. The new *Directory for Catechesis* (2020), from Rome, continues the honourable tradition of the two previous General Directories in this area (1971, 1997), of highlighting adult catechesis, that is assisting the faithful to maturity of faith, as essential in the life of the Church and its people. The Directory offers a clarification as to why the ongoing education of adults is deserving of greater concern and interest today:

> In comparison with the past, this stage of life is no longer understood as an already completed state of stability, but as a continual process of restructuring that takes into account the evolution of personal sensibilities, the interweaving of relationships, the responsibilities to which the person is called. (par. 257)

The relationship of adult Christians to their faith is highly varied, the Directory notes, insisting that, 'every person should be welcomed and listened to in his [sic] uniqueness' (par. 258). Research with adults as to what their needs are and how they might see themselves participating in adult conversations about faith, and learn to grapple with theological concepts, is therefore of increasing importance. The formation and ongoing faith development of adults should be recognised as gradual and progressive, the Directory offers, such that the gospel message 'may be received in its transformative dynamism', and make its mark on personal and social life:

> In the final analysis, catechesis with adults reaches its goal when it makes the adults themselves capable of taking their own experience of faith in hand and desirous of continuing to journey onward and to grow. (par. 260)

Formal, Informal and Lifelong

This book is the fruit of an academic conference that was convened in order to address the relationships between formal, informal and lifelong Catholic education. This international conference took place in October 2019, organised by the Network for Researchers in Catholic Education (NfRCE) and hosted by the Mater Dei Centre for Catholic Education (MDCCE), Dublin City University (DCU). The NfRCE had approached MDCCE to be the host for this gathering of researchers and practitioners, the first of its kind to be held outside Great Britain, because of growing collaboration with the Centre which was already taking seriously the importance of adult and informal Catholic education. Indeed, MDCCE, at that time, already had commenced an innovative research project, exploring Adult Religious Education and Faith Development (AREFD). The conference, under the title, 'Catholic Education: Formal, Informal and Lifelong', was a resounding success, bringing together researchers and experts in Catholic education from the Republic of Ireland and from the UK. In excess of sixty papers were presented. In this volume sixteen of the most significant and thought-provoking papers on the theme have been developed into carefully crafted chapters, offering a variety of reflections which together confirm the importance of an integrated approach unifying all areas of Catholic education. They help to demonstrate in an accessible manner the variety of ways in which Catholic education is to be encountered across a lifetime. Catholic education can be transformative in the lives of people who are interested, and indeed in the lives of those who *might* be interested given a real, open and invitational opportunity to become involved. This publication is a way of sharing this important insight beyond those who participated in the original conference and beyond the world of academic discussion. We hope it will contribute to the initiation of a wider conversation about the contribution Catholic education can make to families, in parishes, and for society generally, as well as acting as a catalyst for further research and reflection around the fullest possible understanding of what Catholic education can be.

Facing Significant Risks

Keeping the spotlight firmly on the richness surrounding the variety of meanings of Catholic education is helpful. If we do not challenge our tendency to focus just on formal Catholic education in schools we face some significant risks. One of these is the danger of assuming that all our eggs are safe in one basket, the Catholic school. The pressing needs of the day-to-day realities of school life can make attending to these needs the overriding and sometimes only education priority. If, however, Catholic education is reframed to fully include informal, non-formal and lifelong approaches, this will create a space in which to see Catholic schools as the starting point for something broader, and not simply consider it as confined to the first two decades of a person's life.

A second risk is the potential failure to properly ground Catholic education in the theology of baptism. In the context of state-funded mass education, the link between attendance at Catholic schools and being baptised is evermore challenged, particularly so in the UK and in the Republic of Ireland. For example, in England and Wales an increasing proportion of students attending Catholic schools are not baptised Catholic Christians. In the Irish Republic school admissions policies no longer give weight to baptism as the typical criteria for admission to a Catholic school as they did up until recently. The state, in both jurisdictions, whilst willing to fund Catholic schools, is seeking to ensure a significant uncoupling of the relationship between baptism and attending a Catholic school. It is, of course, relatively easy to frame Catholic education according to the paradigm of 'hospitality', seeking to provide for those in need, regardless of baptism. Through reaching out to the poor, Catholic schools witness to a sense of care and compassion, something deeply rooted in the charism of the religious congregations and orders who originally founded Catholic schools in Great Britain and Ireland. Catholic schools are however defined in the first instance by their response to the baptised in their locality and then to the wider community, rather than simply providing schooling for the sake of it.

The third risk is that we would be satisfied that all that could be done for a person's faith education would be completed before they left school. All that we have been saying here negates such a view. Within the Catholic community a lifelong journey begins at baptism, whether as an adult or a child. There is a contemporary need to find ways of reinforcing the relationship between baptism, initiation, sacramental celebration and lifelong religious education and faith development. We can never be content as we might have been in the past that the young person leaving school has been fully formed religiously, spiritually, morally. In our time it has become clearer than ever that the journey of faith is a lifelong journey which takes place in a world of fluid relationships and contexts, and is often supported within small groups of one kind or another. The Christian person must learn to say yes again and again to God, to the support of the Christian community, to a renewed understanding of faith and of ourselves as people on a voyage of discovery through all that life presents, challenges us with and gifts us. This volume seeks to alert us to the many questions that people of faith, and indeed people without religious belief live through, and to suggest possibilities for developing the educational space that can be made available in which to help formulate responses that can engage head, heart, hands, as well as spirit. It is an education journey we have only just begun.

Learning through Covid-19

Since the conference, and during the editing process, the Covid-19 pandemic has stretched across the world and blighted the lives of many. Who would have known what we would have to face and how people have had to deal with it together or fall? Reflection is already taking place as to what this experience will mean for formal, informal and lifelong learning across the education spectrum. Certainly the movement toward digital and mobile learning has come to the fore as online and social media platforms have encouraged meetings, lectures, lessons, interviews and gatherings of one kind or another to take place virtually. In-person teaching and learning will no doubt be preferred where possible, but when it is not possible, or now not favoured, and people must, or chose to, work at a distance, new efforts, new arrangements, new design will be put in place. Who knows what new modes of learning are in store? Formal, non-formal and informal education will all be rethought. Adult education is already moving forward in leaps and bounds, with self-directed and distance learning all considered quite the norm on one type of screen or another. Whether the Church can fully grasp this opportunity remains to be seen, providing future generations with creative avenues into discussion of the mystery of God and the mystery of humankind, and ever new opportunities to grapple with the deepest and most profound of questions. Pope Francis in his call during the pandemic for universal fraternity, social friendship, religious dialogue, respect for all especially those in greatest need, and a deepening care of the environment (see *Fratelli Tutti*, 2020), reveals a whole agenda around which adults of all age groups in our world today must converse and educate themselves and learn to act decisively and intuitively in solidarity for the good of all.

Research Themes

The chapters in this book are organised into five sections, each contributing in different ways to a fuller understanding of formal, informal and lifelong approaches to Catholic education needs and possibilities. The opening section, 'Catholic Education: Formal, Informal and Lifelong', presents three significant contributions offered originally as keynote presentations at the NfRCE conference at DCU. They deserve to be read as a whole, because taken together they introduce central facets useful in grasping the informal and lifelong aspects of Catholic education while acknowledging their relationship with more formal approaches.

The opening chapter, by Ros Stuart-Buttle, focuses on the nature of adult learning in relation to theological education and faith formation. Drawing on recent research in association with the Catholic Certificate in Religious Studies offered in England and Wales, the author reflects on what kinds of theological education might best serve adult learning today. Adults learn for a variety of reasons, in a variety of ways, and in a variety of settings. The chapter observes that adult theological learning is a complex phenomenon, something expressed in an underlying tension between core academic, spiritual and practice-based objectives. The findings that emerge offer initial suggestions about what sort of theology and what kind of adult faith-based learning might best serve people today.

In Chapter 2, Bernadette Sweetman reflects on the need to pick up Jesus' encouragement to 'push the boat out' in terms of adult religious education and faith development today. Her chapter reports on research underway at DCU into the current situation and possible future opportunities for adult religious education and faith development in Ireland and beyond. Noting the intersection between research participants' understanding of being religious and being spiritual, the discussion touches on their interest in ongoing formal, non-formal and informal education opportunities. Grounded within the Catholic context, the questions and conversations emerging also engage with learning in other contexts, and with people of other faiths and worldviews. The research reported upon here confirms that adulthood is a spectrum and that no single approach will suffice to cover the needs of all. One of the outcomes envisaged is a self-reflective toolkit to assist those involved in adult religious education and faith development, supporting a variety of needs and requirements.

Gareth Byrne, in Chapter 3, puts the focus on significant challenges for Catholic education across the life cycle in the Republic of Ireland today. The changing landscape and rapid rate of adjustment within the school system in Ireland is noted. In response, the unique identity and contribution of Catholic schools is considered, taking the Irish Episcopal Conference's seminal document *Share the Good News* as foundational. The case of recent changes to Religious Education as a school subject at Junior Cycle (for 12- to 15-year-olds) in the Republic of Ireland, and its implementation in Catholic schools, is taken as a particular example. Returning to the larger question, the future of Catholic education, formal, informal and lifelong, is addressed. The suggestion here is that it is time to breathe in deeply of the tradition and experience to which the Catholic education community belongs, acknowledging the power of the Holy Spirit to encourage honest reflection, serious conversation, and concrete action in those who are open and available.

In Part II, four chapters are grouped together under the theme 'Religious and Spiritual Underpinnings', highlighting key questions that contribute in different ways to an understanding of the religious and spiritual foundations of Catholic education whatever the context.

In Chapter 4, Anne Hession ponders the models of human and spiritual development that help inform Catholic education today. It is argued here that Catholic educators require a critical conceptual framework that will enable them to evaluate whether emerging models of human and spiritual development are supportive of Catholic faith. The classic Christian spiritual path must be re-presented, the author argues, in a way that is consistent with the insights of modern psychology if it is to appear relevant for today's students. However, the touchstone for the Catholic educator must be the *Christian* concept of maturity and humaneness. This chapter draws attention to the danger for Catholic educators of presenting the gospel only to the extent that it has therapeutic potential, downplaying the prophetic and counter-cultural elements of the message.

In Chapter 5, David Kennedy presents the case for recognising religious enquiry as a valid pathway to human knowledge. Reason and enquiry in the context of religious education, he maintains, as is the case in other areas of education, are reliable routes to meaning, knowledge and truth. There has been a failure to appreciate, however, the author argues, the claim to truth of religious education, particularly in terms of the validity of religious belief. This chapter argues that while religious truth claims are certainly different from that of science, such claims are not inferior. Religious education, understood in its own terms, is a valid pathway to human knowledge.

Attention is given by John Sullivan in the next chapter to a broad analysis of lifelong learning in the Church, something that is integral to the Church's life locally and pivotal to promoting mature Christian discipleship. If Christian faith is to lead to an ongoing transformation of people's lives so that these have a recognisable Christ-like character and display a reading and response to reality as God-given, then education in the Church must provide a multifaceted experience of learning that engages with, listens to, illuminates and integrates the totality of each person's experience. The chapter proposes a set of questions that could help Church members, at all levels, develop a richer and more realistic understanding of the complex dynamics at work in teaching and learning in the Church, and draw more focused attention to the lifelong nature of that teaching and learning.

Chapter 7 focuses on the place of small groups in fostering faith development. In this chapter Paul F. Perry picks up on the reality of decline in recent decades in terms of religious practice, vocations to priesthood and religious life, and of the influence of traditional forms of the Christian Church. The challenge, in Ireland as in other parts of Europe, is highlighted, and the new environment within which all Christian traditions must witness to the gospel is acknowledged. Examples of small group engagement, historically and more recently, are cited to encourage reflection on the importance of smaller groups within bigger congregations and parishes, facilitating both experience and dialogue around the meaning of the Christian heritage for today. A radical revisioning, both spiritual and ecclesial, of the Church is recommended, with small groups at its heart, opening up new ways of presenting Christ and encouraging genuine and ongoing adult faith development.

The three chapters in Part III, entitled, 'Presence, Accompaniment, Transformation', are juxtaposed because each draw heavily on key themes associated with the Emmaus narrative. It is a welcome insight to be reminded how fruitful this resurrection narrative is and how it can be used creatively in addressing practical questions related to Catholic education.

In Chapter 8, Thomas G. Grenham explores the role of the chaplain in Catholic education using the question, 'to be or not to be a pastoral presence'. The author argues that developing an empowering pastoral presence is a journey, a pilgrim journey, in becoming more mindful of self and others. A lifelong journey in discovery of self, others, God and the created world is recognised here as essential. Building on the Emmaus story, the writer presents the role of chaplain as that of being present to and encountering people of various worldviews and religious beliefs in the multiplicity of their needs. An effective chaplain learns to be a helpful and meaningful presence to all. From the discussion, five idea are highlighted as significant in fostering good chaplaincy practice into the future.

In Chapter 9, John J. Lydon and James G. Briody focus on Salesian education, which spans both the formal and non-formal aspects of Catholic education. The authors argue that accompaniment constitutes a perennial theme in a Christian context, best encapsulated in the Emmaus story when Jesus accompanies the two disciples on a journey of discovery. Saint John Bosco (1815-1888), the founder of the Salesians, was concerned with the transformation of the lives of *every* young person with whom he came into contact. This concern resonates with 'the uniqueness of the individual', one of the key principles of Catholic education set out by the English and Welsh Bishops' Conference. The chapter explores the concept of Salesian accompaniment in a contemporary context. It emphasises the kind of presence and encounter which involves the teacher or pastoral worker and the accompanied meeting each other and having frequent conversations, taking place in informal ways and in a variety of environments, marked by openness, trust and availability.

In Chapter 10, Raymond Friel draws on insights that emerge from the pastoral cycle 'See-Judge-Act' in order to propose a basis for a distinctively Catholic pedagogy in schools and as the basis for lifelong formation in the faith. The author explains how See-Judge-Act, endorsed by Pope St John XXIII, had been developed, in its modern form, by Joseph Cardijn, the Belgian priest who founded the Young Christian Workers at the beginning of the twentieth century. Friel explains that

Pope John's desire that this approach should be part of the curriculum in Catholic schools (*Mater et Magistra*, 1961) was not realised, at least not in Europe and North America, apart from in a small number of stand-alone examples. It was in the soil of South America that See-Judge-Act took root in the post-Vatican II era, and the next phase of its evolution unfolded. The papacy of Pope St John Paul II did not hold out much encouragement for this approach, perhaps because of its association with liberation theology and the lingering suspicion of the latter's proximity to Marxism. The chapter seeks to reignite interest in the relevance of this approach for Catholic education, formal, informal and lifelong.

In Part IV, attention moves to the place of 'Religious Education and Faith Formation' in relation to young people, and to primary and second-level schools. The five chapters, three from an English perspective and two from Ireland, set out the web of relationships experienced in formal Catholic education school contexts and beyond, focused particularly on the role and remit of Religious Education in the differing jurisdictions.

In Chapter 11, Ann Casson introduces an empirical study of Catholic primary school pupil accounts of their exploration of faith at home. The author argues that in the Catholic faith tradition, the home is seen as the primal space for the child's religious socialisation, supported by the Catholic school and parish. There is, however, a paucity of research on how the three work together to facilitate a child's exploration of faith. This chapter, focused on the perspective of the child, considers how Catholic primary school pupils describe their explorations of faith at home, and investigates the stimulus for this activity. It employs the lens of French sociologist Danièle Hervieu-Léger's (2000) concept of 'religion as a chain of memory', to illuminate the changing patterns of influence between the three pillars of home, school, and parish.

In Chapter 12, Sean Whittle, a serving Religious Education teacher in Catholic second-level school for over twenty-five years, explains that change is on the horizon for Religious Education in English and Welsh Catholic schools. Since the autumn of 2018, planning led and overseen by the Catholic Education Service of England and Wales, an agency of the Bishops' Conference of England and Wales, has been underway. Despite the effects of the Covid-19 pandemic, the hope is to begin implementing the revised *Religious Education Curriculum Directory*, designed specifically for Catholic schools, primary and second level, from September 2022. The impending change to the Religious Education curriculum in Catholic schools provides an apt opportunity to reflect on some challenging questions about what ought to be the nature and scope of this part of the curriculum within the context of Catholic education in England and Wales taken as a whole.

In Chapter 13, Philomena Clare investigates some key learning to emerge from the provision in the Republic of Ireland since 2000 of optional state-examined Religious Education syllabuses at the end of Junior Cycle (12- to 15-year-old students) and Senior Cycle (16- to 18-year-old students). Catholic schools choose, along with other schools, whether to facilitate participation in state certification of student learning in Religious Education. The author, using material provided by the Department of Education and Skills and the State Examinations Commission, highlights a number of issues worthy of particular attention: levels of participation in the Religious Education syllabus examinations; attainment across Religious Education examinations; gender and Religious Education achievement; and the particular example of engagement with the biblical studies elements provided in the syllabuses. Significantly, girls out-perform boys and Bible-centred units have been the least positively engaged with by students.

The second Irish perspective here is provided by Aiveen Mullally who offers a challenge to the leaders of Ireland's Catholic second-level schools, asking, 'why are Catholic schools afraid to be Catholic schools?' This chapter discusses empirical findings from research conducted by the author with the Joint Managerial Board of second-level schools in Ireland and the Association of Management of Catholic Secondary Schools, on the challenges facing leaders of Catholic secondary schools regarding religious diversity. Mullally discusses here her findings on the reality of nominal Catholicism in Ireland, on young people not identifying with any religion, and the on the pressures felt by Religious Education as a school subject. The question as to how Catholic schools approach faith formation in an increasingly plural society also emerge. This chapter invites leaders of Catholic schools to consider their identity in a new way and not fear the credibility of the Catholic voice in the public square. It argues that Catholic schools can create spaces for reflection and faith formation while also engaging with religious difference and indifference.

In Chapter 15, Robert Bowie considers the overlapping space between the formal and intellectual dimension of religious education in schools and the more affective faith formation frame. To clarify this he draws on some personal reminiscences of conversations over the kitchen table with his mother, who was serving as RCIA (Rite of Christian Initiation of Adults) catechist. From there we are given an insight into Bowie's own awakening to the study of theology as an adult through the Catholic Certificate in Religious Studies. His early conversations with his mother about the interpretation of scripture are recalled as a point of realisation about how best to study the Bible in the formal setting of school with young people today. It is taken as a given that faith is part-and-parcel of the multidimensional nature of life, seen as a whole. It follows that the binary approach to questions of religious beliefs that characterise exam questions in formal Religious Education lessons in school needs to be seriously called into question. Young people deserve more.

In Part V, 'Lifelong Catholic Education: A Personal Reflection', a stand-alone chapter provides an eloquent personal reflection weaving through the inter-relationship between formal, informal and lifelong Catholic education. Chapter 16 is a reflective discourse from Gerry O'Connell as he considers fifty-five years of involvement in Catholic education, as a child, as a student, as a teacher, as a lecturer and as a researcher. Autobiographical in nature, and coming at the end of this book, it encourages readers to reflect, firstly, on their own story and, secondly, on the broader question of vision and ethos in Catholic education, continuously seeking out reflective space for living with these questions. O'Connell recalls his earliest experiences as a child through to primary, secondary and third-level education. He reflects on twenty-five years teaching in Catholic primary schools, on his parallel ongoing engagement in informal Catholic adult education, on studying for a Masters' in religious education, and on the lecturing role in religious education in a teacher education college that followed all this. The key findings from the author's doctoral thesis, examining past students' perceptions of his practice in Religious Education in teacher education, along with his thoughts on the role of vision and ethos in Catholic education, and on the enormous importance of teaching in teacher education colleges, provide further food for thought. This piece of reflective writing is a contribution that will help readers consider their own education story.

Gratitude for the Opportunity and Support Provided

As editors of a collection of sixteen chapters, we understand that readers will inevitably want to dip in and out of the differing contributions. We would, however, encourage readers to engage with the volume as a whole. In this way something of the conversation and dialogue of the original conference will be encouraged to stay alive and helped to flourish.

This book provides a powerful case for broadening and enriching our everyday understanding of Catholic education, to include both formal and informal dimensions, across a lifetime of questions and engagement, and through all the new horizons and transitions we experience. Catholic education holds out the possibility of transformation in the lives of those who willingly participate in the variety of its contexts and offerings, for at its heart, Christ is present and available, ever encouraging us on our journey.

We are grateful to each of the contributors. They have given generously of their time and efforts to develop and enhance their papers, taking on board the discussion and learning experienced at the October 2019 conference at DCU Institute of Education. Without their willingness to dig deep we would not be presenting the scholarship they have engaged with for our nourishment and ongoing consideration.

We would like to offer a special word of thanks to Susan Dwyer who provides enthusiastic administrative assistance at MDCCE and who oversaw a great deal of the preparation and administration of the conference. Her able and personable encouragement and support for all involved was remarked on at the time as pivotal to the success of the conference, contributing significantly to the easy sense of collaboration and camaraderie that developed over those days and has continued since.

We would particularly like to express our gratitude to Veritas in helping us to bring this publication to fruition and for making it so easily accessible to a wide readership, and affordable. Academic research and writing is as good as the impact it has on reflection and practice in its field of study and among those who work on the ground. The dedicated contribution that Veritas makes to Catholic education on these islands is powerful, opening up in so many ways 'a light for all the world to see' (Lk 2:32), encouraging ongoing conversation, and providing an outlet for timely research and reflection.

Part I:

~~~~~~~~~~~~~

Catholic Education:
Formal, Informal and Lifelong

Chapter 1

〰〰〰〰〰〰〰

Adult Learning, Theology and Faith Formation

Ros Stuart-Buttle

Introduction

This chapter focuses on adult learning in relation to theological education and faith formation. It firstly considers the role and importance of adult education within lifelong faith-based learning and discusses some models and approaches for this. The chapter then presents recent research findings from a programme of adult theological education across England and Wales, the Catholic Certificate in Religious Studies (CCRS), to offer further reflection about the nature of adult learning and what form of adult learning might work best for today.

Adult theological education runs across the categories of formal, non-formal and lifelong learning. The discourse is complex, not least because of the three meta-concepts involved – adulthood, theology and education – each of which carry myriad meanings and practices that lie beyond the scope of this chapter. Adult learning encompasses a multiplicity of learners and a variety of theories, methods and contexts. It can include academic programmes of theological or religious studies at university, training courses for professional or vocational roles such as working in a Catholic school, or lay ministry formation for chaplaincy, catechesis, liturgy, youth work or parish mission. It also includes adults who follow non-formal parish or diocesan activities such as sacramental or liturgical programmes, as well as those who wish to learn for self- interest or personal reasons concerning religion, faith and spirituality, either independently or with others in study groups and networks.

Adult learners bring diverse characteristics, skills, backgrounds, goals and reasons for learning. They include those in vocational and voluntary roles as well as the paid and the professional. Some carry ecclesial authorisation or mandate and have funding or employment for this; others seek learning opportunities out of their own sense of vocation, on their own initiative, under their own time and financial cost, and often while negotiating jobs, relationships, families, work responsibilities and other life commitments. Some want initial formation to grow in knowledge and understanding of the Christian tradition. Others undertake continuing education while engaged in specific work or ministry. Others again seek to further their own journey in faith. Adults learn for a variety of reasons, in a variety of ways and in a variety of settings.

Adult theological education and faith formation presents, therefore, a rich and complex landscape. It has developed from different historical influences, is conducted through diverse pedagogies and expressed in varied theological approaches. It is affected by changing Church structures and contemporary demographics as well as the multifarious religious, educational, economic and socio-cultural situations of postmodern Britain and Ireland. This is the backdrop for the landscape of adult faith-based learning today.

Why Is Adult Learning Important?

Human learning and development is a lifelong process. This is well established across major fields including biology, physiology, psychology, anthropology, sociology and education. In educational terms, John Elias reminds us that,

> To be human means to learn. To be fully human entails a lifelong effort in acquiring knowledge, attitudes, skills, and behaviours. The complexity of life and the constant changes that persons face, increasingly demand that adults continue to learn throughout their lives. (1993, p. 93)

We see that learning is something that we do all our lives; it is a long arc as practical theologian Craig Dykstra noted (Bass & Dykstra, 2008).

Furthermore, adult learning takes priority in Christian tradition. Historically it was adults who received the attention of the early Church. Adult formation primarily was the way for the Church to grow and hand on its faith and beliefs. This understanding was renewed at the

Second Vatican Council (1962-65) and many documents of Vatican II re-emphasised its priority. For example, the *Decree on the Apostolate of the Laity* (1965) confirmed the mission and vocation of lay people in the Church and called for their 'diversified and thorough formation' (par. 28). The *Decree on the Pastoral Office of Bishops* (1965) made a specific call for catechesis and education to be extended to adults (par. 13-14). The *Decree on the Ministry and Life of Priests* (1965) saw the need for 'educating adults in the attainment of Christian maturity' (par. 6). The *Decree on Missionary Activity* (1965) called for the revival of adult formation and promoted the role of the catechist or educator for this purpose.

Key documents from Rome from the 1970s further contributed to a growing vision for adult learning in faith. The *General Catechetical Directory* (1971) strongly asserted the priority of adult continuing education for Christian growth and maturity for people of all ages, recognising their diverse needs and experiences. The *Rite of Christian Initiation of Adults* (1972) recognised that conversion to and growth in faith belongs to a gradual process and spiritual journey that continues into adulthood and once again affirmed adult education as the norm. *Evangelii Nuntiandi* (1975) considered the lay vocation and stressed the need for theological formation for all Christian adults engaged in the evangelising task of the Church in the modern world. *Catechesi Tradendae* (1979) repeated that adult education is both essential and lifelong. The *Code of Canon Law* (1983) reasserted the right and duty of adult formation while *Christifideles Laici* (1987) spoke of adult formation as an essential and collaborative task of the Church for all baptised persons. Later initiatives including the publication of the *Catechism of the Catholic Church* (1992, Eng. trans. 1994) and the revised *General Directory for Catechesis* (1997) gave clear impetus to the priority of adult formation and laid down a systematic theological exposition of what this should look like in practice.

Furthermore, the critical formation of adults who contribute to the life of their local Church in distinct roles, vocations and ministries has been called for by local Bishops' conferences:

> Discipleship in the Gospel is life-long, a journey of faith coming to complete fulfilment only in the presence of God in heaven. The entire life of the disciple is marked by learning and growth. Life-long growth in faith is to be a characteristic of Catholic life. An understanding of the educative task of the Church must start from this perspective, and increasingly opportunities for life-long learning need to be developed for every member of the Church. (Catholic Bishops' Conference of England and Wales, 2000, p. 1)

More recently, the emphasis by Pope Francis on mission and the new evangelisation has called for adult renewal with a deepening understanding of faith across the life of the Church and in dialogue with a pluralised world. This comes, however, at a time when shifts in religious identity, alongside declining belief and practice, are increasingly the norm within a Western culture of faith denial. For many people in today's post-secular world, opportunities for faith education have been either non-existent, limited, or ended prematurely at adolescence. This means that many adults no longer have knowledge or understanding of Christian faith and tradition as was the case in times past, and so the questions that challenge us all to find meaning and values in life, or face up to life and death issues, or find answers to problems of suffering and moral issues, remain unanchored and adrift or else pieced together in a world of many options. So, the task of adult formation is urgent, not least for those working in Catholic schools and other professions, or serving as lay ministers, chaplains or parish catechists, or parents accepting their responsibility as first educators for their children in faith. Opportunities for some form of adult engagement with the Church's faith and theology, that are credible and relevant for today, are surely essential. But what form should such opportunities take?

Some Theories and Approaches

A wide body of theory on adult learning, commonly referred to as 'andragogy' in contrast to pedagogy whose strict etymological connection lies with the child learner, can be drawn upon. Knowles (1980) noted the particular characteristics of the adult learner as self-directed or self-motivated, possessing a unique resource or reservoir of life experience, as more disposed to active or practical problem-solving than to theoretical learning, who learns best in collaborative dialogue with others, and who seeks both to reflect on and apply their new learning to concrete life-work contexts and situations. Kolb (1984) acting on the earlier ideas of John Dewey, stressed the importance of the cycle of experiential learning, in other words the ways in which adult learners experience life in its many situations and acquire new forms of knowledge, understanding and/or skills from and in relation to that experience. These ideas, pointing to the integration of learning with prior knowledge, skills and understanding, have become a key part of adult learning theory alongside thinking about transformational learning based on a learner's ability to acquire new understanding through reflection as critical dialogue, emerging from thinkers such as Mezirow

(1991) and Freire (1997). Such theories, among others, have contributed to a re-evaluation of adult learning in recent years (Wickett, 2005).

The classical understanding of theology as knowledge of God interacting with human experience (Anselm's 'faith seeking understanding') belonged to the Church more or less until the time of the Enlightenment. It involved both education in a body of Christian teaching as well as the formation of Christian wisdom, virtue and character. In the West, theology was long understood as both *scientia* and *habitus* (Vanhoozer, 2002). However, as theology became rooted in Enlightenment thinking, it was increasingly viewed as a rational object of systematic inquiry, usually the preserve of those preparing for ordained ministry. Theology became primarily intellectual, viewed as a set of doctrines, separated from practice. Over time, this became the model which universities and seminaries adopted. It led to a prioritising of theological education that depended on knowing the 'text' of scripture and tradition over and above other more embodied, affective and relational ways of knowing (Iselin & Meteyard, 2010).

More recent models of theology have brought a diversity of forms and categories, discussion of which lies beyond the scope of this chapter. Inevitably such new directions have impacted on adult faith-based learning. One approach has brought recognition of the importance of inculturation, seeing that significance must be given to the context of lived practice and establishing critical connection and engagement with the socio-cultural realities of everyday life. Groome's (1991) shared praxis is an example of this approach, which has influenced adult learning as it takes people through movements starting with initial and then deepening reflection on their own life experience into an engagement with the 'story' of the Christian scripture and tradition and then back into critical reflection and action response. Indeed, the shared praxis model has taken root in many adult education contexts and across different denominational settings.

Other approaches to adult theological education have centred on a need to recast the disparity between faith and learning, with an emphasis on integration of the two, especially in a time of secular crisis and non-practice of faith. Concerns over how to relate Christian epistemology with Christian faith practices seek to overcome any schism or dichotomy between theological education viewed, on the one hand, as primarily gaining intellectual knowledge about the content of Christian tradition and, on the other hand, as practical skills with spiritual and moral formation (Chandler, 2016). Much of this has stemmed from criticism that any theological education that relies on the accumulation of theological knowledge only has failed to provide the practical habits of faith or the vocational skills for ministry, needed to handle the issues and responsibilities of everyday life. By way of response, forms of adult theological education have emerged that pay attention to the importance of habitus and embodied practices (Smith, 2009, 2013) or adopt a missional focus (D'Orsa & D'Orsa, 2013; Banks, 1999) or seek spiritual formation as the main outcome (Stuebing, 1999). Such models are aimed to help people discover and live their identity as those who share in the mission of the gospel in Church, the world, their families, friendships and workplaces. For these proponents, adult theological education can never be a solely cognitive undertaking cut adrift from affective and behavioural dimensions that include spiritual practices, community, prayer, liturgy, sacramental and moral formation.

Although some suggest there is tension and dilemma for both content and method in contemporary theological education between the formal articulation of theology and the practical development of faith and skills to exercise Church roles and ministries (Bryce, 2017; Banks, 1999; Fernandez, 2014) this chapter holds that adult faith-based learning is not about finding one model or framework as a magic bullet for all. Adult theological education and faith formation is not reducible to a single set of positions, theories, contexts or pedagogies. It can, and often does, take intellectual, systematic and critical dimensions as well as seeking pastoral and spiritual approaches that engage the whole person, head as well as heart and hands. Such catholicity, however, deserves further consideration and so the chapter now turns to recent research findings to further reflect about the nature of adult faith-based learning for today.

Recent Research Findings

Research findings from a Catholic Bishops' Conference of England and Wales longstanding programme of adult theological education offers valuable insights and so is presented in this chapter for discussion. It is by no means the only provision of adult faith-based learning across England and Wales and indeed there are opportunities to study in formal higher education settings as well as local diocesan and parish initiatives, teacher in-service programmes, lay ministry workshops, spirituality courses, faith sharing groups and bible study etc. However, the CCRS has played a major part and significant role in Catholic adult education since 1992 across England and Wales. The course is delivered by dioceses and university providers and has seen over thirty thousand people taking part across the years, though not all participants complete the full award. In 2019, a report from a three-year research project examining the CCRS was published (Stuart-Buttle, 2019). The project had gathered both quantitative and qualitative data across a two-phase study among adult course participants and key stakeholders responsible for providing and delivering the course, the latter including senior Church leaders, primary and secondary school head teachers and diocesan religious directors. Questions across both research phases enquired about the role and purpose of CCRS, the reasons why people study, what sort of theological learning occurs and the impact that CCRS has made. The aim was not only to evaluate the CCRS as a programme of adult education but to stimulate national conversation and theological reflection about adult faith-based learning in light of changing religious, socio-cultural and educational contexts.[1]

Research data shows that the adult learners taking the CCRS are predominantly female, aged between twenty-six and fifty-five years. The majority are teachers, either pre-service or in-service, working in the Church school sector but representing a range of roles. Other adult participants are in parish or lay ministry roles or taking the course for personal interest or spiritual formation. Almost two-thirds state they have not previously studied Catholic theology. In terms of religious affiliation, most self-identify as practising Catholics but a small number are either non-practising, from another Christian denomination, another religious background or follow no religion at all. Their reasons for taking the CCRS indicate an overwhelming demand for theological knowledge and understanding of the Catholic faith tradition. For those with a role in a Catholic school or parish, this is their main reason for taking the course. Participants speak strongly in terms of the CCRS enabling them to gain theological literacy alongside growing in personal faith, spiritual or professional-vocational development. When put together with findings from the phase two stakeholder interviews, the CCRS is clearly affirmed as a rich and valuable resource for adult education and faith formation across England and Wales.

However, this chapter has already identified differing understandings and expectations about the goals and pedagogies of adult faith-based learning. The CCRS research echoes this and raises questions about what sort of theological learning is most needed and most relevant for adult Catholics today. Findings from both research phases, i.e. participant surveys and stakeholder interviews, disclose an underlying tension between what are perceived as the core objectives of the CCRS and these vary between academic, spiritual and practice-based directions. There is some disagreement among both participants and providers over whether adult theological education should be aligned with formal theology (head knowledge), faith-spiritual development (heart), or its function or usefulness for professional or pastoral activity (hands). Some proponents see one of these aspects as demanding priority; others see the need for an integration of all three.

For example, one reading of the research data gives strong articulation that the purpose of CCRS is to provide theological knowledge and understanding to enable participants to make sense of God, his Word and his Church, highlighting this as *the* real need for today in light of the fact that many adult Catholics, including those in Church schools and parish ministries, lack familiarity with the faith tradition. This set of data sees that establishing a theological vocabulary, understanding and worldview is needed first and foremost. This largely supports the current shape of the CCRS curriculum, which explores the foundational disciplines of biblical studies, systematic theology, Church history and moral theology through six core compulsory modules, with two specialist electives offered in areas of practical theology such as liturgy or Catholic education. So, in presenting the Christian tradition through the life, history, worship and mission of the Church together with the meaning of God's revelation in Word and in Christ, with some insights into pastoral ministry and human culture, the CCRS largely supports a paradigm where adult theological education involves primarily knowing the 'text' of scripture, creed and Church and then being able to connect, critique or apply this to one's personal worldview with vocational or professional insight.

However, not all CCRS research findings reflect this approach. Another reading of the data, from other respondents across both research populations, views adult learning less as theological knowledge acquisition or arrival into a set of beliefs or worldview, and more as integration of the role of human experience in making sense of theology for the local professional, pastoral or personal context. These respondents do not deny the need for knowledge and understanding of Catholic theology and tradition; indeed, this is their overwhelming motive for taking the course. But they call for a going beyond 'just knowing about or just knowing that' to seek a more deliberate personal interpretation, inner reflection and appropriation, as well as practical application or outer engagement with real-life contexts and contemporary situations such as the school classroom or the parish workplace. When this is deemed to be missing then they report limited opportunities for growth and development and the risk of detachment or lack of relevance for the value of adult learning in faith and theology. This reading of the CCRS research data, therefore, sees that both the theological curriculum and its pedagogy must bring together intellectual, spiritual and practical components to serve the needs of adult learners today. This can be framed as a shift from an epistemological to a contextual and hermeneutical paradigm to better integrate theology with contemporary life and praxis. The final section of the chapter now reflects further on this.

What Sort of Adult Theological Education for Today?

The issue of contextual relevance is not new to the Church or to theology. As the early Church moved from a predominantly Jewish setting into a Roman world steeped in Greek philosophy, staying faithful to apostolic teaching amidst competing philosophies and allegiances became a significant challenge. The question of how one can teach sound theology and communicate the gospel in different times and contexts has occupied attention ever since. Migliore writes,

> Confession of Jesus Christ takes place in particular historical and cultural contexts ... Our response to the question of who we say Jesus Christ is ... is shaped in important ways by the particular context in which these questions arise. (2004, p. 205)

It is supported by Bevans (2002, p. 3) who suggests that 'there is no such thing as "theology"; there is only theology in context'. This invites further thinking about how to do adult education in ways that are sensitive and faithful to past tradition yet relevant to real-life situations and our contemporary world (Das, 2016). Proponents of contextual theology suggest that formal models that expect people to learn theological categories to understand God and his interaction with the world and then absorb this for practical or functional application, have limited impact due to a lack of importance placed on the socio-cultural context within the educational process.

Emerging in more recent theological thinking is the idea of recontextualisation. The work of Boeve (2007) has been particularly influential here, suggesting that in the face of changing cultural boundaries that have brought pluralism in religious belief together with a devaluing of Christian tradition, there needs to be a reformulating or reinterpretation of the tradition in light of new experiences and understandings if it is to be meaningful for today's complex and post-secular world. This means developing theological frameworks that can 'help people examine their lives, figure out what's going on and distil the issues, and prepare the seedbed where real theological learning and application can occur' (McNeal, 2009 p. 105). But while attention has been given to the recontextualisation of Catholic education in the school setting, for example in the KU Leuven Enhancing Catholic Schools Identity Project,[2] there has been less consideration of how this might look for adult faith-based learning. We have already seen in this chapter that adult formation is essential for the articulation of Christian beliefs, mission, identity and practice, especially to make sense for those who think in a different frame of reference or who need to deal with secular and professional elements of Christian life in complex circumstances. The message of faith that once spoke in a different era, now needs to be recontextualised if it is to speak meaningfully to adults in a contemporary situation of many faith options and life choices.

This approach to adult theological education recognises learning that is situational, participatory, empowering and transformational. The CCRS research data confirms that adult learners carry their hopes, dreams, challenges, opportunities, everyday situations and presuppositions about God, Church, family, work and society into their learning. The diversity of the adult population and their motivations for learning means that they seek programmes that best fit their learning needs for such things as life transitions, employment demands, personal benefits or spiritual growth, and that they do this in line with their preferred mode of learning and time, circumstance or lifestyle constraints. The theological curriculum and pedagogy on offer, therefore, must recognise what is going on in their lives as well as their (non)faith positions and worldviews. This suggests the importance of building on prior knowledge and experience through a range of learning styles and methods to invite reflection and insight that can relate to participants' vocational, personal, professional and community lives. 'Paying attention to what is on the hearts and minds of adults, what is going on in their lives, is crucial and cannot be overstated' (Riley & McBride, 2006, p. 28). It means embracing approaches to adult learning that are less an impartation of already formulated doctrine or pre-packaged theological content and more as a hermeneutical process that recognises the characteristics, prior experiences and 'cultural texts' of the people of God.

The CCRS research confirms that authentic adult learning happens in environments that invite first-hand active participation rather than dispassionate reception. Adult learners are often led into new questioning and unanticipated changes in views about self, God, the Church and the world. Engaging with theology and faith formation can mean crossing thresholds of language, concepts, culture and worldview. When such thresholds are negotiated successfully then there is a journey through pre-liminal, liminal and post-liminal stages, which moves from catalyst encounter to dialogue and integration with Christian tradition, to arrive eventually at new understandings and transformed perspectives or praxis (Chandler, 2016). But this journey is never automatic nor guaranteed as it requires leaving behind one's accepted frame of reference to open up to new ways of interpreting, mediating or analysing the understanding and experience of God, self and others. Hauerwas (1983, p. 27) asserted that, 'We know who we are only when we can place ourselves – locate our stories-within God's story'. To do this with authenticity for adult learners requires both theological curriculum and pedagogy to invite critical reflection and dialogue to enable them to find real meaning in the Christian narrative and in their own and others' personal and cultural experiences.

The CCRS research data suggests that this happens most effectively in adult learning communities, through collaborative and communicative processes. It confirms that adults are generally motivated to learn by settings that are interactive, communal and that respect and treat them as adults. As Iselin & Meteyard (2010, p. 43) state, 'Knowing and learning within this context are essentially relational and interactive, participatory rather than accumulated, shared rather than merely personalised.' The adult learning environment needs to model a contextual and critical form of dialogue, open to reflection about God, Church, oneself and the world, in order to challenge and re-think, to negotiate between different faith experiences and contexts, to respect other traditions and alternative worldviews. It is well recognised that as adults mature, there is progressive acceptance of diversity, tolerance of ambiguity, and the realisation that knowing is linked to doing (D'Orsa & D'Orsa, 2020). Adult theological education, in this sense, must bring the Christian tradition into conversation with human culture and experience. This is what Freire (1997) referred to as a dialogical and empowering pedagogy of possibility and action.

To Conclude

Adult theological education and faith formation belong to the ministry of the Church. A holistic understanding seeks to develop and engage the whole person in learning, service, commitment, and action, both in the life of faith and in the world. Adult theological education can, and should, be both educational and formational; it 'is possible to induct students into critical thinking at the same time as inviting them to be mediators of and witnesses to the faith tradition' (Sullivan, 2011, p. 97). Without attention being given to developing spiritual practices and faith formation alongside building theological knowledge and cultural understanding, there is risk of forming 'detached intellectuals', i.e. those with no practical engagement with the Church or a life of faith, but also a risk of forming 'inconsequential bystanders' or 'impotent pragmatists', in other words those who lack theological depth and any practical or faith commitment (Easley, 2010). The recent CCRS research findings confirm that adult learners themselves want to go beyond solely intellectual or cognitive activity aimed at just knowing the 'text' of the Church's tradition, to include contextual understanding and relevance through critical dialogue with contemporary life and human experience, illuminated by hermeneutical processes that encompass the richness of prayer, liturgy, scripture, sacraments, community and spiritual practices. This is seen as best supporting the lifelong journey of adult participants today.

Adult theological education, therefore, can be understood as a practice that integrates faith, life, learning and culture. It can take diverse approaches and distinctive forms that speak to a particular context or prioritise specific adult constituents such as teachers in Catholic schools, parish catechists or lay ministers. But it should incorporate cognitive, affective and behavioural domains to engage head, heart and hands for contemporary life and praxis, to involve the whole person and invite intellectual, spiritual and pastoral-practical formation. If the CCRS research study rings true, then adult learning in faith and theology is never a 'one-size-fits- all' approach.

To summarise what sort of adult learning and theological education might be faithful, relevant and effective for today, the following principles are offered. Adult faith-based learning should

- recognise multiple backgrounds, interests, levels of faith maturity, learning characteristics and lifelong needs of adult learners themselves;
- ensure a welcoming, supportive and affirming learning environment;
- build effective relationships to collaborate and team-play within a learning community that is social, dialogical and relational;
- encourage theological knowledge and understanding that speaks of God, revelation and Church tradition but that simultaneously values human contexts and life experiences;
- invite opportunities for critical and reflective engagement, among other learning styles and intelligences, to deepen knowledge, understanding, worldview, habits and skills;

- speak to the whole person and creatively engage with mind, body, heart and spirit;
- commit to learning that integrates knowing, being and doing – in other words, that seeks to foster intellectual growth, practical involvement and personal/spiritual (trans)formation.

Postscript

This chapter developed from a conference keynote paper given in Dublin in October 2019. Since then, Covid-19 has hit our world with sudden force and the contours that have up-to-now underpinned Catholic thinking about education, faith, liturgy, spirituality, community and so much more have changed. This is not only due to the uncertainty of the pandemic for the health and well-being of societies and individuals but to an urgent reliance on online technology for everyday living, work practices, faith activities and human relationships. The role of online adult theological education and faith formation has previously received some attention (Stuart-Buttle, 2010, 2013, 2014) but the recent explosion of online learning and its impact for adult faith education will require significant future focus.

ENDNOTES

1 The full report can be downloaded at: www.brs-ccrs.org.uk/images/CCRS-Twenty-Five-Years-On-WEBSITE.pdf

2 See https://www.schoolidentity.net/introduction/

References

Banks, R., *Reenvisioning Theological Education: Exploring a Missional Alternative to Current Models*, Grand Rapids, MI: Eerdmans, 1999.

Bass, D. & Dykstra, C. (eds), *For Life Abundant: Practical Theology, Theological Education, and Christian Ministry*, Grand Rapids, MI: Eerdmans, 2008.

Bevans, S., *Models of Contextual Theology*, Maryknoll, N.Y: Orbis Books, 2002.

Boeve, L., *God Interrupts History: Theology in a Time of Upheaval*, London: Continuum, 2007.

Bryce, B., 'Theology in Practice: Context for Minister Formation', in *Restoration Quarterly* 59/2, (2019), pp. 105-115.

Catechism of the Catholic Church, London: Geoffrey Chapman, 1994.

Catholic Bishops' Conference of England and Wales, Committee for Catechesis and Adult Christian Education, *The Priority of Adult Formation*, London: Catholic Media Trust, 2000.

Chandler, Q., 'Cognition or Spiritual Disposition?', in *Journal of Adult Theological Education* 13/2, (2016), pp. 90-102.

Code of Canon Law, London: Collins, 1983.

Congregation for Divine Worship, *Rite of Christian Initiation of Adults*, 1972. Available at: http://www.vatican.va

Congregation for the Clergy, *General Catechetical Directory*, Vatican City: Libreria Editrice Vaticana, 1971. Available at: http://www.vatican.va

Congregation for the Clergy, *General Directory for Catechesis*, Vatican City: Libreria Editrice Vaticana, 1997. Available at: http://www.vatican.va

Das, R., 'Relevance and Faithfulness: Challenges in Contextualizing Theological Education', in *InSights Journal for Global Theological Education* 1/2, (2016), pp. 17-29.

D'Orsa, J. & D'Orsa, T., *Leading for Mission: Integrating Life, Culture and Faith in Catholic Education*, Mulgrave: Garratt Publishing, 2013.

D'Orsa, J. & D'Orsa, T., *Pedagogy and the Catholic Educator: Nurturing Hearts and Transforming Possibilities*, Mulgrave: Garratt Publishing, 2020.

Easley, R., 'Taking Stock of Our Work as Theological Educators: An Essay on the Context, Meaning and Future of Theological Education', 2010. Available at: www.academia.edu/9897901/Taking_Stock_of_Our_Work_ as_Theological_Educators

Elias, J., *The Foundations and Practice of Adult Religious Education*, Florida: Krieger Publishing Company, 1993.

Fernandez, E., 'Engaging Contextual Realities in Theological Education: Systems and Strategies' in *Evangelical Review of Theology* 38/4, (2014), pp. 339–349.

Freire, P., *Pedagogy of Hope: Reliving Pedagogy of the Oppressed*, New York: Continuum, 1997.

Groome, T., *Sharing Faith: A Comprehensive Approach to Religious Education and Pastoral Ministry*, San Francisco: Harper, 1991.

Hauerwas, S., *The Peaceable Kingdom*, Note Dame; University of Notre Dame Press, 1983.

Iselin, D. & Meteyard, J., 'The "Beyond in the Midst": An Incarnational Response to the Dynamic Dance of Christian Worldview, Faith and Learning', in *Journal of Education and Christian Belief* 14/1, (2010), pp. 33–46.

Knowles, M.S., *The Modern Practice of Adult Education: From Pedagogy to Andragogy*, Wilton, CT: Association Press, 1980.

Kolb, D., *Experiential Learning: Experience as the Source of Learning and Development*, Englewood Cliffs, NJ: Prentice-Hall, 1984.

McNeal, R., *Missional Renaissance: Changing the Scorecard for the Church*, San Francisco: Jossey-Bass, 2009.

Migliore, D., *Faith Seeking Understanding: An Introduction to Christian Theology*, Grand Rapids, MI: Eerdmans, 2004.

Mezirow, J., *Transformative Dimensions of Adult Learning*, San Francisco: Jossey-Bass, 1991.

Pope John Paul II, *Catechesi Tradendae*, 1979. Available at: http://www. vatican.va

Pope John Paul II, *Christifideles Laici*, 1987. Available at: http://www.vatican.va

Pope Paul VI, *Evangelii Nuntiandi*, 1975. Available at: http://www.vatican.va

Riley, D. & McBride, J., *Best Practices in Adult Faith Formation: A National Study*, Washington, DC: NCCL, 2006.

Smith, J., *Desiring the Kingdom: Worship, Worldview and Cultural Formation*, Grand Rapids, MI: Baker Academic, 2009.

Smith, J., *Imagining the Kingdom: How Worship Works*, Grand Rapids, MI: Baker Academic, 2013.

Stuart-Buttle, R., 'Communicating Faith and Online Learning', in J. Sullivan (ed) *Communicating Faith*, Washington, DC: The Catholic University of America Press, 2010, pp. 328-343.

Stuart-Buttle, R., *Virtual Theology, Faith and Adult Education: An Interruptive Pedagogy*, Newcastle upon Tyne: Cambridge Scholars, 2013.

Stuart-Buttle, R., 'Interrupting Adult Learning through Online Pedagogy', in *Journal of Christian Education and Belief* 18/1, (2014), pp. 61-75.

Stuart-Buttle, R., *CCRS Twenty Five Years On: One Size Fits All?*, Stockport, UK: Rejoice Publications, Matthew James Ltd, 2019.

Stuebing, R., 'Spiritual Formation in Theological Education', in *Africa Journal of Evangelical Theology* 18/1, (1999), pp. 47-70.

Sullivan, J., 'Promoting the Mission: Principles and Practice', in *International Studies in Catholic Education* 3/1, (2011), pp. 91-102.

Vanhoozer, K., *First Theology: God, Scripture and Hermeneutics*, Downers Grove, IL: InterVarsity Press, 2002.

Vatican II, *Ad Gentes: Decree on Missionary Activity*, 1965, in Abbott W. (ed), *The Documents of Vatican II*, New York: Herder and Herder, 1966.

Vatican II, *Apostolicam Actuositatem: Decree on the Apostolate of the Laity*, 1965, in Abbott W. (ed), *The Documents of Vatican II*, New York: Herder and Herder, 1966.

Vatican II, *Christus Dominus: Decree on the Pastoral Office of Bishops*, 1965, in Abbott W. (ed), *The Documents of Vatican II*, New York: Herder and Herder, 1966.

Vatican II, *Presbyterorum Ordinis: Decree on the Ministry and Life of Priests*, 1965, in Abbott W. (ed), *The Documents of Vatican II*, New York: Herder and Herder, 1966.

Wickett, R., 'Adult Learning Theories and Theological Education', in *Journal of Adult Theological Education* 2/2, (2005), pp. 153–161.

Chapter 2

$\sim\!\!\sim\!\!\sim\!\!\sim\!\!\sim\!\!\sim$

Adult Religious Education in Ireland: Pushing the Boat Out

Bernadette Sweetman

Introduction

This chapter focuses on the current situation and possible future avenues for adult religious education and faith development in Ireland. It will touch upon formal, informal and lifelong teaching and learning. While grounded in the Irish Catholic context, it is hoped that questions and conversations may emerge that engage other contexts and faiths or worldviews.

A short piece of scripture will serve to evoke three images that will be used to illustrate the three main sections of this chapter:

> Once while Jesus was standing beside the lake of Gennesaret, and the crowd was pressing in on him to hear the word of God, he saw two boats there at the shore of the lake; the fishermen had gone out of them and were washing their nets. He got into one of the boats, the one belonging to Simon, and asked him to put out a little way from the shore. Then he sat down and taught the crowds from the boat. When he had finished speaking, he said to Simon, 'Put out into the deep water and let down your nets for a catch'. Simon answered, 'Master, we have worked all night long but have caught nothing. Yet if you say so, I will let down the nets.' When they had done this, they caught so many fish

that their nets were beginning to break. So they signalled
to their partners in the other boat to come and help them.
(Lk 5:1-7)

Reading the passage from Luke's Gospel, three images stand out.
These might be useful when attempting to grasp the intricacies of
engaging in adult religious education. The images are:

1. The fishermen before Jesus intervenes.
2. Pushing the boat out.
3. Partners in the other boat.

The Adult Religious Education and Faith Development Project (AREFD): Background and Rationale

The content of this chapter is situated in the context of a particular
research project currently underway from 2018–2021 at the MDCCE at
DCU – the Adult Religious Education and Faith Development project
(AREFD). The importance of progressing adult religious education in
Ireland has been highlighted in recent years and this project is borne
out of that movement. *Share the Good News: National Directory for
Catechesis in Ireland* (SGN; Irish Episcopal Conference, 2010) affirms
the education of adults in religion as 'one of the urgent religious needs
in Ireland in our time. An educated world needs an educated faith'
(SGN, par. 70). This immediately raises questions including my personal
favourite question: Why? What is the value of education in faith as an
adult? Is education in religion the same as education in faith? Is it about
planning for opportunities to educate in religion, in a formal way? Or
is it about empowering adults to be open to educational experiences in
their faith, in a more informal, and perhaps non-formal way? What might
be particular to this creature, the adult, which makes the task different
in comparison to the religious education and/or faith development
of children? These are some of the questions in the milieu as we work
through the AREFD project. They are questions that are not necessarily
new, nor particular only to Catholic education or indeed Ireland.

The genesis of the AREFD project was twofold. Firstly, there was
the awareness of existing work being carried out in communities, in
both formal and informal contexts that, in different ways, offers adults
the opportunity to reflect on their faith, their religious understanding,
their identity and their role in society. At first thought, one might
recall the more formal examples such as courses of study, Bible study

groups, parish events, guest speakers and so on. These usually have an explicit religious focus and belong within a particular denomination. Formal education in religion and faith for adults is often associated with training for ministry. Terms such as theological education are also frequently used. This may take place in seminaries or schools of theology (Stache, 2014). There are also ecumenical initiatives in some localities, both formal and informal. Other instances might involve adults working together, engaging in discussions and practical projects that might not be seen as purposefully religious, spiritual or related to belief or faith. They may have an element of belonging, or community, and could perhaps be predisposed to an openness to faith-based questions. The literature shows a recognised trend of a growing number of adults seeking spiritual answers to their questions outside of formal religious institutions (Zeph, 2000; Ó Murchú, 1998).

Secondly, the project also has its roots in the understanding that there is a thirst and a hunger among adults to find new ways to deal with new questions as they emerge. The formal education within primary and post-primary school is insufficient in itself as we encounter both good and bad times in our lives as we grow older; challenges as well as opportunities. Adults both need and deserve age-appropriate educational experiences. We also recognise the great wisdom that comes with adulthood. Experience is a great teacher and many adults wish to share their wisdom in some way and help others, especially younger generations, when they encounter the different transitions and milestones in their lives. The term 'religious education' in Ireland is usually associated with the formal educational activity in primary and post-primary schools. State-sponsored syllabuses at post-primary level were introduced from 2000 (Junior Cycle level) and 2003 (Senior Cycle level). These were designed to 'equip students to understand their own religious tradition or non-religious worldview and also to reflect on the religious traditions and worldviews of others' (Byrne, Francis & McKenna, 2019, p. 204). Do adults not need these skills too, in different ways across the vast and diverse spectrum of adulthood? Knowles (1973), often referred to as 'the father of adult education in America', called the adult learner 'a neglected species'. In devising the AREFD project, the team were aware of similar possible shortfalls for Irish adults. When it comes to existing opportunities, such as parish groups, community projects and courses on offer, are people aware of and/or in a position to avail of them? Is the value of such work celebrated and publicised? Are they accessible? Are they welcoming? Are they 'doable' in the busy schedules of Irish adults with increasing responsibilities? What about the personnel currently involved? How can they be assisted in evaluating present practice, in order to improve the experience of future generations? How might such work be presented as a model of best practice to other contexts wishing to get involved?

The First Phase: A Listening Exercise

Returning to the images evoked by the scripture passage above. Envisage the fishermen before Jesus intervened. All were individuals with different stories to tell but together at this moment. The first phase of the AREFD project was a listening exercise. The respondents are represented by the fishermen. The purpose of this survey was to listen. Respondents were invited to provide basic demographic information, to articulate their particular beliefs and values, to indicate the positive influences on their faith development, and to comment on belonging to a faith community. They were also given the opportunity to relate both the content of and possible ways through which they could deepen their faith and explore religious education further.

An online survey consisting of seventy-seven items was constructed by the research team and made available on the MDCCE website for six weeks in May/June 2019. Items were either multiple choice, five-point Likert scales or open questions that gave the participant the option to provide text responses. Consequently, data analysis is both quantitative (frequencies, correlations and factor analysis using SPSS) and also qualitative (thematic analysis and interpretative phenomenological analysis). The survey was open to all adults living on the island of Ireland aged 18 or over. A snowball self-selecting sampling strategy was employed with the survey publicised via university communication networks, social media, national print media and radio. It amassed a total of 738 respondents from all thirty-two counties.

Demographic Profile

Of the 738 respondents, 77% were born in the Republic of Ireland, with almost equal proportions being born in Northern Ireland (11%) or elsewhere (10%). Almost two-thirds hailed from Leinster (64%), followed by 16% from Munster, 12% from Ulster and 8% from Connacht. Respondents were given the same categories of religious affiliation as per the 2016 National Census. Over four-fifths identified as Roman Catholic (87%), with the next highest proportion being those of 'No religion' (8%). No one identified as Muslim or Orthodox. Of those who selected 'Other', many indicated that they were 'formerly Catholic' or 'non-practising', in addition to 'Christian', 'pagan', 'humanist' and 'atheist'. Almost two-thirds were female (61%). Forty-six per cent of the 738 respondents were aged between 40 and 59, while 41% were aged 60 or older.

The National Census 2016 figures paint a different picture. Just over half of the total population were female (51%). One-quarter (25%) of the total population were aged between 40 and 59, and 18% were aged over 60. The figure for those self-identifying as Roman Catholic was 78% (Central Statistics Office, 2017).

Given the difference in the profile of respondents in the survey contrasted to National Census 2016 figures, it is acknowledged by the research team that volunteer bias may have played a role. More women, and those more positively disposed to religion and faith were more likely to participate. Therefore, while not taking the responses as representative of the general population, it is nonetheless worthwhile to examine the differences between the responses of those who chose to participate.

Beliefs and Values

Going beyond demographic details, the participants were invited to respond on a five-point Likert scale with a number of statements regarding their beliefs and values, the positive influences on their faith development, and the extent to which they belong to a faith community. As with the image of the fishermen, who were all individuals with their own stories to tell, though together in that moment, the research team sought to know more about the respondents and 'where they were at' in relation to religious education and faith development. During data analysis, Strongly Agree and Agree responses were combined for reporting purposes.

Faith and religion were important to the majority of respondents (84% and 81% respectively). There was a notable gap between the percentages of respondents identifying as 'religious' (64%) and those identifying as 'spiritual' (79%). In this regard, it was noteworthy that of those strongly agreeing that they were 'religious', 79% also strongly agreed to being 'spiritual'. In contrast, only 47% of those who strongly agreed with being 'spiritual' also strongly agreed with being 'religious'. This suggests that the adults who responded distinguish between the two terms, with the term 'spiritual' appearing to be more user friendly to some extent. Perhaps unsurprisingly, much greater proportions (over 20%) of those aged 60 or over strongly agreed with statements such as 'Religion is important to me' than the average of the entire set of respondents. This pattern is repeated elsewhere with the older generations strongly agreeing with such statements in greater proportion than younger generations.

Influences on Faith Development

Returning to the image of the fishermen before Jesus intervenes, we recall that they were skilled people. Some may have loved their job, others not so much. Fishing may well have been a tradition, following in the footsteps of parents and significant others. What influenced them? The AREFD survey included a section on the different positive influences on the respondent's faith development using the same five-point Likert scale as previously mentioned. Again, the following results are the combination of Strongly Agree and Agree.

Parental influence on faith development has been well-documented in the literature (Byrne, Francis, Sweetman and McKenna, 2019). In the AREFD survey, 73% of respondents identified their mother as being the most positive influence on their faith development. This was greater than that of the father (58%) which was slighter higher than the influence of the school (56%). There was a positive correlation between the positive influence of the school on the faith development of respondents and their age, the older population suggesting a more positive connection between school and faith. This may suggest that school was a greater influence on older adults than has been the case for younger adults. It is acknowledged, however, that older adults may have the benefit of hindsight having had a greater number of influences over their longer lives, perhaps, than younger people. There was a negative correlation between the positive influence of friends on the faith development of respondents and their age. Thirty-three per cent of all respondents indicated that friends were a positive influence on their faith development, but the younger respondents rated friends as a positive influence in greater proportions than their older counterparts. It should be remembered that older adults may have different experiences of their peers than the younger generations. A stand-out result was that the media was seen as a positive influence on faith development by just 9% of all respondents. Given the oft-contentious nature of public debate in the media concerning religion and education, this is a thought-provoking statistic.

Belonging to a Faith Community

What led those particular fishermen to be in that boat on that morning may have varied, but it is probable to assume that they, like the adults in Ireland today, have particular strengths and weaknesses, different skills and roles to play, as well as varying motivations. Together, they were a crew. Similarly, adults in faith are called to be a community. The AREFD survey contained a section, using the same five-point Likert scale, on 'Belonging to a faith community'. When reviewing these responses, we might compare the community with the fishermen, including their partners in the other boat. Collectively, they can prompt conversation about the relationship between personal and communal faith.

A smaller percentage of respondents (75%) agreed that belonging to a faith community was important to them than those who agreed that religion was important to them (81%). Respondents rated the importance of praying on one's own (78%) more highly than praying with others (68%). While belonging to a faith community was important to three-quarters of the respondents (75%), slightly lower percentages rated the importance of weekly worship and/or going to Church on Sunday (both were 69%). In relation to active and tangible community involvement, 70% of respondents agreed with 'I feel I have gifts/talents to offer to my local faith community', yet only 45% of respondents have 'a particular job' in their local faith community, with 42% indicating they were a minister. Just over three-fifths felt they belonged to their local faith community (61%) or enjoyed it (61%). While 59% of respondents are aware of ways to be actively involved in their local faith community, only 49% would like to be more actively involved.

The gap between rating the importance of personal or private prayer to that in a community setting is highlighted even more when only the Strongly Agree responses are reported. Just 36% of all respondents strongly agreed with 'Praying with others is important to me' – the highest (44%) being those aged 70 and older and the lowest (21%) being those in their 20s. Even among the older generations, communal worship and prayer is less important than personal or private prayer. For example, 54% of all respondents strongly agreed that going to Church on Sunday was important to them. This ranged from the highest (68%) aged 70 and older to the lowest (36%) aged in their 30s. A pattern is evident among the respondents to this particular survey that there is greater stability and confidence perhaps in the personal faith of the participants but that this stability and confidence wanes somewhat when called to engage with others.

Pushing the Boat Out

Up to this point, we have used the scripture image of the fishermen to examine their identities and what may have influenced and shaped them so far. We have looked at the identity of and influences upon the adult participants of the AREFD survey in a similar vein. Thus far, the sections of the survey reported upon here were largely retrospective. The respondents were giving an account of themselves up to now, looking back as it were. One observation on the data as a whole is that there was a lot more information given by respondents in the earlier sections than was offered in the later open sections. The later questions invited suggestions as to how to develop adult religious education or what new ideas or approaches they thought might work. For some, it seems, there was a gap of some kind, or perhaps a barrier preventing them from expressing opinions about next steps.

One might wonder why, in the scripture passage, some of the fishermen did push their boat out and others remained on shore. Was motivation a factor? Hope? The prospect of a valuable outcome? Peer pressure? Furthermore, how might the fishermen who pushed out their boat after a long night of catching little feel about those 'partners' who stayed behind? Did they feel like leaders or lemmings, left out or let down? This may sound unkind but the data from the survey showed a strong emotional connection in the respondents with religious education and faith development, evident in the open text responses. Some participants indicated a very strong drive to protect and progress religious education, to preserve traditions and pass on the faith. Others indicated a sense of being restricted, that involvement in religious education in schools had felt like it was imposed, and that they would like to explore issues, as adults, at their own pace. Others again expressed resentment that some avenues of being involved were not, they felt, open to them. A concern that prompted the research study as a whole was echoed by the survey participants, namely that despite the current efforts to provide opportunities for adult religious education and faith development (mainly the examples given were courses and various parish teams), uptake and long-term engagement was not as strong as they would have desired. Somewhere there is a discrepancy between need and the provision of appropriate opportunity. It is not dissimilar to the fishermen being out all night and returning with little or nothing.

Amongst a number of barriers against adult Christian education, according to Goodbourn (1996), is the failure of the provider 'to take account of motivation and preferred method', the 'belief that adults don't want to learn' and the 'uncertainty as to how it is to be done'. Wickett (2005) advocates that theological education must 'consider the issues from the learner's perspective' (p. 154).

In the scripture passage, after listening to Jesus, the fishermen pushed the boat out. They pushed it out, not Jesus. Jesus was the catalyst, the inspiration. Indeed, the person of Jesus should be a central in Christian religious education and faith development. However, the agency of the adult in religious education and faith development is very important. Rather than in the culture of provision that has prevailed for so long, when efforts with varying success have been made to 'pull' and 'keep' adults in religious education and faith development scenarios, how might we move forward to enabling adults to 'push out the boat of their own religious education and faith development'. How might we do so in community, where 'partners' are not left behind if they do not wish to be?

A Variety of Content and Approaches

In the AREFD survey, respondents were given a list of topics and asked to select which ones they would like to learn about as an adult. Similarly, they were offered a list of skills to choose from. In both cases, they were given the option to select 'other' and to elaborate as they saw fit. The lists of topics and skills was generated in light of a research study conducted in DCU on 'CPD and RE: What Do RE Teachers in Irish Catholic Schools Say They Need?' (Byrne & Sweetman, 2019). The three most popular topics selected were 'Faith in the future' (56%), 'Scripture' (54%) and 'Other worldviews and religions' (51%). The top three skills selected were 'Passing on the faith' (54%), a concern often expressed; 'Dealing with challenges to my faith' (49%) and 'Living in a pluralistic society' (44%). In both categories, there was a broad spread of selections across the various suggestions and respondents also indicated the 'other' option in sizeable proportions. Such a spread indicates that there are many topics and skills that should be included in initiatives for adult religious education and faith development. This may influence either the redesigning of existing formal opportunities such as courses of study, or the creation of new modules.

Bernadette Sweetman

The Importance of Agency in Adult Religious Education and Faith Development

In the survey, when asked to indicate what would encourage them to engage more in adult religious education, respondents highlighted the 'atmosphere of respect' (48%), feeling a sense of 'contributing to the "bigger picture"' (48%), and 'meeting people of similar interests' (46%). Forty-three per cent opted for 'blended learning', 43% chose 'evenings during the week' and 42% selected 'discussion groups in my local area' when asked to indicate preferred modes of education. With no one leading factor in what would encourage greater involvement, it is all the more significant to recognise the role played by the motivations of the adult learners themselves. In other words, helping them to push out their own boat. The work of Schaeffler (2015) in the American context is very insightful for this purpose.

The responses to the survey show a clear preference for more opportunities in religious education in non-formal contexts. This is to say beyond the formal structures of a course or training, and opportunities that might be short-term and learner-led in nature. Non-formal religious education, as defined by Simojoki (2019) is 'any organized, systematic, educational activity carried on outside the framework of the formal system to provide selected types of learning to particular subgroups in the population, adults as well as children' (p. 236). Those currently involved in providing formal education opportunities could compare this area to the planned learning experiences that we increasingly encounter in our curricula. How might we create more opportunities for such learning experiences specifically for adults both in and beyond formal religious education?

Connected to this, we ought to also consider informal education. Simojoki (2019) defines this as 'the lifelong process by with every person acquires and accumulates knowledge, skills, attitudes and insights from daily experiences and exposure to the environment – at home, at work, at play' (p. 236, citing Coombs & Ahmed, 1974, p. 8).

Conclusion

As the research continues, it is increasingly evident that adulthood is a spectrum and no single approach will suffice the needs of everyone. Over time, approaches will need to be revisited to examine their ongoing efficacy. One of the intended outcomes of the project will be a self-reflective toolkit to assist those involved in adult religious education and faith development in this regard. Additionally, in later phases of the project, the research team will engage with established groups and individuals who have been working in different ways in adult religious education and faith development. Through such consultations, interviews and focus groups, and informed by their ongoing reflection, further rich qualitative data will be obtained. This will contribute to the literature from a current Irish context and also provide some lived wisdom for those aiming to adapt existing opportunities on reflection. Later phases of the project will also include pilot projects using new models and approaches.

References

Byrne G. & Francis, L.J. (eds), *Religion and Education: The Voices of Young People in Ireland*, Dublin: Veritas, 2019.

Byrne, G., Francis, L.J. & McKenna, U., 'Exploring the Social Benefit of Religious Education in Post-primary Schools in the Republic of Ireland: An Empirical Enquiry among 13- to 15-year-old Students', in G. Byrne & L.J. Francis (eds), *Religion and Education: The Voices of Young People in Ireland*, Dublin: Veritas, 2019, pp. 203–221.

Byrne, G., Francis, L.J., Sweetman, B. & McKenna, U., 'Sustaining Churchgoing Young Catholics in the Republic', in G. Byrne & L.J. Francis (eds), *Religion and Education: The Voices of Young People in Ireland*, Dublin: Veritas, 2019, pp. 223–246.

Byrne, G. & Sweetman, B., 'CPD and RE: What Do RE Teachers in Ireland Say They Need?', in M. Buchanan & A. Gellel (eds), *Global Perspectives on Catholic Religious Education in Schools*, Singapore: Springer, 2019, pp. 231–243.

Central Statistics Office, *Census 2016 Summary Results – Part 1*, Dublin: The Stationery Office, 2017. Available at: www.cso.ie/en/media/csoie/newsevents/documents/census2016summaryresultspart1/Census2016SummaryPart1.pdf

Central Statistics Office, *Census 2016 Results Profile 8: Irish Travellers, Ethnicity and Religion*, Dublin: The Stationery Office, 2017. Available at: https://www.cso.ie/en/releasesandpublications/ep/p-cp8iter/p8iter/

Goodbourn, D., 'Overcoming Barriers to Adult Christian Education', in *Ministry Today*, 7, (1996). Available at https:/www.ministrytoday.org.uk/magazines/issues/7/28/

Irish Episcopal Conference, *Share the Good News: National Directory for Catechesis in Ireland*, Dublin: Veritas, 2010.

Knowles, M.S., *The Adult Learner: A Neglected Species*, Houston, TX: Gulf, 1973.

Ó Murchú, D., *Reclaiming Spirituality: A New Spiritual Framework for Today's World*. New York: Crossroad, 1998.

Pontifical Council for Promoting New Evangelisation, *Directory for Catechesis*, London: Catholic Truth Society, 2020.

Schaeffler, J., 'Motivation for Adult Faith Formation', in *Lifelong Faith*, 8/2, (2015), pp. 34-39.

Simojoki, H., 'Researching Confirmation Work in Europe: An Example of Research on Non-formal Education', in F. Schweitzer, W. Ilg & P. Schreiner (eds), *Researching Non-formal Religious Education in Europe*, Münster: Waxmann, 2019, pp. 235-250.

Stache, K., 'Formation for the Whole Church: A New/Old Vision of Theological Education in the 21st Century', in *Dialog: A Journal of Theology*, 53/4, (2014), pp. 286-292.

Wickett, R., 'Adult Learning Theories and Theological Education', in *Journal of Adult Theological Education*, 2/2, (2005), pp. 153-161.

Zeph, C., 'The Spiritual Dimensions of Lay Ministry Programs', in *New Directions for Adult and Continuing Education*, 85/Spring, (2000), pp. 77-84.

Chapter 3

〰〰〰〰〰〰〰

Catholic Education: Breathing In and Out the Spirit of God's Love

Gareth Byrne

Introduction

In this presentation significant challenges for Catholic education in the Republic of Ireland today, and a way of thinking about how to respond, are considered. The changing landscape (Anderson, Byrne & Cullen, 2016) and rapid rate of adjustment within the school system in Ireland is leaving school management and many teachers breathless (Byrne 2018a, 2018b, 2018c). What do we mean by Catholic education today and what can it contribute to a deeper sense of who we are, any of us, into the future?

This review seeks to understand key points of departure for a renewal of Catholic education in Ireland today. It considers what may be useful in preparing a considered response, taking *Share the Good News* (SGN; Irish Episcopal Conference, 2010) as its foundational document. It will highlight as a particular case the changes to Religious Education as a school subject at Junior Cycle in the Republic of Ireland (National Council for Curriculum and Assessment [NCCA], 2019) and its implementation in Catholic schools there (Council for Catechetics of the Irish Episcopal Conference, 2019). Using what can be learned from this example, it will return to the larger question and ask how Catholic education, formal, informal and lifelong, might look to the future, engaging dynamically and proactively to the benefit of all. It will suggest that it is time to breathe in deeply of the tradition and experience to which the Catholic education community belongs, allowing the Holy Spirit space in which to encourage reflection and engagement. This conversation, while often focused on Catholic schools, can speak, too, to the bigger picture of Catholic education broadly conceived of, and to, those concerned with Catholic education in other jurisdictions.

Breathing In and Out

Among the many changes ongoing and being considered for implementation in the Irish education system are the request for divesting of some Catholic primary schools, the arrival of Wellbeing as a school subject, the innovative new Junior Cycle Framework (12–15 year-olds), the recently-launched specification for Religious Education within that Framework, new requirements in relation to school admissions policies, the restructuring of the primary school curriculum, the reshaping of Relationships and Sexuality Education across all levels, and the upcoming review of Senior Cycle (16–18 year-olds). Are such changes a threat to Catholic education in schools or can the challenges presented in the Republic of Ireland be understood as opportunities?

The Scottish composer James MacMillan premiered his newest work at the Edinburgh Festival on 17 August 2019 (MacMillan, 2018). It opens not with music but with the choir breathing audibly, in and out, in and out. Breathing is relevant because the symphony is inspired by and centred on the third person of the Holy Trinity, sometimes referred to as God's breath, the Holy Spirit. It is a musical examination of what the Spirit, that hard to personify manifestation of God's presence, mysterious, challenging as well as comforting, might mean, signify and require of us. 'The quickest way to change your state of being in any moment couldn't be simpler,' Joanna Moorhead comments in a review of the piece, 'You breathe.' In and out, quietly, deeply, more self-consciously, taking your time, in and out. Emotionally and psychologically, as well as physically, breath-work is tremendously effective (Moorhead, 2019, p. 18).

Catholic education, this paper argues, breathes in the breath of God, the life of God, the Spirit of God, the love of God, and breathes it out again for the building up of our world and all its peoples. That is what makes it different (a question that is often posed), gives it its fundamental character, and helps to define what Catholic education offers its participants and the world. Catholic education is always renewing and reinventing itself, under the impulse of the Holy Spirit, in order to contribute to the growth and wellbeing of individuals, their community and society, caring for the common good, and now more explicitly too for the common home within which we live and move and have our being. Concerned for the environment in which we live, and with the conviction that all things are connected, Pope Francis is convinced that by playing our part responsibly we can contribute to a new beginning: 'The Spirit of God has filled the universe with possibilities and therefore, from the very heart of things, something new can always emerge' (Pope Francis, 2015, par. 80).

Share the Good News

Share the Good News: National Directory for Catechesis in Ireland provides a framework indicating principles and guidelines for evangelisation, catechesis and religious education, seeking to make one piece of Catholic education in Ireland, in schools and beyond (Byrne, 2011). Ten years since its publication in December 2010, this catechetical directory is still having an increasing impact. The issues the Irish Catholic bishops were, even then, seeking to address have come to dominate the discourse about Catholic education in Ireland. The bishops recognise the struggle of large numbers of Irish Catholics to find a correlation between faith and life, acknowledging that young people are becoming generally absent from Church. As Cullen puts it more recently: 'Religion has not gone away in the lives of many young people but for an increasing number of other young people religion does not play any part in their experience or worldview' (Cullen, 2019, p. 279). The bishops set themselves and the local faith community the task of seeking, 'in love and with respect, to open up a dialogue about all these things with those who are committed, with those who are alienated, and with those who are coming to consider these questions for the first time' (SGN, par. 8). *Share the Good News* encourages members of the Christian community to express in contemporary ways the great hope the Christian message offers the world and its peoples, presented in language that is accessible, inclusive and respectful (Byrne, 2013a).

Faith Development

Allowing for the complexity of needs, 'faith development' is used as the overarching term for education in faith in *Share the Good News*. It brings together under one umbrella term all the different approaches that one may encounter and engage in across the journey of faith and life, personally and within a faith community, while allowing each their own significant space for engagement: initial proclamation, Christian initiation, catechesis, religious education, new evangelisation, theological reflection (SGN, pars. 30 p–43):

> Faith development includes initial faith formation, but suggests that formation in faith is lifelong and does not achieve its end except finally in Jesus Christ. It acknowledges that a person's faith can evolve and mature, guided by the Holy Spirit, throughout the experience of life. (SGN, par. 43)

Share the Good News 'is not a "quick fix"', Aidan Ryan acknowledges. Faith development needs a variety of approaches according to the variety of people's faith needs: 'I suspect the solution may be very much about the long haul of addressing basic issues of faith – how it begins, how it does or does not develop, what diminishes it, what nourishes it' (Ryan, 2019, p. 41).

Celebrating Adult Faith

Share the Good News takes up the oft repeated affirmation that the ongoing catechesis of adults be seen as the chief form and model for catechesis and faith development at every level in the Church (Congregation for the Clergy, 1971, 1997): 'Christians are continually invited to develop the intensity of their faith, the intimacy of their friendship with Christ and the strength of their love for God and for their neighbour' (SGN, par. 43).

Adult faith development is not understood simply as the investigation by adult Christians of their own faith, but also as a drawing of them into their faith community for their own further education and growth, and for the enhancement and development of the community (Byrne, 2008): 'This is more than an individual undertaking, but belongs properly to the local Christian community, drawing the adult Christian into fuller communion and enriching the community in the process' (SGN, par. 70).

Sharing the Gift of Faith with Young People

Share the Good News notes, too, that when Catholic adults recognise the significance of their Christian faith in their own lives, they offer their children the gift of Baptism into that faith, and gladly accept the responsibility, with the encouragement of the Holy Spirit, of bringing them up in the faith (SGN, par. 92). They are not on their own in so doing: 'Family and parish support for parents/guardians, godparents and grandparents as they foster the human and spiritual growth of their child is essential' (*SGN*, par. 92). The local Catholic school, too, understands itself as supporting the efforts of parents and family and parish, such that it 'contributes generously to the children's faith development' (*SGN*, par. 91).

Ongoing Religious Learning Experiences

First indications of findings from the Adult Religious Education and Faith Development survey conducted in May/June 2019 by Byrne and Sweetman (Sweetman & Byrne, 2019; Sweetman, 2019) give some indications of how adults continue to connect with religious learning experiences they have had during their lives. Adults were asked in this survey to choose from a list of those who might, as appropriate to their circumstance, have influenced them most in regard to religion. Taking 'strongly agree' and 'agree' responses together, from the five-point Likert scale offered, Catholic participants signalled their highest influencers as mother (77%), father (62%), schooling (62%), and parish/faith community (60%). These came in, generally, higher than grandparents, children, spouses or friends. Early thematic analysis of open answer responses indicates the importance often, now, too, of newer contemporary influencers, such as spiritual writers, YouTube clips, and social media, especially tweets from Pope Francis and parish social media feeds. How adults understand Catholic education, formal and informal, both for themselves and their young people, in schools and elsewhere, may well be a changing dynamic.

Four Signs of Gospel Living

Share the Good News recognises fours characteristic of gospel living which lie at the centre of any efforts to encourage members of the Christian community to develop their faith:

- Learning about and witnessing to the gospel (*kerygma/martyria*)
- Building up a caring Christian community (*koinonia*)
- Celebrating faith in worship, prayer and through liturgical participation (*leitourgia*)
- Service of neighbour, particularly the most poor, the work of justice (*diakonia*)

(*SGN*, par. 36)

Sometimes one of these four signs of commitment will be the focus or starting point for faith development. All four, however, need to be attended to in the life of the adult or young person if the full significance of adopting Christ, and his revelation about life and love, is to be fully understood and, prompted by the Spirit of God, put into practice in the life of the Christian and in the life of the Christian community. All four then, we shall see, are also the concern of the Catholic school in building itself up as a Catholic community, supporting its young people and their families, and positioning itself in relation to all of its students, whatever their family traditions and worldview.

The Characteristic Spirit of Schools

The *Education Act, 1998*, and all documentation from both the state and the churches in Ireland recognise that education in school takes place within the ethos and characteristic spirit of the particular school (Government of Ireland, 1998). The Catholic school, for example, seeks to give generously of its Catholic ethos. This ethos is expressed through the characteristic spirit of the school, built on the tradition of its trustees, and on the specific manifestation of this in the particular school, something which is not static but grows and develops year-in, year-out. The changing context of Ireland, the variety of students, their various cultural identities and nationalities, and the plurality of their religious and other belief systems, means that Catholic schools are changing too, something recognised in their student admissions policy (Government of Ireland, 2018). The needs of the students and the characteristic spirit of the school together open up the context within which the school addresses faith development generally and religious education more specifically:

> The young person's religious experience is welcomed and supported. Young people are helped to know and belong to their religious tradition and to know about other faiths ... Those of no faith are encouraged to develop spiritual and moral foundations upon which to engage with the world, its religions and particular faith communities. (SGN, par. 107)

Catholic schools in Ireland are dealing with the plurality of their student population because of, and not despite, their Catholic ethos. Each school constantly seeks to articulate its mission, vision and aims anew, using language that speaks to and can engage young people today, their parents, family and community (Le Chéile, 2019). This ongoing reflection, we might say, is a clear example of what it means to be open to the signs of the times, to breathe in and out the Spirit of God's love, and allow the Spirit to guide us along.

Catholic School Mission

Arising from this understanding, it can be said that the mission and ethos of the Catholic school is knowingly and purposefully Catholic (CEIST, 2017). At the same time it is embracing of the variety of young people that become part of its community. *Share the Good News* makes a strong case for this understanding, stating on the one hand that, 'The Catholic school will operate according to a Mission Statement and Ethos Policy that openly reflects its Catholic spirit' (SGN, par. 147). On the other hand, it is clear that this also means that, 'the Catholic school, primary or post-primary, will be characterised by respect, generosity, justice, hospitality, and critical reflection', and specifically that, 'the Catholic school will be known to be open to pupils from all cultural and religious backgrounds ... utterly respectful of everyone's belief system' (SGN, par. 148). The Catholic school hopes to support all its young people on their journey toward a full and mature life at home and in society, and specifically seeks the full inclusion of students of different belief systems in the Catholic school (Joint Managerial Body/ Association of Management of Catholic Secondary School, 2019). At the same time, the Catholic school has a duty of care to the young Catholics who attend and to their parents or guardians, supporting Catholic parents as catechists of their children, toward initiation into and personal development of their young people within their faith community (SGN, par. 91). The Catholic school sees itself as being at the service of family, parish and the wider community as it establishes the deepest of connections with young people (SGN, pars. 110-111).

Religious Education and Religious Diversity

Religious Education, as a subject at second-level, offers a particular example of the developments that have taken place and are continuing to evolve in response to the needs of young people today. Religious Education has, since 2000, been provided as an optional examination subject in the Republic of Ireland, as designed by the NCCA in conjunction with interested parties. This initiative was introduced at Junior Certificate level, for 12- to 15-year-olds, at the beginning of the process in 2000, and at Leaving Certificate level, for 16- to 18-year-olds, in 2003 (Department of Education and Science, 2000, 2003). These syllabuses have underpinned developments in Religious Education in all second-level schools, including Catholic schools, whether students take the state examination or not. All such programmes, *Share the Good News* acknowledges, are limited but should be understood 'as useful tools for the religious education and faith formation of Catholic students, opening them up to critically significant questions and to the profound in daily life' (*SGN*, par. 107).

A survey of 13- to 15- year olds in the Republic of Ireland, conducted between 2013 and 2015 across all school types, reported on in Byrne & Francis (2019), highlights a very positive appreciation among the 3,000 young people surveyed of the learning that comes from Religious Education. 85% of them indicated that studying religion in school helped them understand people of other religions; 84% agreed that we must respect all religions; 71% said that studying religion in school had shaped their views about religion (Byrne, Francis, & McKenna, 2019).

There is no need to review the detail of the 2000 and 2003 state syllabuses here now (see, Byrne, 2018a; 2017; 2013b). They are being renewed at this time as we shall see in the next section of this presentation. Brendan Carmody, however, has observed: 'Much has been achieved in giving the subject an improved academic status'. At the same time, more, he says, can be asked of the Religious Education classroom:

> To be truly educational, however, it is proposed that it needs to adopt the kind of self-reflectivity that moves to more authentic 'learning from' religion, thereby facilitating an intelligent, rational, and responsible student choice of worldview, religious or not. (Carmody, 2019, p. 561)

Framework for Junior Cycle, 2015

The *Framework for Junior Cycle, 2015* (Department of Education and Skills, 2015) underpins the innovative curriculum that has been gradually introduced for 12- to 15-year-olds across subjects and other learning experiences in all schools, including Catholic schools, in the Republic of Ireland. The Framework highlights the importance of 'valuing, acknowledging and affirming all the students' learning opportunities and experiences' (Department of Education and Skills, 2015, p. 8). It seeks to encourage a balance between the learning of subject knowledge and developing a wide range of skills and thinking abilities: 'In particular, learners will be enabled to use and analyse information in new and creative ways, to investigate issues, to explore, to think for themselves, to be creative in solving problems and to apply their learning to new challenges and situations (Department of Education and Skills, 2015, p. 7). With regard to the significance of the characteristic spirit of a school in implementing the Framework, the Minister for Education in a circular letter to schools at the time, and subsequent Ministers in each succeeding year, employing the same language, could not be clearer:

> Each school should use the Framework to plan a programme for the three years of junior cycle that meets the requirements set out in this circular, is informed by the particular learning needs and interests of the students, and reflects the characteristic spirit of the school. (Department of Education and Skills, 2016, 2.1)

A full range of new subject specifications, and assessment procedures, classroom-based and formative as well as summative, have now been completed. The final group of subject specifications, including Religious Education, have been made available for use in schools from September 2019 (NCCA, 2019). Without Religious Education it is very difficult to see how any school can fulfil its obligation to provide students with learning opportunities around all twenty-four Statements of Learning set out in the Framework (particularly SoLs 5, 6, 7 and 8). The background paper for Religious Education establishes the brief:

> To be an educational pursuit, religious education offered by the State has to go beyond simply offering information and facts about religion(s) and worldviews in a detached manner. It should facilitate young people engaging with their learning in ways that offer insights and wisdom for the student's own life. (NCCA, 2017, p. 6)

Junior Cycle Religious Education Specification

The new *Junior Cycle Religious Education Specification* (NCCA, 2019) fits directly within the Framework, helping 'to equip students with knowledge, understanding, skills, attitudes and values to support their life journey and enable them to participate in their communities and in the world as informed, respectful, responsible and caring members of society.' (NCCA, 2019, p. 6). As the rationale for the subject explains, it contributes in a unique way to the holistic development of the young person: 'It facilitates the intellectual, social, emotional, spiritual and moral development of students' (NCCA, 2019, p. 6). Religious Education, it suggests, has an irreplaceable role to play in the school curriculum for all young people whether they belong to a faith tradition or not:

> Religious Education provides a particular space for students to encounter and engage with the deepest and most fundamental questions relating to life, meaning and relationships. It encourages students to reflect, question, critique, interpret, imagine and find insight for their lives. (NCCA, 2019, p. 6)

While other subjects may sometimes venture into this territory, second-level Religious Education, adapted to the needs of adolescents, is at home here, engaging wholeheartedly and in a consistent and coherent manner with the questions young people have about the deepest things in life:

> Religious Education supports the development of students by helping them to explore how religious and other beliefs are expressed; engage with life's big questions; and reflect on moral values for life. (NCCA, 2019, p. 6)

Without the opportunity to engage with this dimension of life, the interior, spiritual and moral perspective within the human person is in danger of remaining underdeveloped. The important thing, Cullen suggests, is inviting young people into a conversation about what really matters to them (Cullen, 2017). The subject, therefore, must not only provide information about religions and other worldviews but also draw the young person into reflection on what is really important for them in the broad scheme of life, love, respect, responsibility, and care. 'The student's own experience and continuing search for meaning is encouraged and supported' (NCCA, 2019, p. 6).

Religious Education at second-level provides a genuinely broadening learning experience for young people whatever their family experiences and traditions. It encourages 'students to engage critically with belief systems and principles of moral behaviour which can serve as a foundation for decisions', and opens up a whole series of ways of understanding our relationships with others and with the world (NCCA, 2019, p. 6). Religious Education expands the horizons of adolescents, and ensures that their education engages them holistically and at so many levels beyond their own imagining.

Three Underpinnings: An Approach to Teaching and Learning

Before looking at the content around which the Religious Education specification unfolds, three methodological underpinnings at the heart of the specification need to be highlighted. Without these the depth of the engagement that is envisaged could be missed and the remit of the specification itself misunderstood. 'Enquiry', 'Exploration', and 'Reflection and Action' are three approaches to learning that lie deeply embedded in the tradition of religious education that is acknowledged here. These are built in as cross-cutting elements to be engaged with within and around topics, themes and material set-out in the specification. 'Enquiry' stimulates students' curiosity and prompts their engagement; 'Exploration' asks for a fuller examination of detail, 'questioning, probing, discussing, listening, imagining, interpreting and drawing conclusions, for the purpose of discovery.' (NCCA, 2019, p. 12). 'Reflection and Action' asks for more: it 'encourages students to examine what they have learned in order to gain deeper insight and understanding. It also enables students to consider how the learning relates to their lives and/or to the lives of others, thus prompting active and responsible citizenship' (NCCA, 2019, p. 12).

Building on Three Inter-connected Strands

There are three strands in the Junior Cycle Religious Education Specification. The first of these, 'Expressing beliefs', enables young people to reflect on and appreciate how people live out their beliefs, religious and others. This strand invites students to develop their 'ability to understand, respect, and appreciate how people's beliefs have been expressed in the past and continue to be expressed today though lifestyle, culture, rites and rituals, community building, social action and ways of life' (NCCA, 2019, p. 16). Students are encouraged for example, in Learning Outcome 1.6, to 'examine and appreciate how people give expression to religious belief in religious rituals, in formal places of worship and other sacred spaces.' 'Exploring questions' introduces the questions of meaning, the mystery and wonder at the heart of life, and the response people have made down through time: 'It focuses on students developing a set of knowledge, understanding, skills, attitudes and values that allows them to question, probe, interpret, analyse and reflect on the big questions, in dialogue with others' (NCCA, 2019, p. 18). The emphasis here is not just on posing deep questions. The impact the responses people make might have in their lives is emphasised, asking students, for example, to 'present stories of individuals or of groups in the history of two major world religions that have had a positive impact on the lives of people because of their commitment to living out their beliefs' (LO 2.8). In the third strand, 'Living our values', students are enabled 'to understand and reflect on the values that underlie actions and to recognise how moral decision-making works in their own lives and in the lives of others based on particular values and/or beliefs' (NCCA, 2019, p. 20). Leaning Outcome 3.8, for example, requires that students be able to 'explain how an understanding of care for the earth found in a major world religion promotes the wellbeing of all people and the planet and discuss its relevance for today.' Here, the teaching of Pope Francis in *Laudato Si'* comes quickly to mind. When appealing for care for the earth as our common home, he envisages the possibility of a unified and unifying approach that can put new practices in place in support of the planet and all its peoples:

> Today ... we have to realize that a true ecological approach always becomes a social approach; it must integrate questions of justice in debates on the environment, so as to hear both the cry of the earth and the cry of the poor. (Pope Francis, 2015, par. 80)

Junior Cycle Religious Education in the Catholic School

The Council for Catechetics of the Irish Episcopal Conference has led the response of the Catholic education sector to the Junior Cycle Religious Education specification, publishing firstly a document entitled *Religious Education and the Framework for Junior Cycle* from the Bishops' Conference in 2017 and then in September 2019 another, from the Council for Catechetics itself, with the title *Junior Cycle Religious Education in the Catholic School*. The first document sets out a positive response from the bishops to the framework:

> Religious Education has a positive role to play in supporting young people as they ask significant questions, begin to express their responses, and seek to formulate a caring and responsible way of living so that they can be at peace with themselves, with others, with creation and with God. (Irish Catholic Bishops' Conference, 2017, p. 7)

The more recent document assists trustees/patrons, boards of management, and senior management teams, as well as religious educators, to explore how Catholic schools can best respond to the new approach to Religious Education as part of its whole-school teaching and learning activities. Whether a school chooses for its students to avail of the subject as a fully state-assessed subject, the Bishops' Conference is clear that Religious Education will continue to be a two-hundred-hour subject in all Catholic schools.

Best practice in Religious Education (RE) is understood here, as in *Share the Good News*, as key: 'Excellent RE is at the very heart of a Catholic school's life and mission.' (Council for Catechetics of the Irish Episcopal Conference, 2019, p. 5; *SGN*, par. 147). The richest possible experience of Religious Education is championed, providing for, 'a solid educational, religious educational and Catholic understanding to underpin the teaching of RE in a Catholic school' (Council for Catechetics of the Irish Episcopal Conference, 2019, p. 4). Concerning the crucial issue of responding appropriately to the needs of Catholic students and all students, the Council could not be more transparent:

> Catholic schools have a responsibility to assist in providing for an interesting and richly-educative experience of RE for all students, including those of other faiths and those who have no religious faith. It should also be remembered that Catholic parents who send their children to Catholic schools have an expectation that their children's faith will be deepened in and through RE and the wider lived faith of the school. (Council for Catechetics of the Irish Episcopal Conference, 2019, p. 5)

What is always important is that whether in the Religious Education classroom, or as part of the liturgical and prayer life of the school, or when it comes to community building and outreach in justice to those in need (*SGN*, par. 36, noted above), faith is proposed rather than in any way imposed (Pope Francis, 2013):

> In a Catholic school, the faith tradition is presented to students in an open and invitational manner as a rich resource that can bring meaning to the young person's life.' (Council for Catechetics of the Irish Episcopal Conference, 2019, p. 6)

The 2019 document from the Council for Catechetics is brief and accessible and offers substantial guidance on how very many themes and resources from the Catholic faith community and its tradition can be used in bringing the Religious Education specification to life for Catholic pupils and for others. Teachers are reminded, here, of the very many ways in which they can, through investigation of Catholic faith, help young people enquire, explore, reflect and act in the world, becoming agents of their own formation and development (*SGN*, par. 104). As Amalee Meehan says:

> Good religious education is a well from which we can draw. It is a well that can help sustain young people of today in this age of identity, learning and wellbeing.' (Meehan, 2019, p. 515)

Catholic Education: Formal, Informal and Lifelong

The learning from this discussion of educational developments in second-level Religious Education is crucial. There is a conversation that needs to take place within Catholic education, in schools and beyond. It is not a case of the Catholic school in Ireland, primary or post-primary, simply doing what it always did. That might be a good starting place, but it must do what it does well in the world of today and for tomorrow, engaging with the needs of its young people and their families, in accord with a constantly reflected upon and ever-renewing characteristic spirit. Conversation with the school's young people and their families is indispensable. Belief in what the Catholic school seeks to offer all who belong within its community, for their own good and for the common good, locally and globally, is essential too. All this is held constantly alive within the school community by promoting openness to the inspiring presence of the Spirit and encouraging a response always focused on the young people in the school and their needs.

Additionally, the discussion around the new Religious Education specification suggests the need for ongoing conversation about Catholic education not only in schools but also among Catholic adults to equip themselves to participate more fully in the variety of settings, formal, informal and lifelong, where Catholic education can make a significant contribution to their lives. Adult and ongoing reflection is crucial so that members of the Catholic community can make themselves available to engage in discussion with young people and engage themselves fully in their own faith development. This is a good time to ask significant questions about our understanding of the role of Catholic education in the broadest sense into the future.

Catholic education, it seems, in order to offer its continually unfolding and unique gift to coming generations, will need to engage ever more fully:

- in promoting ongoing life-long consideration of the interior, spiritual and religious aspects of life, within the local Catholic community and beyond

- in encouraging personal enquiry, exploration, reflection and action, whatever the context
- in insisting on the dialogue between faith and reason, and embracing inter-religious and intercultural dialogue
- in demanding recognition of participants, and who they are, and of the journey they are on to discover truth and meaning and hope
- in respecting and developing appropriate approaches and resources for participants according to their age, stage of development and personal needs
- in establishing committed engagement with the living tradition, rediscovering the healing peace and the challenge set out by Jesus
- in requiring the Catholic school, and other Catholic environments to look at the whole-school/whole-community nature of their characteristic spirit
- in continuing to build up the theological as well as educational expertise of its teachers, school leaders, boards of management, trustee boards, parents and students, catechists, ministers, and members of its faith communities
- in seeking not just a renewal of the approach to religious education but also to prayer and liturgical celebration, community-building and service of neighbour in schools
- in supporting intergenerational engagement, between parents and family, teachers and students, parish leaders and ministers and members, in new and transformative ways for all
- in invoking always the Holy Spirit in prayer and in planning such that all enterprises are imbued with a Spirit-filled and forward-looking dynamic.

Coming Back to the Big Picture

And so we come back to how adult Catholics, reflecting on their own faith lives and on the questions they have, can contribute actively to the building up of the school family their young people belong to, and to the faith community they inhabit. Rediscovering the importance for their young people and for themselves of their home family, their faith family, their school family and their world family is key (Byrne, 2018d). Everyone involved has much to contribute in gathering up all that Catholic education can be.

It is essential, too, that Catholic education be understood as more than the provision of schools despite the enormous contribution they make. Catholic education is a lifelong process, which can be provided for in formal, non-formal and informal contexts, offering itself as a boon in the lives of those who engage with it. All of this requires committed, open, informed and forward-looking conversation – conversation in the academy, conversation among adults, conversation in Church, and conversation between home, parish and school. Catholic education is a space in which the mind and the heart is continually reawakened to the working of the Holy Spirt, who encourages reflection and action in the Church and in world for the good of all:

> Ask the Holy Spirit each day to help you experience anew the great message. Why not? You have nothing to lose, and he can change your life, fill it with light and lead it along a better path. He takes nothing away from you, but instead helps you to find all that you need, and in the best possible way. (Pope Francis, 2019, pars. 130-131)

Breathing In and Out God's Holy Spirit

To stay alive and energetic, Catholic education must continually breathe in and breathe out again. Catholic education breathes in and out the Spirit of God. It inhales the Spirit of God's love and exhales wisdom, joy, love, hope, and the peace that God gifts us within our lives. It gathers in all the challenges. Catholic education helps people enquire, explore, reflect, act, act again, and begin again. It breathes in the Spirit of love of God and love of neighbour, and breathes out respect, justice, truth, generosity, care, service, and loving kindness. Catholic education breathes in and out the Spirit of faith, hope, and love for the transformation of the whole world and its peoples.

References

Anderson, B., Byrne, G. & Cullen, S., 'Religious Pluralism, Education, and Citizenship in Ireland', in E. Aslan., R. Ebrahim, & M. Hermansen (eds), *Islam, Religions, and Pluralism in Europe*, Dordecht: Springer, 2016, pp. 161–172.

Byrne, G., 'Lifelong Religious Education in Home, Parish and Other Educational Environments', in A. Hession & P. Kieran (eds), *Exploring Religious Education: Catholic Religious Education in an Intercultural Europe*, Dublin: Veritas, 2008, pp. 35–41.

Byrne, G., 'Communicating Faith in Ireland: From Commitment, through Questioning to New Beginnings', in J. Sullivan (ed), *Communicating Faith*, Washington, DC: University of America Press, 2011, pp. 261–276.

Byrne, G., 'Pluralism, Dialogue and Religious Education in "Share the Good News: National Directory for Catechesis in Ireland"', in G. Byrne & P. Kieran (eds) *Toward Mutual Ground: Pluralism, Religious education and Diversity in Irish Schools*, Dublin: Columba, 2013a, pp. 147–155.

Byrne, G., 'Encountering and Engaging with Religion and Belief: The Contemporary Contribution of Religious Education in Schools', in G. Byrne & P. Kieran (eds) *Toward Mutual Ground: Pluralism, Religious Education and Diversity in Irish schools*, Dublin: Columba, 2013b, pp. 207–224.

Byrne, G., 'Religious Education in Catholic Second-level Schools in Ireland Today: An invitation to Love, Understanding, Commitment, Hospitality and Dialogue', in M. Shanahan (ed), *Does Religious Education Matter?* London/New York: Routledge, 2017, pp. 114–129.

Byrne, G., 'The Place of Religious Education in the Changing Landscape That Is Ireland Today', in S. Whittle (ed), *Religious Education in Catholic Schools: Perspectives from Ireland and the UK*, Oxford: Peter Lang, 2018a, pp. 33–50.

Byrne, G., 'Religion and Education: A Changing and Challenging Relationship', in B. Mooney (ed), *Ireland's Yearbook of Education 2018/2019*, Dublin: Education Matters, 2018b, pp. 32-38. Available online at: https://issuu.com/educationmattersie/docs/irelands_yearbook_of_education_2018_fd142f04af68b3?e=36219384/66963017

Byrne, G., 'Religious Education in Catholic Second-level Schools in Ireland: Drawing on Our Heritage, Living in the Present, Anticipating New Directions', in S. Whittle (ed), *Researching Catholic education: Contemporary perspectives*, Dordrecht: Springer, 2018c, pp. 205–217.

Gareth Byrne

Byrne, G., 'Catholic Schools Engaging with Family Today: Inspiration from the World Meeting of Families 2018', in L. Franchi (ed), *Catholicism, Culture, Education*, Paris: L'Harmattan, 2018d, pp. 25–33.

G. Byrne & Francis, L.J. (eds), *Religion and Education: The Voices of Young People in Ireland*, Dublin: Veritas, 2019.

Byrne, G., Francis, L.J. & McKenna, U., 'Exploring the Social Benefit of Religious Education in Post-primary Schools within the Republic of Ireland: An Empirical Enquiry among 13- to 15-year-olds', in G. Byrne & L.J. Francis (eds), *Religion and Education: The Voices of Young People in Ireland*, Dublin: Veritas, 2019, pp. 201–221.

Carmody, B., 'Ecclesial to Public Space: Religion in Irish Secondary Schools', in *Religious Education* 114/5, (2019), pp. 551–564. DOI: 10.1080/00344087.2019.1643273.

CEIST: Catholic Education, an Irish Schools Trust, *CEIST Strategic Plan 2017-2020: Living Out Our Founding Mission and Catholic Ethos*, 2017. Available at: www.ceist.ie

Congregation for the Clergy, *General Catechetical Directory*, Vatican City: Libreria Editrice Vaticana, 1971.

Congregation for the Clergy, *General Directory for Catechesis*, Vatican City: Libreria Editrice Vaticana, 1997.

Council for Catechetics of the Irish Episcopal Conference, *Junior Cycle Religious Education in Catholic Schools*, Dublin: Veritas, 2019.

Cullen, S., 'Interpreting "Between Privacies": Religious Education as a Conversational Activity', in M. Shanahan (ed), *Does Religious Education Matter?* London/New York: Routledge, 2017, pp. 37–47.

Cullen, S., 'Turn Up the Volume: Hearing What the Voices of Young People are Saying to Religious Education', in G. Byrne & L.J. Francis (eds), *Religion and Education: The Voices of Young People in Ireland*, Dublin: Veritas, 2019, pp. 271–283.

Department of Education and Science, *Junior Certificate Religious Education Syllabus*, Dublin: The Stationery Office, 2000.

Department of Education and Science, *Leaving Certificate Religious Education Syllabus*, Dublin: The Stationery Office, 2003.

Department of Education and Skills, *Framework for Junior Cycle, 2015*, 2015. Available at: www.education.ie/en/Publications/Policy-Reports/Framework-for-Junior-Cycle-2015.pdf

Department of Education and Skills, *Circular Letter 0024/2016*, 2016. Available at: https://www.education.ie/en/Circulars-and-Forms/Archived-Circulars/cl0024_2016.pdf

Government of Ireland, *Education Act, 1998*, Dublin: The Irish Statute Book, 1998.

Government of Ireland, *Education (Admission to Schools) Act, 2018*, Dublin: The Irish Statute Book, 2018.

Irish Catholic Bishops' Conference, *Religious Education and the Framework for Junior Cycle*, Dublin: Veritas, 2017.

Irish Episcopal Conference, *Share the Good News: National Directory for Catechesis in Ireland* [SGN], Dublin: Veritas, 2010.

Le Chéile: A Catholic Schools Trust, *Living Our Le Chéile Charter*, 2019. Available at: https://lecheiletrust.ie

MacMillan J., 'Symphony No. 5: "Le Grand Inconnu" (The Great Unknown)', for Chamber Choir, Chorus and Orchestra', Boosey & Hawkes, 2018.

Meehan, A., 'Wellbeing in the Irish Junior Cycle: The Potential of Religious Education', in *Irish Educational Studies* 38/4, (2019), pp. 501–518. DOI: 10.1080/03323315.2019.1656100.

Moorhead, J., 'Into the Unknown: A New Work by Britain's Leading Catholic Composer Draws Breath from the Holy Spirit', in *The Tablet*, 31 August 2019, p. 18.

Mullally, A., *Guidelines for the Inclusion of Students of Different Beliefs in Catholic Secondary Schools*. Dublin: JMB/AMCSS Secretariat, 2019.

National Council for Curriculum and Assessment, *Background Paper and Brief for the Review of Junior Cycle Religious Education*, 2017. Available at: www.ncca.ie/media/3432/re-background-paper-for-website.pdf

National Council for Curriculum and Assessment, *Junior Cycle Religious Education Specification*, 2019. Available at: https://ncca.ie/media/3785/junior-cycle-religious-education-specification.pdf

Pope Francis, *Evangelii Gaudium: On the Proclamation of the Gospel in Today's World*, 2013. Available at: http://www.vatican.va

Pope Francis, *Laudato Si': On Care for Our Common Home*, 2015. Available at: http://www.vatican.va

Pope Francis, *Christus Vivit: Apostolic Exhortation to Young People and to the Entire People of God*, 2019. Available at: http://www.vatican.va

Ryan, A., *Pastoral Ministry in Changing Times: The Past, Present and Future of the Catholic Church in Ireland*, Dublin: Messenger Publications, 2019.

Sweetman, B., 'Dominant Public View of Religious Persons as Less Intelligent is Lamentable', in *Irish Times*, 25 June 2019. Available at: www.irishtimes.com/opinion/dominant-public-view-of-religious-persons-as-less-intelligent-is-lamentable-1.3935842

Sweetman, B. & Byrne, G., 'What Does a Religious or Spiritual Irish Adult Look Like?', *RTÉ Brainstorm*, 2 Sept 2019. Available at: www.rte.ie/brainstorm/2019/0830/1071822-what-does-a-religious-or-spiritual-irish-adult-look-like/

Part II:

～～～～～～

Religious and Spiritual Underpinnings

Chapter 4

~~~~~~~~~~~~~~~~

What Models of Human/Spiritual Development Should Inform Catholic Education in Our Time?

Anne Hession

Introduction

Over the past fifty years, Catholic religious educators have drawn on various models of the human from the psychology of religion for their understanding of the human and spiritual development of their students. James Fowler's stage theory of faith-development has probably had the most influence among Catholic educators and Erik H. Erikson's account of the formation of personal identity in the life cycle has been widely adopted, particularly his account of the tension between basic trust and basic mistrust in infancy as the basis for all religious development in later life (Astley, 2009; Wright, 1982; Zock, 1990). In recent years, there has been a broadening of the psychology of religion to include the study of the psychology of spirituality (Hood, 2012; Watts, 2017). Furthermore, while the distinction between transpersonal psychology and the psychology of religion is fading, there is a call to broaden the psychology of religion by engaging in a more meaningful way with new methodologies that enable more precise study of the contemplative domain (Friedman, Krippner, Riebel, & Johnson, 2012). From this standpoint, it is important that the psychological models of human and spiritual development that currently inform Catholic education are enriched by new developments in this field. However, Catholic educators require a critical conceptual framework that will enable them to evaluate whether emerging models of human and spiritual development are supportive of Catholic faith.

Why Is This Important?

As a Catholic educator working in religious education and theology at university since the turn of the millennium, it has become increasingly difficult to connect with students using the typical language(s) of Catholic theology. This breakdown in communication has emerged from the fact that students have begun to think through a different framework, a different language. In short, students think and speak in psychological terms in order to express their understanding of their own human and spiritual development. Hence it is reasonable to conclude that Catholic education must interact increasingly with the language of psychology or it will struggle to attract the attention of students who are growing up in a psychological (in the sense of psychologising) culture. The challenge for Catholic educators today, is how to properly communicate about how Christians experience and understand what it means to be human, with students who have begun to think in terms which are deeply couched with psychological assumptions.

Western Spirituality: A Psychological Model

A quick perusal through the psychology, spirituality or well-being section in your local bookstore will confirm that psychology provides the most common conceptual framework for spirituality in our time. However, since the rise of psychology as a science within the academy over the past century, more or less disassociated from philosophy and religion, the Christian concept of humanity has increasingly been side-lined by a number of new concepts of humanity. Phillip Rieff was one of the first to write of the cultural moral revolution set in train by the advent of science-based, academic psychology in the nineteenth and early twentieth centuries and its significance for the history of Western culture and personality. Rieff's book – *The Triumph of the Therapeutic* – offered the intriguing thesis that the language of faith previously controlled by the religions has been taken over by the language of psychology which is now proposing an alternative language of faith (Rieff, 1987 [1966]). This psychological language has now become the source of many of our collective habits and actions. According to Rieff, the surrounding culture of our Western societies, now proffers an ideal character type, designated by him as the 'therapeutic'. The therapeutic is one whose personality is organised around the anti-cultural predicate of the letting go of all settled convictions; whose ethics are based on releasing oneself from the inherited religious controls; whose gospel is self-fulfilment; and whose primary goal is 'an intensely private sense of well-being to be generated in the living of life itself'. As such, the therapeutic revolts against all doctrinal traditions which advocate the salvation of self through identification with the purposes of the community. For him or her, salvation is amplitude in living itself. Rieff's final words, written over fifty years ago, seem extraordinarily prescient when viewed through the lens of our contemporary culture:

> That a sense of well-being has become the end, rather than a by-product of striving after some superior communal end, announces a fundamental change of focus in the entire cast of our culture – toward a human condition about which there will be nothing further to say in terms of the old style of despair and hope. (1987, p. 261)

Throwing the Baby Out with the Bathwater?

Clearly, the process of identity formation in postmodern cultures is much more complex than in the late twentieth century, when Rieff announced the rise of his 'therapeutic man'. Students in Catholic schools are constructing their identities out of a wide variety of resources in twenty-first century pluralistic societies, with the internet assuming a huge role in the process of identify formation for teenage students in particular. However, it could be argued that many of the primary sources for students' identity, and for their inner life in particular, continue to be framed by psychological assumptions. For example, the infiltration into school curricula and popular magazines of the psychological concept of 'well-being' is one way in which students are now being invited to think about their own development and overall health. As a result, Catholic educators must continue to re-present the classic Christian spiritual path in a way consistent with the insights of modern psychology, if it is to appear relevant to today's students.

This reality notwithstanding, the touchstone for the Catholic educator should be the *Christian* concept of maturity and humaneness. This is because, ideally, the Christian vision of personal development is the cornerstone of the Catholic school, shaping the kind of personal formation offered to students there. But is that always the case? Is it not true that student teachers study a considerable amount of developmental psychology in their professional education, without much analysis of whether this knowledge is compatible with the vision of the human from a Christian perspective? And is it not the case that educators adopt theories of psychological, spiritual and faith development without interrogating whether these models are fully compatible with the Christian vision of the person and of the central role that religion should play in the development of a Christian's self- identity? This essay will outline three areas where a hermeneutic of suspicion about such theories is in order.

Three Cautions

A first caution concerns the individualist bias in the field of psychology of religion and spirituality (PRS). All inquiry in PRS involves methodological, epistemological, ethical, and ontological assumptions that influence the shape of the work produced. In their review of the philosophical assumptions that inform PRS today, Nelson and Slife found that most mainstream PRS researchers still work from a set of assumptions that are drawn from the philosophies of naturalism and positivism. They call the combination of these philosophies 'positivistic naturalism' and discuss its effects on the scientific practice of PRS, noting that 'alternative philosophies of science for investigating religion and spirituality are rarely acknowledged' (Nelson & Slife, 2012, p. 27). This means that positivist naturalism, while under some attack, still remains 'the core philosophy for most of psychology' (Nelson, 2009, p. 65). One important implication from this approach to research is that positivist naturalism will tend to pit the individual against the social. This is termed 'individual essentialism'. As Nelson and Slife explain:

> ...individual essentialism is the Positivist Naturalism position that in the human realm the primary reality is that of the individual. Relationships and group membership may be important but do not make up what is essential about the human person. (Nelson & Slife, 2012, p. 26; Benhabib, 1992)

As a result, the ethical slant of many PRS theories will tend to be individualistic: they tend to interpret spirituality in an exclusively 'inner' way, and will therefore lend support to individualist rather than communal models of spirituality. For example, the focus on consciousness as the key to spiritual development in many transpersonal theories may support an individualistic conception of spirituality, as the relational and communal aspects of spirituality are not given the attention they deserve. Rothberg argues that this latter emphasis reflects the general modern appropriation and marginalisation of spirituality, in which spirituality has been relegated to the private domain thus removing it from the public square (Rothberg, 1993).

A second caution relates to the role religion is thought to play in the development of the self or self-identity in some of the psychological theories currently used by Catholic educators. More specifically, there is a need to examine the extent to which religion is deemed to be an adequate basis for the achievement of personal identity *throughout* the life cycle in some of these theories. Schweitzer has demonstrated, for example, that for writers such as Erik H. Erikson and Jürgen Habermas, while religion has a role to play in the early stages of human development, their vision of a more mature post-conventional self is not necessarily supported by religious worldviews or by religious traditions (Schweitzer, 2003). In other words, this kind of framework encourages the perception that one's religious tradition is redundant once one becomes an adult. The question then emerges as to why one would bother to remain immersed in the creed, code and cult of one's own religion? The formative role of the narratives of Christian faith *throughout* the Christian life cycle seems to be cast aside.

A third caution relates to the common discourse surrounding the idea of spirituality in contemporary Western societies, in particular, the way in which some conceptions of 'spirituality' and 'well-being' may have been co-opted by neoliberal forces, aided precisely by the discipline of psychology. In this regard, the thesis of Carrette and King is worth examining, although it does need to be balanced with other perspectives. In their challenging book – *Selling Spirituality: The Silent Takeover of Religion* – they argue that the concept of the spiritual was shaped in the modern period by a process of *individualisation*, linked to the rise of psychology as a discipline and then, more recently, by the rise of neoliberalism which has led to an increasing *corporatisation* of spirituality in Western culture. Examining the growing commercialisation of religion in the form of the popular notion of 'spirituality', as it is found in education, health-care, counselling, business training, management theory and marketing, they claim that in advanced capitalist societies, the market mentality of neoliberal capitalism is now infiltrating the human expression of spirituality. Such infiltration has culminated in domesticating religious traditions, practices and communities 'in terms of an increasingly homogenised, sanitised and socially pacifying conception of spirituality' (Carrette & King, 2005, p. x). There is a danger, they insist, that such psychologised discourses of spirituality encourage people to conceptualise their spirituality in an individualist manner and in a manner that fits the corporatist values of a consumer society, which effectively displaces questions of social justice. As they explain:

> With the emergence of capitalist spirituality we are seeing ... an erasure of the wider social and ethical concerns associated with religious traditions and communities and the subordination of 'the religious' and the ethical to the realm of economics, which is now rapidly replacing science (just as science replaced theology in a previous era), as the dominant mode of authoritative discourse within society. (2005, pp. 4–5)

One of the features of these newly emergent conceptions of spirituality that Carrette and King wish to challenge is what they term 'their essentially accommodationist orientation'. This means that instead of challenging people, capitalist spiritualties encourage passive acceptance of the reigning social, economic and political mores of society and do little to upset a lifestyle of self-interest and consumption. This contrasts with many religious spiritualties which tend to be more subversive to the status quo, especially when it supports social inequality.

Carrette and King's thesis that contemporary psychological theories of spirituality both shape and are directed towards the ideology of the neoliberal world is probably overstated. It could be argued that their sociological critique of the modern psychologies and of modern conceptions of spirituality fails to appreciate the extent to which many of these psychological conceptions of spirituality are *responses* to the forces and trends of capitalist societies (Browning & Cooper, 2004). Nevertheless, their thesis does challenge us to reflect on whether the integration of psychological discourse into the realm of contemporary spirituality does offer support to models of humanity that over-emphasise the idea of an isolated, consuming self to the detriment of an awareness of social interdependence and social justice.

What is Particular to the Catholic View?

The Catholic approach to a dialogue between psychology, religion and spirituality is that any knowledge that we can discover about human development or spirituality from the sciences should actually help us to know Jesus Christ and, in turn, know humanity in the light of faith in him (O'Callaghan, 2016). Through his incarnation the Son of God has united himself with every person; hence, to be fully Christian implies and necessitates that one become fully human. As Hans Küng has explained, being Christian 'is not an addition to being human' but 'an elevation or – better – a transfiguration of the human' (1977, p. 601). Therefore, there should be no inherent contradiction between good scientific knowledge about human development and the insights of Christian faith. However, a Catholic approach to PRS will always be mindful of the fact that the norm for Christian development or spiritual maturity is the unique theological anthropology made possible through Christian faith.

Catholic theology starts from the conviction that human development is shaped by a very particular type of spiritual transformation – a project of grace entirely directed to the Father through the Son in the Holy Spirit (Balswick, King & Reimer, 2005). In other words, the path of personal or spiritual development undertaken by the Christian ultimately has its basis in God's transcendent grace. The personal depths of every person and their vocational call to a particular life in the world has its source in the Spirit of Jesus Christ. This means that while the terminology of conventional academic psychology may be very useful in describing human development, it cannot be expected to take account of the role of the Holy Spirit, in the process of personal transformation. Furthermore, as Nelson reminds us, transcendence, 'typically manifests itself in the different rather than the uniform' (Nelson, 2009, p. 196). This means that all theories that postulate common patterns of development in the psychological domain will be used with great caution by Catholic educators and with an appreciation that what such theories offer should never be used as a framework within which to pigeonhole people or groups.

Catholic spiritualties offer a unique set of lenses within which to approach life. For example, many Catholic spiritual practices are concerned with developing the freedom of human persons, releasing them from the prison of self-made patterns, so as to open up the mental space in which the Holy Spirit is able to operate. Within this space, the human mind is shaped by something additional to the patterns that conventional psychology holds valid for humankind. Therefore, while religious spiritual activities may enhance our well-being and health, this is not the primary goal of these practices. The goal is to reach a level of humaneness in which the person is continually open to being healed, transformed and empowered by the Spirit of Jesus.

The Christian concepts of divine providence and of vocation suggest that full Christian maturity is having the ability to stand in the integrity of one's own unique selfhood in dialogue with God's revelation throughout one's life. In other words, Christian spirituality is understood as a *life-long journey* to unity with God in which God reveals God and the person reveals their self through the mediation of the unique and specific context of their own life. In this understanding, life is about the fullness of human and divine freedom coming together in partnership, as each person makes their unique journey to God.

The self-identity of the Catholic will therefore be based on immersion in their religious tradition in infancy, in adolescence and right throughout adulthood. In other words, the constitution of the self at every stage depends on the great Christian narratives and traditions, whose meaning engender a new self-understanding of oneself as a follower of Christ. In the course of normal Christian development then, children and adults will be introduced to the narratives of the Bible, and the narratives of Christian faith as lived by believers down through the ages. In this way, religious educators in Catholic schools gift their students with a framework within which to develop their unique identity as Christian *throughout their lives* (Schweitzer, 2003, Nelson 2009).

Towards a Critical Conceptual Framework

In 1987, Don S. Browning published his *Religious Thought and the Modern Psychologies: A Critical Conversation in the Theology of Culture,* in which he articulated the thesis that modern psychologies are not strictly scientific but are instead mixed disciplines blending strictly scientific psychological insights with both ethical and metaphysical assumptions. Browning proposes that the modern psychologies are best treated as practical moral philosophies rather than as strictly scientific psychologies. The distinction between scientific psychologies and philosophy is easy to maintain in the case of experimental psychology; it is a distinction that is more difficult to maintain in the case of the clinical psychologies which are concerned with the interpretation of patterns, modalities, themes and narratives in human experience. Browning explains that to do this, clinical psychologies often proceed by 'correlating internally perceived introspective knowledge with externally observed patterns, themes, and modalities', such that the clinical psychologies are more properly understood as '*interpretive*' rather than 'explanatory' disciplines. This helps us to appreciate that that both religion and psychology make their interpretive judgments from differing frameworks of meaning (Browning & Cooper, 2004, p. 5). This understanding does not mean that we overlook what is scientific about these psychologies: they do yield some objective insights into the human condition. However, it is important to distinguish what is scientific from what is moral and quasi-religious in these theories so as to critically evaluate the contribution of each of these perspectives.

In the second edition of Browning's book (2004) Browning draws on Cooper, to argue in support of a method of 'critical hermeneutics' or 'hermeneutic realism' in order to judge whether or not the philosophies that underpin modern psychologies are compatible with Christian faith. This involves a 'critical correlational' analysis, comparing and contrasting the implicit images of the human offered by psychology with Christian perspectives of the human condition. While Browning and Cooper take a moral approach to the critical conversation between theology and modern psychologies, they maintain that a more metaphysical approach to the philosophical claims behind any psychological model is not only valuable, but also necessary (Browning & Cooper, 2004).

Browning and Cooper propose that any adequate hermeneutical dialogue between Christian theology and scientific psychological models of religion and spirituality will require a critical analysis of the ethical and metaphysical horizons of such models. Catholic educators will interrogate, for example, the narratives of salvation that lie behind any particular theory. What does the theory propose as the goal of human development and is this compatible with the Christian ideal of loving one's neighbour as oneself? Furthermore, Catholic educators might explore the deep metaphors (e.g. control, detachment, care, joy, self-regard, and regard for the other) and views of human nature in psychological models and discern whether there are points of contact between Christian thought and the metaphors lying behind such models. A primary question, for example, is the extent to which the deep metaphors in any psychological theory support the degree of freedom and self-transcendence necessary for Christian faith.

Browning and Cooper incorporate 'mutually critical correlations' in their use of theories from the psychology of religion and spirituality. In other words, they propose that a critical conversation between the vision and experience of Catholic spiritual maturity and the implied cosmology, metaphysical system and ethical framework of psychological theories should be a *two-way* conversation. On the one hand, educators working in a Catholic school will bring a Catholic theological lens to scientific psychological/spiritual models. On the other hand, critical hermeneutics will examine the ways in which psychological/spiritual models can potentially critique and enhance the Catholic understanding of human and spiritual development.

Where the Catholic Tradition
Speaks to PRS Models

Catholic theological anthropology plays a mediating role in relating scientific theories of psychological development and spirituality to Christian doctrine. It affords a meeting ground where the connections and disconnections between the model of spirituality proposed and the requirements of an explicitly *Christian* spirituality can be discerned (Watts, 2017). For example, where there appears to be a simple correlation between the language of psychology and the language of theological anthropology, careful discernment may be required. For example, O' Callaghan explains how in modern discourse 'soul language' is often reflected upon not in metaphysical, but in subjectivistic terms. In other words, most psychological models will use the term 'soul' to describe the subjective experience of a level of consciousness (i.e. phenomenological language) or simply the subjective experience of oneself as having depth or an inner drive toward relatedness. Note for example, Moore's description of soul: 'Soul is not a thing, but a quality, or a dimension of experiencing life and ourselves. It has to do with depth, value, relatedness, heart and personal substance' (1992, p. 6). This contrasts with the metaphysical language of ontology that can be used in Catholic systematic theology and in which the distinction between the natural and the supernatural is maintained (O' Callaghan, 2016).

The perspective of Christian theology also means that Catholic educators will favour a socially engaged construction of the term 'spirituality' in contrast to the individualist conceptions that dominate the modern psychologies. This means that Catholic educators will seek out contemporary social models of the person, where the self is understood to be inherently relational and interdependent. This leads to an ideal of human flourishing that includes care for people on the margins and a concern for the well-being of the created environment as an integral part of what it means to have a *Christian* spirituality in our time.

Where PRS Models Might Speak to
Catholic Educators

Contemporary PRS theory and models offer rich resources for the work of religious education in Catholic schools. Essentially, PRS enables a greater understanding of the psychological dynamics within which the process of grace works in the self-transcending, transformative process of human development. In recent years, for example, advances in modern neuroimaging techniques have contributed extremely valuable data which enables a greater understanding of the human response to meditative experiences (Newberg & d'Aquili, 2001). This has led to a regeneration of interest in the Christian contemplative tradition and the rediscovery of traditional meditative techniques for a new generation. Similarly, some contemporary models of spiritual development are immensely helpful for educators concerned with identifying pathological elements in religious understanding and practice (Wilber, 2017). This should be of particular interest to educators who encounter students who may have difficulty moving beyond their present level of psychological and spiritual development and who need understanding and help.

Summary and Conclusion

The discipline of PRS is an essential resource for religious educators in Catholic schools tasked with explaining the vision of humanity offered by Christian theology to twenty-first century students. Nevertheless, Catholic educators need a robust method for interpreting emerging psychological models: to understand the insights they give them, to comprehend the proper area of their competence, and most importantly of all, to discern their limits in helping them convey the vision of transformation by being 'in Christ' that is their gift to the next generation. This chapter has drawn attention to the danger for Catholic educators of presenting the gospel only to the extent that it has therapeutic potential, and to downplay the prophetic and counter-cultural elements of the message. Catholic education will always strive to enable students to respond to a character ideal that necessitates the integration of the self into communal purposes, and to develop a faith that in all our spiritual development it is Christ who does the transforming and who leads us onwards to unity with God at the end of our lives.

References

Astley, J., 'The Psychology of Faith Development', in M. De Souza, L.J. Francis, J. O'Higgins-Norman & D.G. Scott (eds), *International Handbook of Education for Spirituality, Care and Wellbeing*, Dordrecht: Springer, 2009.

Balswick, J., King, P. & Reimer K., *The Reciprocating Self: Human Development in Theological Perspective*, Downers Grove, IL: InterVarsity Press, 2005.

Benhabib, S., *Situating the Self: Gender, Community and Postmodernism in Contemporary Ethics*, New York: Routledge, 1992.

Browning, D.S., *Religious Thought and the Modern Psychologies: A Critical Conversation in the Theology of Culture*, Philadelphia, PA: Fortress Press, 1987.

Browning, D.S. & Cooper, T.D., *Religious Thought and the Modern Psychologies*, 2nd edition, Augsburg: Fortress, 2004.

Carrette, J. & King, R., *Selling Spirituality: The Silent Takeover of Religion*, London & New York: Routledge, 2005.

Friedman, H., Krippner, S., Riebel, L. & Johnson, C., 'Models of Spiritual Development', in L. J. Miller (ed.), *The Oxford Handbook of Psychology and Spirituality*, New York: Oxford University Press, 2012.

Hood, R.W., 'The History and Current State of Research on Psychology of Religion', in L.J. Miller (ed.), *The Oxford Handbook of Psychology and Spirituality*, New York: Oxford University Press, 2012.

Küng, H., *On Being a Christian*, trans. E. Quinn, London: Collings, 1977.

Moore, T., *The Care of the Soul: A Guide for Cultivating Depth and Sacredness in Everyday Life*, New York: Walker, 1992.

Nelson, J.M., *Psychology, Religion and Spirituality*, New York: Springer, 2009.

Nelson, J.M. & Slife, B.D., 'Theoretical and Epistemological Foundations', in L. J. Miller (ed.), *The Oxford Handbook of Psychology and Spirituality*, New York: Oxford University Press, 2012.

Newberg, A. & d'Aquili, E., *Why God Won't Go Away: Brain Science and the Biology of Belief*, New York: Ballantine, 2001.

O'Callaghan, P., *Children of God in the World: An Introduction to Theological Anthropology*, Washington, DC: The Catholic University of America Press, 2016.

Rieff, P., *The Triumph of the Therapeutic: Uses of Faith after Freud*, Chicago: University of Chicago Press, 1987 [1966].

Rothberg, D., 'The Crisis of Modernity and the Emergence of Socially Engaged Spirituality', in *REVision*, 15, (1993), pp. 105-14.

Schweitzer, F., 'The Religious Dimension of the Self', in R.R. Osmer & F. Schweitzer, *Religious Education between Modernization and Globalization*, Grand Rapids, MI/Cambridge, UK: William B. Eerdmans Publishing Company, 2003.

Watts, F., *Psychology, Religion and Spirituality*, New York: Cambridge University Press, 2017.

Wilber, K., *The Religion of Tomorrow*, Boulder, CO: Shambhala Publications, 2017.

Wright, J.E., *Erikson, Identity and Religion*, New York: Seabury, 1982.

Zock, H., *A Psychology of Ultimate Concern: Erik H Erikson's Contribution to the Psychology of Religion*, Amsterdam: Rodopi, 1990.

Chapter 5

∿∿∿∿∿∿∿∿

Religious Enquiry: A Valid Pathway to Human Knowledge

David Kennedy

Introduction

Is there no truth in religion? Do religious encounters not contain a claim to truth which is certainly different from that of science, but just as certainly is not inferior to it? This chapter makes the claim that religious education is a valid pathway to human knowledge. It argues that reason and enquiry in the context of religious education, as in other areas of education, are reliable routes to meaning, knowledge and truth. While it must be acknowledged that there is more to religious education than the pursuit of religious knowledge and truth by way of religious or spiritual enquiry, this chapter argues that at a fundamental level there has been a failure to appreciate the claim to truth of religious education, particularly in terms of the validity of religious belief in any objective sense. The chapter demonstrates that such neglect is evident in contemporary programmes such as the recently proposed *Education about Religions and Beliefs and Ethics* programme for primary schools in the Republic of Ireland (National Council for Curriculum and Assessment [NCCA], 2015). It is argued that such positions are a consequence of the contemporary context in which religious education is taking place, a context which has ultimately led to the erosion of objective truth in terms of religious belief. Consequently, such an erosion has significant implications in terms of which religion(s), if any, young people are introduced to or *how* they are introduced to it.

A 'Post'-Secular and 'Post'-Christian Context?

When it comes to matters of truth and knowledge within religious education, there is an ongoing debate (Hand 2004; Wright 2004; Wright 2007; Boeve 2012; Aldridge 2017; Hannam 2019). One must, however, at one and the same time put aside such angst and recognise that it is reasonable to expect that any traditional academic subject should be capable of being made good sense of as a rational form of knowledge or enquiry focused upon the discernment of truths of one sort or another concerning the world or human affairs. For a variety of epistemological, social, ethical and pedagogical reasons, the curricular area of Religious Education has been somewhat problematic in this regard (Carr, 1994; Hand, 2004). Such problems arise from the fact that there has been significant confusion, prompted by the work of empiricists, positivists and deconstructionist thinkers, which has been allowed to obscure the nature of religious enquiry as a viable rational enterprise.

Furthermore, the validity of ultimate truth claims as well as the manner in which one engages with them has been influenced dramatically by accelerated secularisation, de-traditionalisation and pluralism of belief; particularly the perspective of absolute or radical pluralism, the view that moves towards the domestication of religions and other stances for living by treating all truth claims as being equally valid responses to the 'Real', which has been facilitated by the insights of both modernist and postmodernist thinkers. In this context, the realm of religious knowledge and the essence of its relationship to religious experience has become a highly contested area. In fact, theologians such as Lieven Boeve (2012) describe the contemporary context in which educational discourse is taken place across Europe as being 'post-Christian and post-secular'.

It is important not to misinterpret the term 'post', here. The term 'post' does not infer 'after', that is that both realities and their effects have disappeared. Rather, in Europe, there has been a significant shift in the way in which people relate to religion and to the secularisation thesis. Within this cultural context, the above categories, and the use of the term 'post', are attempting to convey that our relation to the Christian faith and to secularisation has changed (Boeve, 2012).

Boeve (2012) states that the category 'post-Christian' suggests that,

> although the traces of Christian faith in our society and culture, in our collective and individual identity formation, are still present in abundance, at the same time the Christian faith is no longer the obvious, accepted background that grants meaning. (p. 145)

Similarly, the category 'post-secular' directs attention to the fact that 'the presuppositions of the secularisation thesis no longer apply' (p. 145). In other words, the central presupposition of the secularisation thesis, that modernism in society leads to the almost inevitable disappearance of religion, has emerged as being an erroneous position. However, it is important to clarify that the categories 'post-Christian' and 'post-secular' have not escaped criticism. Writers such as Dermot Lane (2013) have expressed a discomfort with such categories. Lane argues that to talk about a 'post-secular-society' is problematic insofar as 'it implies a chronological development where religion went away for a time and has now come back (p. 8). Whilst expressing this concern Lane explains that one can empathise with writers in using such categories, particularly when the complexity of the reality that they are attempting to mediate is recognised.

The emergence and complexity of this new European context has a direct correlation with the growing influence of postmodern culture during the late twentieth century and the early twenty-first century. Postmodern culture is characterised by a worldview that is sceptical of explanations claiming to be valid for all groups, cultures, traditions or races (Touhy, 2013, p. 177). Rather, it emphasises the importance of the relative truths held by each person. Consequently, there is a dismissal of metanarratives and an elevation of the concrete experience of each individual. Put simply, from a postmodern perspective there is no validity to claims of 'Ultimate Truth'. Rather, each person interprets reality for themselves and it is through this hermeneutic, this 'construct', that the human person 'creates' meaning. Such a position gives rise to fallible and relative understandings by negating abstract principles and universal truths as valid knowledge.

According to David Tuohy (2013), the effects of this postmodern approach can be observed in four aspects of modern culture: (1) pluralism of beliefs, (2) individualisation, (3) secularisation, and (4) radicalisation. In this context, social theorists such as the German philosopher Jürgen Habermas, particularly in his later writings (Cf. Habermas, 2010; Mendieta & Van Antwerpen, 2011), have called for a 'new dialogue between religious reason and secular reason' (cited in

Lane, 2013, p. 13). Habermas proposes such dialogue in light of what he perceives as the ethical decline of modernity, liberal democracies, the excesses of the later hyper-capitalism and an emerging self-questioning within secular reason itself' (Lane, 2013, pp. 13-14).

Other theorists such as Judith Butler et al. (Butler, Habermas, Taylor & West, 2011), however, have reservations about the conditions laid down by Habermas for such dialogue in that the translation between the religious and the secular appears to be only one way. Such writers claim that Habermas proposes a context for dialogue that fails to recognise that religion cannot be translated into a secular language without a remainder. Anglican theologian, Nigel Biggar reaffirms this point, stating that 'the translation proposed [by writers such as Habermas] eliminates the strangeness, difference and otherness that religion brings to the table' (2009, p. 317).

The translation proposed by Habermas gives expression, however, to a narrowing of reason. Such a narrowing of reason, according to Jean-Luc Marion (2008), is 'the most profound crisis of our era' as this restricted rationality has little to say about the human condition, about what we are, what we can know, what we must do, and what we are allowed to hope for. While many writers have reservations regarding the conditions for dialogue proposed by Habermas, it is important that the proposition of such dialogue is welcomed if a contemporary society is to be understood as diverse, pluralist and inclusive. It is important, however, to be aware that a truly inclusive horizon in such a pluralist context is not always achieved. Marie Céline Clegg observes, 'an understandable tendency to focus on minority or alternative groups' that can often times lead to 'lesser emphasis on the rights of long-established groups' (2019, p. 21).

The Erosion of Objective Truth in Religious Education

The conditions laid down for dialogue between religious reason and secular reason present significant implications for religious education. The insights raised above suggest that the objective character of religious truth is being seriously eroded. The position that the truth(s) of a particular faith tradition may actually be true, at least in some substantial objective sense, is being clouded by the view that such truth(s) is (are) merely some non-cognitive attitude or emotional response to the deep mystery of the created order (Carr, 1994). The wider genesis of this dispute can be found in: (1) Schleiermacher's claim that religious beliefs are merely expressions of religious experience as opposed to realistic cognitive propositions, and (2) Kant's position that knowledge is determined by the mind acting in response to phenomenal experience (Wright, 2004).

An example of how such an erroneous approach may be taken up can be seen in the context of recent developments and proposals set out in Irish education in the name of a more liberal and enlightened perspective (NCCA, 2015, 2018; Department of Education and Skills, 2018a, 2018b). Such initiatives seem to be animated by a deep current of scepticism concerning religious belief and its place within the public sphere. It can be argued that such actions give voice, consciously or less so, to the positivist claim that religious statements are meaningless because they are unverifiable (Wright, 2004). Hence, it is not surprising that such scepticism is directed at those implications of religious belief that appear to be at odds with rational scientific knowledge. Yet, it must be recognised too that such scepticism is animated by a principal opposition to those implications of faith-formation which appear to be at variance with contemporary social views about the freedom of the individual (Carr, 1994).

It is evident that ethical, social, political and religious differences frequently have socially divisive, even combative consequences – not least in social contexts in which a high degree of plurality and diversity is attained among the value preferences of their members (Carr, 1994). In this manner, liberal democratic forms of political administration and organisation can be regarded as strategies for what it is hoped might be impartial arbitration and negotiation between different potentially conflicting moral, social and religious perspectives (Carr, 1994). Such strategies are often designed to limit and curtail what might be understood as the clamorous demands of particular sectarian interest groups within a given society. All of this is achieved by the adoption of a particular stance of 'detached neutrality' with respect to what may be believed in substantive terms by different social, political and religious parties (Carr, 1994, p. 226). Briefly stated, such detached neutrality insists that the claims of one party to a knowledge of what is true, right or good in the realm of socially significant beliefs or opinions are treated as no more or less worthy of a serious hearing than those of another.

A consequence of this strategy is that it can all too easily become a procedural agnosticism that routinely dismisses the truth value of religious claims and beliefs. In the setting of public schooling the liberal state's desire for neutrality, or to minimise offence, means that religious beliefs are treated with scepticism (Department of Education and Skills, 2018a, 2018b). A similar point is made by Michael Hand in his treatment of whether non-confessional religious education is logically possible. Hand identifies himself with the realistic turn in contemporary religious education accepting the premise that 'understanding a unique form of knowledge involves holding certain presuppositions of that form to be true or false' (2004, p. 25). In other words, to understand religion is to hold particular propositions to be either true or false. In this context, Hand is speaking of truth claims such as the reality of God, or some other transcendent being or ultimate reality, as such claims are either affirmed or rejected by the religious believer or the atheist (Wright, 2010).

Hand's (2004) work is significant in that it challenges any restriction of religious education in the public sphere to the study of religion as some historical, psychological and socio-cultural phenomena (Wright, 2010). In this way, Hand argues against an approach that either completely ignores the realistic truth claims affirmed by religious traditions or at best merely offers a description of them. This even greater agnosticism about whether there can in fact be any rational basis for articles of religious faith beyond the disposition of the faithful to confess them is fortified further by the old empiricist distinction between 'facts' and 'values'. Empiricist philosophers work out of the theoretical tradition know as empiricism. This philosophical tradition argues that sensory experience is the foundation of all knowledge (Cottingham, 2008). This distinction (i.e. between facts and values), which operates within the context of liberalism with particular ease, is commensurate in empiricism to a distinction between what is rational and objective in human enquiry and preference (i.e. fact) and what is, by contrast, subjective and non-rational (i.e. value) (Carr, 1994, p. 226).

The culmination of all of the above is that it has come to be quite commonly held that religious views should not be taught in schools in any way which suggests they might be true for what would usually appear to be a confused mixture of two reasons: (1) on the liberal ground that particular religious beliefs are matters of personal preference rather than common interest concerning which individuals are entitled to their own, potentially opposing opinions, and (2) on the epistemologically sceptical basis that such beliefs are the sort of personal opinions for which there can be no reasonable or rational foundation (Carr, 1994; Hand, 2004). When one takes the above discussion into account, it becomes clear that it has become inevitable that the critiques of realist epistemologies, and the emergence of non-realist theories of knowledge, such as those of pragmatists and coherentists (James, 2019; Thagard, 2019), would come to exercise influence on the work of educationalists with regard to the nature of teaching and learning. It is not, however, the purpose of this chapter to delve into the whole narrative of this influence.

Yet, it is important to highlight that this post-modern or new age marriage of philosophical and psychological views has led to what is commonly referred to as a 'constructivist' concept of knowledge acquisition. Of particular interest here is the epistemological perspective of a radically 'thick' postmodern constructivism (Barkin, 2010, p. 26). Such a position emphasises the Nietzschean slogan that 'there are no facts, only interpretations' (Nietzsche, 1968, p. 267). It is important to recognise here too that such a perspective presents a very limited understanding of hermeneutics, the science of interpretation, by reducing it to a mere methodology – failing to appreciate that hermeneutics is far more than simply a methodology. Furthermore, contrary to realist epistemologies which view knowledge as being based on what's out there in the world, i.e. the world is real and not constructed, the epistemological perspective of a radically thick constructivism moves that all knowledge, including that of science, is constructed. In a wholly postmodern constructivist horizon of knowledge-acquisition any meaningful criterion of objective enquiry and truth such as the kind considered by classical epistemological realists evaporates. A wholly constructivist approach is predominately an exercise of the creation of personal models of reality. As such, these models possess little in terms of supporting an appeal to any manner of objectivity beyond that of the internal coherence of the experiences of what constructs them.

It is important for educationalists to be clear about the pitfalls and dangers of such constructivist thinking, i.e. a thick postmodern constructivism (Barkin, 2010), about knowledge acquisition, pedagogy and initiation into religious enquiry – particularly as it is common to encounter an apology or defence of something akin to a notion of Religious Education that is perhaps best accounted for under the generic rubric of 'personal search'. For example, no unique issues emerge concerning the objective truth of religious knowledge from a constructivist position, at least not in realist terms. This point follows from the fact that no such problems can emerge within a thick constructivist horizon, not only about religious knowledge but about *any* form of knowledge. Put simply, even those so-called 'precise' forms of scientific knowledge such as physics and mathematics are to be considered as mere social constructs. Such social constructs are no more answerable to some independent order of objective reality than any of the allegedly less exact moral and social sciences (Carr, 1994). On this point one must at least raise the following question: is it not a rather exorbitant cost to incur for the apology of religious enquiry as a valid pathway to human knowledge to call into doubt the objectivity of all those forms of natural scientific investigation that have come to be commonly considered as being so successful concerning the explanation and understanding of an order of independent objective reality? It must be recognised too, however, that constructivist approaches such as those of neo-classical constructivism or even recent attempts to develop a realist constructivism at least signal to the notion of an objective reality by way of the notion of inter-subjectivity (Barkin, 2010, p. 26). Contrary to a 'thick' postmodern constructivism, a neo-classical or 'thin' constructivism speaks of an inter-subjectivity within which there is at least the potential to integrate a mode of philosophical realism, i.e. the world exists independent of our observations of it, while at one and the same time acknowledging that not all parts of this objective reality are directly observable to the human person in any wholly objective manner.

From the above discussion it is evident that if one is to reach any understanding of the difference between knowledge that is capable of speaking to an objective world and that which speaks only to a constructed world, it is of the utmost importance to uphold the distinction, as Carr (1994) explains,

> between subjective human experience as expressed in this or that epistemic state and a world of independent objective reality by reference to which it is possible to judge such states to be true or false, correct or incorrect. (p. 225)

If one fails to uphold this distinction the epistemological subject is confined and constrained within the circle of his or her own thoughts, as Carr (1994) affirms,

> either solipsistically on individualist accounts of knowledge acquisition or, in the case of social or intersubjective conceptions, as the member of a given epistemological community. (p. 225)

In such a context, any possibility of a truly meaningful encounter with the other is removed, and therefore, so too any possibility of being transformed by the other. In this way, then, if any understanding of knowledge is to be considered adequate or at least respectable, it is essential that the notion of objective truth is considered to be a central goal of human enquiry. This point is fundamental to the acceptance of the proposition that a person's enquiries may bring them somewhere by way of an appreciation of that 'which exists beyond the otherwise uncertain contents of one's mind' (Carr, 1994, p. 225). On this point, the folly of embracing a wholly postmodern or 'thick' constructivist position becomes clear – one finds oneself in the grips of relativism thereby utterly eroding the particularity that is so characteristic of religious truth claims.

Faith-based or Non-faith-based Religious Education?

With this in mind, there appears to be an emergent position amongst many contemporary religious educators that in no instance should a child be *intentionally* initiated into a given faith or taught that such a faith might be true because of a fear of indoctrination. Rather, some educators would suggest that children may be taught *about* a faith only as an account of what many people have chosen to believe which should leave it open for pupils to accept the faith only if they so choose. It is important to note that the freedom of the individual to choose to accept faith is a central pillar to a Catholic approach to religious education. Faith *qua* faith is a gift that must be *freely* accepted by the individual. For instance, in *Gaudium et Spes* one reads that humankind is 'from the very circumstance of [its] origin... already invited to converse with God' (Vatican II, 1965, par. 119). This point is emphasised by Karl Rahner in his notion of the 'supernatural existential'. He states that the human being 'possesses an ontic and spiritual-personal capacity for communicating' with God (1963, pp. 240–241).

For example, Rahner speaks of the human person as the hearer of the message and defines the hearer as a person and a subject. Fisher commenting on Rahner notes that the word 'person' signifies, 'that the hearer cannot be reduced to a mere product of the forces that have shaped him or her' (Fisher, 2004, p. 7). In fact, the hearer not only has the ability to listen, 'but to freely respond' to the message (p. 7). As expressed in the Gospel of John, 'No one can come to me unless drawn by the Father who sent me, and I will raise that person up on the last day' (Jn 6:44). Moreover, the word 'subject' also has a technical meaning. Subjects are human beings capable of reflecting on themselves. The human person has the capability to ask himself or herself what they really are and, as Fisher notes, about 'what is their true self' (p. 7). The words of Rahner present human existence as being orientated towards the transcendent. According to Rahner, the hearer or human person is a transcendent being (p. 9). This point infers that humankind recognises that it is limited. However, it is by the virtue of this awareness, that human beings imagine how they can surpass their limitations. It is this transcendence that presents choices. In this perspective, when a person chooses the better alternative, they are not only acting freely and responsibly, but they are realising what God has called them to be. Thus, it is the message which invites human beings to become what God means them to be, which is to be 'agents of salvation' (p. 7). Such an understanding informs a Catholic approach to religious education, in that pupils encounter the message of God revealed in Christ but are free to respond in their own way. However, this is not accommodated in approaches to religious education that bracket out 'learning from' or 'learning into' faith.

Such a bracketing out is evidenced by the introduction of 'Education about Religion and Beliefs' (ERB) programmes across Europe, highlighting the challenges faced by education systems in attempting to accommodate the diversity that is evident within schools (Jackson, 2013). These programmes focus on 'learning *about*' different religions and beliefs, but do not facilitate 'learning *from*' or learning *into* religions and beliefs. Such programmes seek to adopt a neutral stance regarding the validity of truth claims by utilising the approach of ideological pluralism (Donovan, 1993). Such an approach moves that for one to be 'pluralist' they ought to take up an ideological project which strives to neutralise any authentic recognition of diversity by imposing a totalitarian apprehension of truth, i.e. there is only one truth, the truth of pluralism (Merrigan, 2013, p. 66). However, it must be recognised that there is no such thing a value neutral education (Freire, 2005). Furthermore, on this point one is not inferring that pupils should be *indoctrinated* into any particular faith. As outlined above, to force one to belief defeats the very notion of faith that is proclaimed by the Christian tradition. Rather, the above is merely suggesting that to present religious truth as just that, 'truth', is not to move towards indoctrination. This is because, as Boeve points out, it is an appropriate presentation that is fitting to a pluralist context within which 'each identity is structurally challenged to conceive of itself in relation to difference and otherness – especially to the effect of other truth claims to its own claim' (2012, p. 146).

This point can be observed when one recognises that each school community makes a unique contribution to the public square by virtue of the fact that every school educates from a particular worldview. In Ireland, each school is recognised as having its own 'ethos' or 'characteristic spirit'. The ethos of a school has a direct correlation with but is not limited to the way in which a school approaches Religious Education (Hession, 2015). For instance, Catholic schools utilise a particular approach to Religious Education, one that makes an explicit claim to ultimate truth. Further, contrary to an ERB programme, a Catholic approach to Religious Education utilises the perspective of epistemological pluralism (Hession, 2015; Dillon, 2013). Such an approach moves that an authentic understanding of diversity is central if one is to be 'pluralist'. As such, epistemological pluralism recognises the existence of contrary truth claims, and proposes that the cause of truth is best served by way of discussion and argument (Merrigan, 2013, p. 66). This proposition is central to an approach to Religious Education, particularly if it is to accommodate the 'strangeness, difference and otherness' of religion (Biggar, 2009, p. 317).

In taking up the approach of epistemological pluralism, both 'participative knowing' and inter-faith engagement are central to Catholic religious education (Lane, 2011, p. 48; James, [1902] 1974). The transformation of one's 'prejudices' is at the centre of participative knowing and is brought about through dialogue with the other. This relationship between transformation and dialogue signals the value of inter-personal conversation in religious education, particularly in the area of inter-faith engagement. Contrary to an approach to religious education that moves solely towards the acquisition of a detached knowledge about religions or the *accents* of religions, such inter-personal conversation promotes an approach that moves towards facilitating an openness to deeper relationship with the other through participation in a process of interpretation and understanding.

From this standpoint, a case can be made regarding the centrality of religious experience to a holistic Religious Education. For instance, if an approach to Religious Education utilises a mode of reason that operates solely towards the acquirement of 'religious knowledge', which is evident in the approach taken by ERB programmes, the development of 'religious knowing' that is facilitated by religious experience is not accommodated. Rather, it is perceived as somehow irrational, and, therefore, not valid knowledge. Yet, 'religious knowing' is indispensable to one's understanding of religious reason in that 'religious knowing' presents reason as being inseparable from tradition (Gadamer, 2013). This point finds a unique yet clear articulation in the words of Karl Jaspers, 'the thought which breaks with tradition tends to become an empty seriousness' (cited in Ratzinger, 1984, p. 354). This relationship between faith and reason is a unique characteristic of Catholic education and it is at the centre of a Catholic approach to Religious Education (Drumm, 2015). In this way, the Catholic approach to religious education makes a significant effort to give genuine credence to the question of truth while, at one and the same time, recognising the mystery of God. This point is articulated clearly by St Augustine when speaking of the limitations of the human intellect, 'even when he reveals himself, God remains a mystery beyond words: If you understood him, it would not be God' (Sermon, 52, 6, 16). However, this does not infer that we cannot know something of God, just never the totality of the mystery of God.

Conclusion

In conclusion, it is important to make clear that this chapter is not proposing that the pursuit of religious knowledge and truth through religious or spiritual enquiry is *all* that there is to Religious Education. Rather, the point being made here is that it cannot be a matter of indifference for Religious Education which religion, if any, young people are introduced to or *how* they are introduced to it; not, that is, if reason and enquiry are to make the same sort of sense in Religious Education as they undoubtedly should in other areas of education – as reliable routes to meaning, knowledge and truth. However, in taking seriously the realistic truth claims affirmed by religious traditions, a critical openness is sustained within Religious Education. This openness is facilitated by shifting the orientation of Religious Education away from the array of moral challenges encountered by open democratic societies in addressing the existence of a plurality of religious and secular traditions and towards the pursuit of ultimate truth. In this way then, it can be argued that if effective dialogue is to occur between religious reason and secular reason, religious knowing must be understood as being a necessary condition to facilitate an appropriate recognition of the *difference* that exists between religious reason and secular reason. Such an approach enables not only 'learning about' religions and belief, but also 'learning from' and 'learning into' religions and beliefs by being open to the other (Todd, 2003). From this standpoint, it is clear that an approach to Religious Education that facilitates 'religious knowing' by way of encounters with truth presents a richer understanding of religions and worldviews. It also suggests a more dynamic hermeneutic, one that is receptive to revealed truth, by being open to genuine diversity and inclusion in a pluralist society through its accommodation, recognition and openness to difference. Hence, to return to the opening question: is there no truth in religion? The answer is, there is truth in religion. And, while its claim to truth is of a different kind to that of science, this does not infer that its claim ought to be considered inferior to that of science or less relevant in the life of the human person.

References

Barkin. J. *Realist Constructivism: Rethinking International Relations Theory*. Cambridge: Cambridge University Press, 2010.

Biggar, N., 'Conclusions', in L. Hogan & N. Biggar (eds), *Religious Voices in Public Places*, Oxford: Oxford University Press, 2009, pp. 309–330.

Boeve, L., 'Religious Education in a Post-secular and Post-Christian Context', in *Journal of Beliefs & Values*, 33/2, (2012), pp. 143–156.

Butler, J., Habermas, J., Taylor, C. & West, C., 'Concluding Discussion', in E. Mendieta & J. Van Antwerpen (eds), *The Power of Religion in the Public Sphere*, New York: Columbia University Press, 2011, pp. 109–117.

Carr, D., 'Knowledge and Truth in Religious Education', in *Journal of Philosophy of Education*, 28/2, (1994), pp. 221–238.

Clegg, M.C., 'Policy and Partnership', in *Studies: An Irish Quarterly Review*, 108/429, (2019), pp. 20–31.

Cottingham, J., *Western Philosophy: An Anthology*, Cambridge: Blackwell Publishing, 2008.

Department of Education and Skills, *Circular Letter 0013/2018*, 2018a. Available at: www.education.ie/en/Circulars-and-Forms/Active-Circulars/cl0013_2018.pdf

Department of Education and Skills, *Circular Letter 0062/2018*, 2018b. Available at: www.education.ie/en/Circulars-and-Forms/Active-Circulars/cl0062_2018.pdf

Donovan, P., 'The Imbalance of Religious Pluralism', in *Religious Studies* 29, (1993), pp. 218–221.

Drumm, M., 'The Extremely Important Issue of Education', in D. A. Lane (ed), *Vatican II in Ireland, Fifty Years On: Essays in Honour of Pádraic Conway*, Frankfurt am Main: Peter Lang, 2015, pp. 285–303.

Fisher, M.F., *The Foundations of Karl Rahner: A Paraphrase of the Foundations of Christian Faith, with Introduction and Indices*, New York: Crossroad Publishing, 2005.

Freire, P., *Pedagogy of the Oppressed*, trans. M. Bergman Ramos, London: Continuum, 2005.

Gadamer, H.G., *Truth and Method*, trans. J. Weinsheimer & G.G. Marshall (original edition in German, 1960), London: Bloomsbury Academic, 2013.

Habermas, J., 'An Awareness of What is Missing', in J. Habermas et al. (ed), *An Awareness of What is Missing: Faith and Reason in a Post-Secular Age*, Cambridge: Polity Press, 2010, pp. 15-23.

Hand, M., *Is Religious Education Possible? A Philosophical Investigation*, London: Bloomsbury Academic, 2004.

Hannam, P., *Religious Education and the Public Sphere*, London: Routledge, 2019.

Hession, A., *Catholic Primary Religious Education in a Pluralist Environment*, Dublin: Veritas Publications, 2015.

Jackson, R., 'Why Education about Religions and Beliefs? European Policy Recommendations and Research', in G. Byrne and P. Kieran (ed), *Towards Mutual Ground: Pluralism, Religious Education and Diversity in Irish Schools*, Dublin: Columba Press, 2013, pp. 43-56.

James, W., *The Variety of Religious Experience: A Study in Human Nature*, Glasgow: Collins Clear-Type Press, [1902] 1974.

James, W., 'Pragmatism's Conception of Truth', in D. Edwards (ed), *Truth: A Contemporary Reader*, London: Bloomsbury Academic, 2019, pp. 114-125.

Lane, D.A., *Stepping Stones To Other Religions: A Christian Theology of Inter-religious Dialogue*, Dublin: Veritas Publications, 2011.

Lane, D.A., *Religion and Education: Re-Imagining the Relationship*, Dublin: Veritas Publications. 2013.

Marion, J.L., *Le Monde*, 11 Sept 2008, quoted by Stephen England, 'How Catholic is France?', *Commonweal*, 135/19, (2008), pp. 12-18.

Mendieta E. & Van Antwerpen, J. (eds), *The Power of Religion in the Public Sphere*, New York: Columbia University Press, 2011.

Merrigan, T., 'Religion, Education and the Appeal to Plurality: Theological Considerations on the Contemporary European Context', in G. Byrne and P. Kieran (ed), *Towards Mutual Ground: Pluralism, Religious Education and Diversity in Irish Schools*, Dublin: Columba Press, 2013, pp. 57-70.

National Council for Curriculum and Assessment, *Education about Religions and Beliefs (ERB) and Ethics: Consultation Paper*, 2015. Available at: https://ncca.ie/media/1897/consultation_erbe.pdf

National Council for Curriculum and Assessment, *Primary Developments: Consultation on Structure and Time Final Report*, 2018. Available at: https://ncca.ie/media/3242/primary-developments_consultaion-on-curriculum-structure-and-time_final-report.pdf

Nietzsche, F., *The Will to Power*, New York: Vintage Books, 1968.

Rahner, K., *Theological Investigations II*, London: Darton, Longman & Todd. 1963.

Ratzinger, J., 'Faith, Philosophy and Theology', in *Communio: International Catholic Review*, 11 /4, (1984), pp. 350-363.

Thagard, P., 'Coherence, Truth, and the Development of Scientific Knowledge', in D. Edwards (ed), *Truth: A Contemporary Reader*, London: Bloomsbury Academic, 2019, pp. 86-101.

Todd, S., *Learning from the Other: Levinas, Psychoanalysis, and Ethical Possibilities in Education*, in D.P. Britzman (ed), New York: State University of New York Press, 2003.

Tuohy, D., *Denominational Education and Politics: Ireland in a European Context*, Dublin: Veritas Publications, 2013.

Vatican II, *Gaudium et Spes: Pastoral Constitution on the Church in the Modern World*, 1965, in Abbott W. (ed), *The Documents of Vatican II*, New York: Herder and Herder, 1966.

Wright, A., 'Book Review: Michael Hand Is Religious Education Possible? A Philosophical Investigation', in *Theory and Research in Education 8/1*, (2010), pp. 112-113.

Wright, A., *Critical Religious Education, Multiculturalism and the Pursuit of Truth*, Cardiff: University of Wales, 2007.

Wright, A., *Post-Modernity, Education and Religion*, London: Routledge, 2004.

Chapter 6

~~~~~~~~~~~~~~~~

Lifelong Learning in the Church

John Sullivan

Introduction

Education is integral to the Church's life and pivotal to promoting mature Christian discipleship. If Christian faith is to lead to an ongoing transformation of lives so that these have a recognisable Christ-like character and display a reading and response to reality as God-given, then education in the Church must provide a multifaceted experience of learning that engages with, listens to, illuminates and integrates the totality of each person's experience. This chapter reflects on the learning that is picked up within the Church.

First, I focus on two possible and closely connected purposes or goals for promoting life-long learning in the Church – the why. These are having the mind of Christ and becoming a prototype of the gospel. Second, I unpack important features of what is entailed by the phrase 'learning in the Church.' Third, consideration is given to key factors at work which have a bearing on the effectiveness of life-long learning in the Church. Finally, in order to cast light upon our current practice in faith formation, in the final part of the paper I propose a set of questions that could help Church members (at all levels) develop a richer and more realistic understanding of the complex dynamics at work in teaching and learning in the Church.

Purposes

St Paul clearly states: 'Let this mind be in you which was also in Christ Jesus' (Phil 2:5). We acquire this mind of Christ in the context of the Church community and its associated practices. What does 'having the mind of Christ' mean? What does it mean to think Christianly? It does not mean simply thinking about the Bible, prayer, the Church, the sacraments, the saints – necessary though all this might be. For this might be to leave the rest of our thinking – about work, the world of production, politics, taxes, holidays, food, family, sex and relationships, investments, travel – untouched and unconverted. We have to bring into dialogue two kinds of truth: sacred, salvific truth – truth for the sake of our salvation – and all the other kinds of truth that are part of our life. This means that we must bring together and harmonise faith and reason. Harmonise them, not compartmentalise them. When electricity was installed into our houses, all rooms were illuminated, not some. In the house of our lives, all our rooms must be illuminated and all dimensions of our being should be seen differently in the light of faith – intellectual, physical, social, moral, economic, political, artistic, as well as spiritual.

What about becoming a prototype of the gospel as an educational aim for learning in the Church – a prototype for our own particular time and place? We are called, not only to believe in, but also to become the gospel; not just to hear about and approve of, or to vote for it, but personally and actively to participate in the life and work of God in our world. Not only to be familiar with what God was doing in Jesus Christ, but to live our lives, in all their aspects and dimensions, not only the explicitly religious side, in such a way that they are shaped by and permeated with the gospel. What Christ is for us, we have to be for the world, at least for that part of it in which we find ourselves placed. Thus, we are not only to benefit from what God offers to us, but also to bear witness to this, by faithfully embodying the good news in our words and actions. As individuals and as Church communities we should be like a microcosm of the Kingdom, a miniature version, a prototype, a rehearsal; our churches should not be escapes from or hiding places from the world but a sign of what we are all called to become, if we accept God's grace.

We are called to be more than merely beneficiaries of the salvation God has brought about in Christ, though we are that, but also to bear witness to it and to embody it in all we do. Our Church communities are meant to be walking explanations of the gospel, like a living commentary on it. Not all are called to be public preachers or travelling missionaries, but all Christians should become the reflectors of as well as recipients of the gospel. Being, doing and telling, or presence, practice and proclamation through example: these are the three dimensions of our Christian mission and the ways people come to learn the gospel. And the more we *become* the gospel, the more opportunities will open up to *speak* the gospel.

These two purposes, as with other purposes for adult faith-learning, for example, learning how to love, or learning how to find and follow the will of God, require a lifetime to learn and can never be adequately mastered. In addressing such purposes, one has to draw upon and feed into every aspect of our life, not just spiritual, but also intellectual, emotional, physical, social, political and moral.

Features of Learning in the Church

What is the learning that is picked up within the Church? I use the phrase 'picked up' for three reasons. First, to acknowledge the difference between what is deliberately taught and what is actually learned; while these can, in rare circumstances, coincide, more often there will be noticeable gaps between what is promulgated and what is received. Second, to allow for the fact that, even when people are earnestly seeking to learn from the Church, the result may be influenced by a multiplicity of factors that obscure or reinforce that teaching for them, for example, their maturity, motivation and needs, their upbringing, personal experience and intellectual capacity, the company they keep and what else is being taught in the wider culture. These factors come into play with the nature and quality of the range of ways that the Church seeks to educate its members. Third, because faith-learning is an erratic, non-linear, informal and unpredictable process, rather than being an orderly, systematic, logical and progressive development.

Learning in the Church depends on the mutual presence of members, responding to an awareness of, dependence on and openness to the transcendent presence of the divine as known in Christ. Each person in this relationship – God, learners who are also teachers, teachers who are also learners – is a mystery, with none to be manipulated or subject to control.

The Church is made up of Christians seeking together in a school of love the bread of meaning as food and fuel for lives of self-giving. Primary theology occurs in shared reflection on life experience, conscious of being in God's presence. To the extent that we enter in such reflection, we are all theologians – or we can be.

Learning in the Church is not about nouns and concepts but about verbs and joint activity. It is about worshipping together, encountering the Bible, sharing experiences, welcoming, celebrating, questioning, listening, healing, forgiving, reconciling, remembering, serving others, loving, praying and, some of the time, learning and teaching more deliberately and explicitly, instead of doing so implicitly, alongside and as part of all the other activities. Such learning helps us to see with the eyes of faith, interpret in the light of truth and respond with a heart of love.

These are some features of education generally which apply just as much in the Church as in the wider world outside the Church. What gifts or capacities can education give you? How to think clearly; how to analyse ideas; how to weigh up the soundness and significance of claims; how to express yourself convincingly; how to interpret evidence; how to take into account different points of view; how to listen sensitively; how to read intelligently; how to judge carefully; how to appreciate the insights, gifts and works of others; how to relate compassionately and cooperatively; how to know oneself; how to give oneself to commitments and to others; how to love wisely; how to develop confidence and competence in ongoing learning; the discipline and reinforced desire to find truth, beauty and goodness; the capacities to build a good life.

I see the Church as offering formation, training and rehearsal for a life performance – which requires these capacities I have just mentioned – as well as immersion in both the story of God-with-us and in worship, which includes acknowledging, praising, listening, relating and opening up to God.

For all of us, our task is to learn how to love. This is the way to enter into our humanity and to share God's life. The task of education in the Church is to help us develop a Christian imagination and sensibility, the capacity to read and respond to the world in the light of the gospel of Our Lord Jesus Christ – reading and responding to ourselves, our neighbours and to our culture – as we learn *about* Christ, from Christ, learn to live *in* Christ together, *with* Christ, *as* Christ in ourselves, and *for* Christ in others.

Factors at Work

Our relationship to and resonance with what the Church offers is mediated by our past and recent experiences of birth and bereavement, sickness and recovery, suffering and joy, marriage and the breakdown of relationship, success and failure in our endeavours, friendship and betrayal, recognition and isolation and the degree to which we have had positive and negative encounters with the Church.

In communicating faith, factors at work that influence reception include the ability of teachers and learners, affection and warmth, affirmation and encouragement, example, explanation, a space of freedom, safety and exploration, discipline, motivation, commitment and challenge.

Also influential are changing material conditions: entertainment, food, household equipment, holidays, communication and transport – all of which affect our mind-set. There are deep connections between culture and our inner life, influencing imagination, sensitivity, hopes, fears, the expectations of others, our habits, assumptions, priorities, and relationships. These features of our inner life are influenced by, perhaps even framed or constituted by, the culture that surrounds us.

A scholar whose work deserves far more attention than it has received so far on this side of Atlantic from Christians involved in education at any level is Dwayne Huebner (b.1923). Huebner gave great importance to members of educational communities sharing with and learning from each other. He highlighted the importance of language, environment and power-relations in either enhancing or obstructing learning. He strongly emphasised the role of an encounter with 'otherness' (engaging with people who are different from us) in contributing to personal transformation. Huebner influenced many Christian educators who themselves became major figures in that field, such as Thomas Groome, Mary Boys and Maria Harris. His major focus was on curriculum, especially seen in a theological light. Although most of his teaching and writing was intended for teacher education programmes for professionals working in schools and colleges, I believe that his insights apply equally well in the context of adult learning in the Church, a topic to which he gave consideration in some of his addresses. If curriculum is the main focus of his attention, this might at first seem not a promising starting point for reflecting on lifelong learning in the Church, since the term curriculum is rarely used in that context. However, drawing upon Huebner's expansive understanding of curriculum I would claim that every Church does have a curriculum. By curriculum, I intend to refer, not only to what is taught explicitly (for example, through sermons, in catechesis, through talks for parishioners, during spiritual direction, on retreats or in scripture study groups), but also to take into account many other factors. Features other than content are relevant to lifelong learning in the Church. These include all of the following aspects: who teaches, who is taught (in Christian life most people are, at some time, both teacher and taught), the nature of the relationship between teachers and taught, how teaching and learning takes place, the language employed, who decides what is taught and what language is used, as well as how the setting or context influences receptivity and learning and what aspects of people's lives are not included or referred to. All these jointly constitute what I call the Church curriculum (and this should be kept in mind when considering question 8 in the next section of the chapter).

From Huebner (1999) I draw three points that strike me as especially pertinent to learning in the Church. First, we have to be able to tell our story with joy and hear into speech the emerging story of others (p. 180). If each one of us is a word from God, able to hear and utter something unique and indispensable, then we need to hear each one's word about creation. Second, those who have not yet accepted our tradition provide opportunities for us to reflect on what we value and why we think as we do (Huebner, p. 181). Huebner says:

> As the congregation invites the stranger into its forms of life and into its awareness as Church, it also invites newness into its body ... The stranger ... offers an opportunity to rethink the taken for granted of the congregation, and perhaps a new beginning. (p. 335)

This is rather like the effect of having a new baby in your family. For Huebner, 'the stranger is someone who is not at home with us, who does not share our ways, our language, our images and worldview ... The stranger calls us outside of ourselves and our closed interests' (p. 328). And thirdly, Huebner reminds us that education is an aspect of, a fruit of, community life, not separate from the ordinary ways of living in community (p. 328). 'Education within the congregation is a function of the vitality of its life' (p. 331). In these insights Huebner underlines the key roles played by facilitating the expression of personal voice, encountering people whose experience and perspective differs from ours and attention to the quality of congregational life together. In the following section I raise some questions about teaching and learning in the Church that build upon Huebner's insights.

Questions Arising

1. To what degree do clergy (and preachers in particular) share a common education, language and culture with their congregations? Do they have similar or different assumptions and expectations, experiences of life, priorities, concerns and hopes?

2.   To what extent does the experience of congregational members *outside* of Church colour, frame, reinforce or inhibit their reception of what is offered *inside* Church?

3.   How well do clergy and bishops know their people, their lives and outlook? Do the people feel known?

4.   Are the differences (in life-experience, perspective, etc.) among Church members a cause of isolation/separation between them or are such differences drawn upon as a potential source of learning?

5.   To what extent do teachers in the Church (clergy and bishops, but catechists too) have a sense of how their teaching is being received, interpreted, accepted, rejected?

6.   To what extent are Church members expected to be agents in their own faith-learning, rather than recipients of teaching? What scope is given for engagement, responsibility and initiative in Church life, work and learning? Are Church members consulted about decisions in the life of the Church? Is their judgement and evaluation invited?

7.   What is the relative emphasis given to scripture, preaching, sacraments, prayer, liturgy, outreach and service, social bonding among congregational members, catechesis and doctrine, further study/learning opportunities?

8.   What kind of balance is there, within a congregation's experience of the Church's curriculum, between (i) receiving instruction and teaching (in sermons and beyond) by clergy; (ii) individual guidance and mentoring of parishioners by clergy; (iii) peer ministry/teaching by parishioners; (iv) opportunities for sharing experience and giving testimony; and (v) joint action on projects or in serving others?

9.   Is shared reflection on the story of people's faith journeys and their struggles, challenges, questions and insights encouraged and facilitated?

10. Should greater emphasis be put on teaching ability and educational leadership in the Church and her ministries? And, if so, what would this require?

Conclusion

To address these kind of questions adequately, those responsible for promoting learning in the Church need such qualities as imagination and vision, creativity and courage, patience and perseverance, humility and hope, encounter that opens up real and mutual presence, together with attentive accompaniment. If the lofty purposes for lifelong learning in the Church, as proposed in section one, are to have any chance of being properly addressed, and if the factors that influence learning in the Church, as suggested in section three, are to be sufficiently taken into account, there needs to be the patient pursuit of procedures and practices that are both congruent with and commensurate to these purposes and factors. To be congruent with the purposes, mere transmission of doctrine is insufficient (even if necessary), because, by itself, it fails to engage disciples (that is learners) holistically along the lines indicated in section two. To be commensurate to the purposes, more attention needs to be paid to establishing the conditions that render trust, reciprocal learning, personal appropriation and openness to transformation more likely. A major resource is already present; it resides within the hearts and minds, the concerns and the insights of Church members.

Reference

Huebner, D.E., *The Lure of the Transcendent: Collected Essays by Dwayne E. Huebner,* in V. Hillis (ed), Mahwah, NJ: Lawrence Erlbaum Associates, 1999.

Chapter 7

∿∿∿∿∿∿∿∿∿∿

Small Groups and Faith Development: A Historical Exploration of a Contemporary Christian Practice

Paul F. Perry

Introduction

A decline over the last number of decades regarding religious practice, vocations to priesthood and religious life, and of the influence of traditional forms of the Christian Church in Ireland has been chronicled by a number of researchers (Anderson, Byrne & Cullen, 2016; Inglis, 1998; Fuller, 2004). They have highlighted the challenge, represented in Ireland as in other parts of Europe, and the new environment with which all Christian traditions must collectively engage with in ministering the gospel (Murray, 2017). The Irish Catholic bishops in their seminal document on sharing the Christian faith, *Share the Good News: National Directory for Catechesis in Ireland* (SGN), invite dialogue with all people around the meaning of the Christian heritage for today (Irish Episcopal Conference, 2010). Such engagement will involve a 'radical re-visioning, both spiritual and ecclesial, of the church' (Clarke, 2006, pp. 17–18) and a consideration of new ways to present Christ and encourage ongoing adult faith development (SGN, 2010). One of the key areas this will involve is re-engaging with the vision of the Church as the corporate people of God and a place of ministry for all members (McGrath, 2012). However, a pivotal precursor to this will involve considering appropriate ways to see the Christian faith initiated, matured, and continually developed in adults (SGN, 2010).

Such seemingly straightforward questions as how do people begin, grow in and keep the Christian faith have produced a diverse array of answers. Different authors place the emphasis on different areas, whether it be church attendance, worship, scripture reading, serving, reflection (Huebner, 1986), religious education in schools (Buchanan, 2005), spiritual modelling (Oman & Thoresen, 2003; Fowler, 1984), gratitude, thanksgiving and testimonials (Oman & Thoresen, 2003), the Eucharistic celebration (Radcliffe, 2008), charismatic expression (Robbins, 2004), conversion – however defined (Byrne & Kieran, 2013; Ford-Grabowsky, 1987; McGuire, 1982), pilgrimage (Finney, 1996; Turner & Turner, 1978), or preaching (Radcliffe, 2001) to name but a few. In reality, such faith development, in adults, requires a multifaceted approach (SGN, 2010).

An important consideration regarding such adult faith development is the role played by small and often informal groups (Wuthnow, 1994; Byrne & Kieran, 2013; Knabb & Pelletier, 2014; Gallagher & Newton, 2009; Walton, 2011; Williams, 2007; Otero & Cottrell, 2013; Byrne, 2008). This chapter will demonstrate that such an approach is not new but in fact has a significant historical pedigree, and continues to be widely used to promote vitality in the Church's gospel mission.

The Phenomenon of the Small Group Explosion

The proliferation of such 'small groups' (SGs) of various kinds, both within and beyond the Christian Church, and in both the Western and non-Western regions of the world (Wuthnow, 1994; Donahue & Robinson, 2001; Vandenakker, 1994; Cho & Hostetler, 1981; Comiskey, 1998; O'Halloran, 2002), has caused some commentators to speak of the 'small-group movement' (Arnold, 2004, p. 10; Donahue & Gowler, 2014, p. 118; Wuthnow, 1994, p. 4). As far back as 1994, social scientist Robert Wuthnow (1994, p. 4) estimated that in the USA alone, 40% of Americans 'belong to a small group that meets regularly and provides caring and support for its members'. While not all these groups were faith-based, 'nearly two-thirds' did have 'some connection to churches or synagogues', many initiated by clergy and involving prayer and/or Bible study, with the majority of their members saying they joined with a desire to 'deepen their faith' (Wuthnow, 1994, p. 6). A later UK study in 2001 yielded similar results, with 37% of English churchgoers saying they attend a weekly SG and only 1% reporting that there was no opportunity to join such a group. The research highlights the significant role that SGs are playing in the modern Church (Walton, 2011).

Wuthnow's study, however, suggested that such involvement did 'little to increase biblical knowledge' and rather encouraged a more pragmatic and subjective faith (1994, p. 7). So what then was driving such a large-scale movement? In a modern society where family breakdown and community structures are changing, Wuthnow highlights the strong sense of community that such groups offer as a key factor drawing people. People can find support and help in such a tight-knit group and even experience some spiritual development. Notwithstanding this, Wuthnow questions the level of commitment in such communities, when one's involvement is optional and suited to one's whims with the 'weakest of obligations'. He contends that the SG movement is also following the culture in '*adapting* American religion' and creating a type of American 'secularity' that often reduces and domesticates religion to gratify one's own need(s) (Wuthnow, 1994, pp. 6-7, 11-21).

Interestingly, another scholar, John Paul Vandenakker, also published his doctrinal thesis in 1994, the very same year in which Wuthnow's analysis became available. Vandenakker's thesis was completed at the Gregorian University in Rome and focused on the area of small Christian communities. Noting the various names of many such groups, which often reflect a distinctive emphasis of a particular group, Vandenakker uses the name 'small Christian communities (SCCs)' as an overarching term, particularly in his case as it represents the term favoured in North America (1994, pp. 98-99).

Like Wuthnow, Vandenakker highlighted the exponential growth and the wide variety of SGs operating in Western and non-Western countries. Vandenakker generally speaks in glowing terms regarding SCCs. For him, they constitute 'an ecclesiological phenomenon of major theological, pastoral, and institutional import', which have 'proven to be, for the most part, an effective means of both personal and ecclesial renewal' (1994, p. xii). Vandenakker (1994, p. xiii) finds support for some SCCs in the words of Pope Paul VI who calls them 'a great hope for the universal Church' (1975, par. 58), assuming they meet some basic conditions, and Pope John Paul II who similarly calls them 'a sign of vitality within the Church, an instrument of formation and evangelization, and a solid starting point for a new society based on a "civilization of love"' (1990, par. 51). Despite the above Vandenakker does address the potential challenges of SCCs, for example, becoming autonomous in their thinking and separating themselves from being part of the 'local/universal church' (e.g. 1994, pp. xii-xiii, 14-16, 108-114).

The potential of SGs as a means for renewal and evangelism is also enthusiastically promoted within the Anglican and broad Evangelical streams of the Church. As mentioned earlier, the range of such groups can vary considerably, from, for example, two-person discipleship groups to Bible study groups, to various expressions of the cell-group movement (Atkinson, 2018; Wuthnow, 1994).

Small Groups or Separatist Groups?

The potential, Vandenakker noted, for a SG to perceive itself as '*being church*' on its own, is also debated within Evangelicalism (1994, p. xii). This idea constitutes a primary distinction, for example, between the 'house church movement' and cell groups for example. The latter groups 'are always linked to a central church, which provides supervision and sponsorship' (Atkinson, 2018, p. 34; see also, Otero & Cottrell, 2013, p. 61). Thus, Evangelical writer William Beckham (2005) presents what he sees as a Biblical case for a Church organisation consisting of both large (celebration services) and small (cell) groups. Beckham calls this model 'the two-winged church', one wing 'for large group celebration' and 'the other wing ... for small group community' (2005, p. 25).

The Biblical Foundations for Small Groups

Many commentators, in seeking to understand the SG phenomenon, draw from the account of the infant Church in Jerusalem described in Acts 2:46: 'Day by day continuing with one mind in the temple' (larger celebration service), 'and breaking bread from house to house' (SG community meeting; Arnold, 2004, pp. 21, 85–86; Comiskey, 2015, p. 84; Vandenakker, 1994, p. 5). Consequently, Beckham (2005) and many other SG proponents perceive SGs not merely in practical or organisational terms but rather constituting a restoration of an original and valuable dimension of the early Church, long ignored in large sections of the modern Church. For these, the theology of SG communities emerges firstly out of the theology of the Trinity, and with humankind understood as God's image bearers (Donahue & Robinson, 2001; Icenogle, 1994). For example, O'Halloran, drawing upon the Second Vatican Council document, *Lumen Gentium*, notes that the Church is seen to be 'a people brought into unity from the unity of the Father, Son and Holy Spirit' (Vatican II, 1964, par. 4). O'Halloran writes, 'in effect we are asked in the Church to be a community as the Trinity is a community' (2002, p. 14).

Further theological support for building close-knit communities is adduced from the records of the life of Christ. Indeed, it might well be argued that SGs have always been part of the Christian Church. Jesus proclaimed the nearness of the kingdom of God to the multitudes, taught them and ministered to their needs. Indeed if he was not interested in having an impact on a vast amount of people, he could have easily withdrawn more permanently with his disciples to an isolated place (Brondos, 2018). Nevertheless, the gospels also portray Jesus gathering, and spending much of his time with, smaller groups of disciples for individual teaching and attention (Lk 8:1–3; 9:28–36; 10:1–24). One might say, because of his love for the many, he gathered to himself and focused upon disciplining a few (Donahue & Robinson, 2001; Icenogle, 1994; Otero & Cottrell, 2013). They were brought together to 'watch, pray, learn, live, imitate and practice the disciplines and life that Jesus lived with Abba God' (Icenogle, 1994, p. 127; Arnold, 2004).

Some Examples of Small Groups in the History of the Church

Going beyond the Bible, advocates of SGs propose historical precedents for today's SG practices. The space available here will allow us to reflect on three examples only to illustrate some divergent traditions each of which in their own way have facilitated the flourishing of SG communities over time.

Celtic Christianity and Small Groups
The term 'Celtic spirituality' is used in a wide array of ways today, sometimes either too broadly or narrowly (Davies & O'Loughlin, 1999, pp. 3–12, 459 n.1). Care is required to neither overly romanticise or cherry-pick from this area of research to suit one's proposals (Bradley, 1999; Wilkinson, 2000). With this example, and the other historical examples below, one might argue that that is exactly what SG exponents do. While endeavouring to show parallel concepts between the historical and today's SG practices, they ignore the vast differences of context and Christian practice. However, such historical expressions are not presented in this paper because they are perfect models for today, but because they are used by SG proponents to show evidence of a continuation of the SG model they perceive in the scripture and as support for a similar model today. With such cautions in mind, some partial analogies between the approach of the historic Celtic Church expression and modern SG evangelism may be appropriate.

Fifth-century Ireland was entirely dispersed, rural (Edwards, 2008) and tribal. In order to reach such a separated population an innovative church model evolved that generally established monastic communities in, or close to, traditional tribal areas (Aldhouse-Green, 1995; Hunter III, 2000; SGN, 2010; for contra example, see Bradley, 2009), or 'adjacent to medieval thoroughfares' (Stancliffe, 2015, p. 414). Since Irish towns of the time were rarely over three hundred people, a large monastic group could create a town itself, as well as an incredible sense of community (Hunter III, 2000; Sheldrake, 1995; Stancliffe, 2015). Such groups were accommodating, combining 'laxity and rigor, inclusiveness and vocation' (Davies & O'Loughlin, 1999, p. 38). The guests who visited were 'accorded a kind of semi-spiritual status' being 'housed within the sacred enclosure' (Sheldrake, 1995, pp. 43–44), and participating in the community life both spiritually in worship and in learning together, and practically in work and in sharing meals with one another. Significantly, in large monastic groups members were also encouraged to spend time in a smaller community group from within it, consisting of no more than ten people. Finney suggests that such a communal and relational model of evangelism is still relevant, especially in postmodern societies (Finney, 1996; SGN, 2010), such as Ireland today. Such combining of discipleship through personal and SG involvement, along with engagement within the broader faith community aligns closely with the SG and celebration model noted in this chapter.

John Wesley's Three Levels of Groups
Contemporary Evangelical SG practitioners highlight John Wesley as an individual who was able to cut through what he saw as the trappings of Anglicanism and recapture the spirit of *koinónia*, the supportive fellowship of primitive Christianity (Donahue & Gowler, 2014), resulting in the faith development of thousands of individuals in eighteenth-century Britain. A key to the success of his organisation, building on newly developing mass literacy, was the introduction of three different types of group meetings, the class, the bands and the society, combining to accomplish various aspects of discipleship (Henderson, 2016). The class meeting consisted of six to twelve people, meeting in shops, homes, or schoolrooms, and was central to Wesley's vision. The focus of these meetings was on prayer, praise, and the sharing by all about their weekly personal experiences, as distinct from the in-depth doctrinal exposition, reserved for the society (public) meeting. The classes instead focused on explaining, applying and internalising such doctrinal truths, with the goal of personal holiness, all conducted in an affirming atmosphere with others, including the leader, who was on the same journey (Henderson, 2016). The

leader would also carry the pastoral concerns of this sub-group of the church and commitment to this group was a requirement for anybody wanting to be accepted as a member of the society. All this 'provided an environment for behavioural change' (Henderson, 2016, p. 99). Again, for Wesley, such a system was not only effective but represented a return to the characteristics 'of earliest Christianity' (Henderson, 2016, p. 93).

The band meetings added to this an opportunity for affective change with the focus on what Wesley called "close conversation", the 'examination ... of motives and heartfelt impressions' (Henderson, 2016, p. 100). The bands were voluntary and could start with four members, who sought such improvement of their attitudes, intentions and affections. They were separated by sex, marital status and age. They had an egalitarian leadership style with one person starting the meeting but all members sharing based around the injunctions of James 5:14. Because of such intimate sharing, this meeting was closed to visitors.

Finally, the term 'society' was a designation for a gathered public meeting and almost equivalent to the term 'congregation' (Henderson, 2016). Aspects of this model align closely, not only with the general 'two-winged' approach but with other contemporary authors who explore how different size groups may accomplish different levels of transparency and transformation (Harrington, 2016; Ogden, 2016).

Alphonsus Liguori and Adult Faith Formation

Drawing on 'communities of practice' (CoP) theory, Otero and Cottrell suggest a precursor for Catholic SGs is found in another eighteenth-century minister, the Italian priest, Alphonsus Liguori (1696–1787). They specifically point to his use of 'evening chapels' where the impoverished workers of Naples would gather after their day's work and 'engage in adult faith formation'. Further, they draw attention to the fact that the priest functioned as an assistant and trained the lay members as 'adult catechists' within 'these small groups', as well as preparing them to assume the ongoing 'leadership of and responsibility for' the group. Consequently, despite historical and cultural differences, Otero and Cottrell perceive in the 'evening chapels ... an example of a historical precedent of a CoP with respect to the domain of adult faith formation, learning in community, and shared practice' (2013, pp. 59–60).

More Recent Developments

In a similar fashion to the above, we can trace and highlight some key instances from the more recent and contemporary development period of the SG movement. Five examples will be taken here to help clarify the variety of engagements ongoing with the concept of the SG and its contribution to Christian living.

Emergence of the Cell-Church Movement

Beyond the Western Church tradition, David (Paul) Yonggi Cho developed a modern SG or 'cell-church' movement in Seoul, South Korea. From humble beginnings, Yoido Full Gospel Church, started by Cho and his future mother-in-law in 1958, grew to fifteen thousand members by 1971 and would continue to see exponential growth, today numbering in the hundreds of thousands, with Cho 'implementing a cell-group home structure' (Carter, 2018). Cho's inspiration was based on Acts 2:46-47 and other relevant New Testament texts from which he deduced that the way the early Church absorbed three thousand believers after Pentecost and took care of their needs, was through their homes and not the public temple meetings. He also felt that by following the advice of Jethro to Moses, to break up the large crowd into small sections and appoint judges, with delegated authority over each section, to help him govern them (Ex 18), 'he would not wear himself out trying to meet the needs of all those in his charge' (Cho & Hostetler, 1981, p. 18).

Consequently, Cho initiated a 'home cell group consisting of fifteen families or fewer' to meet the needs of church members in their various local regions (Cho & Hostetler, 1981, p. 50). This community context enables members of such a large congregation not to feel 'alienated, lonely, [or] aimless' (Cho & Hostetler, 1981, p. 49). They minister gifts to and pray for one another, care for each other, both practically and spiritually, and discuss their problems together, all leading to a sense of security. The cell leader is a kind of pastor to them and teaches the Bible, but based upon the church-appointed outline' (Cho & Hostetler, 1981, p. 51) or 'standard Bible study course' (Cho & Hostetler, 1981, p. 113). For Cho, the cells form the essential parts of the church, but cell members should also publicly worship and receive instruction from the message preached in this larger setting. Finally, apart from pastoral care, according to Cho, the cell provides a perfect context for evangelism to happen in a non-confrontational way (Cho & Hostetler, 1981).

North America and the Western Church Cell Groups

Drawing upon Cho and other cell-church writings, primarily from the majority world (Comiskey, 2014), key USA leaders such as Ralph Neighbour, Carl George, Lyman Coleman, Gareth Icenogle and others pioneered a comparable movement in North America. However, notwithstanding a few exceptions, the groups were 'more flexible in structure and adaptable to [that] culture', as Cho's pure cell model did not experience the same results in the Western context as it had in Asia (Donahue & Gowler, 2014, p. 120). One such adaption can be seen outworked in the large evangelical congregation of Willow Creek in the USA. As a twelve thousand member church in 1991, it faced a crisis. Their people were having a difficult time making the church part of their lives and their lives part of the church, resulting in them struggling to experience meaningful community. Following the strategy of SG expert Carl George, Willow Creek began to transition their church with a commitment to put community life at its core through the development of a SG philosophy. For them, this meant that 'small groups–once a department–would now become a way of doing life and ministry' (Donahue & Robinson, 2001, p. 13). The result was the church moved from having ten to fifteen per cent of its members involved in SGs, to having eighteen thousand people connected in two thousand seven hundred SGs. For Willow Creek, following George's meta-church model (George, 1991; George & Bird, 1994), the groups can be varied, from task orientated usher groups to recovery groups, to new convert groups. To quote George, 'any time sixteen or fewer people meet together, you have a small-group meeting', which provides an opportunity for care, ministry to one other, and teaching (1994, p. 70). Therefore, Willow recommends that even task-based groups, such as food preparation teams, practice other community-building elements such as prayer or Bible study among its members. Other types of groups include affinity, age/stage, interest or care-based groups (Donahue & Robinson, 2001).

Catholic Examples: The Parishes of St Boniface and St Eustorgio

The contemporary Catholic SG movement draws upon the same Biblical and early Church history for support, and Cho's model also inspired at least one Catholic expression. After visiting Cho's church, Michael Eivers and Perry Vitale spearheaded a large cell-group organisation at St Boniface Catholic Church in Pembroke Pines, Florida, where parishioners gathered to pray, share and reflect on teachings of the Bible. The movement quickly spread among parishes and migrated to

St Eustorgio parish in Milan, Italy, a parish that to this day draws people from many nations, including Ireland (Mac Donald, 2014), to come and explore the cell system. Inspired by the vision of the parish as a 'community of communities' (Pope Francis, 2013, par. 28), and the Church that 'exists in order to evangelize' (Pope Paul VI, 1975, par. 14), the vision of the cells is to grow and when large enough multiply into more cells. This growth strategy is formed around cell members inviting others to join with whom they already have relationships – their '*oikos*' – i.e. family, work, friendship, shared interests (Vandenakker, 1994).

Basic Ecclesial Communities
As noted, Western Catholic SG proponents can also appeal to their heritage in Alphonsus Liguori and, to some degree, the extensive Catholic SG movement elsewhere, such as Latin America and Africa. For example, the Basic Ecclesial Communities (BECs) of Latin America constitute an enormous movement, possibly numbering 1.5 million people in Brazil alone and mainly based in rural and poor locations (Vandenakker, 1994). As already indicated, the tendency of some BECs to see themselves as constituting the Church on their own has been a contentious idea within the Church and has drawn condemnation from bishops and even some liberation theologians (Vandenakker, 1994). However, the original vision of these groups was evangelisation, scripture reading and reflection. Given the poverty where they emerged, and some influence of liberation theology, a strong social action element also developed, in some groups more than others (Cavendish, 1994; Vandenakker, 1994). Again, while variety with commonality exists within this movement, they nevertheless represent a significant SG expression with individual groups ranging in size anywhere from ten to seventy people (Cavendish, 1994; De C. Azevedo, 1985; Vandenakker, 1994).

Small Christian Communities and RENEW
Small Christian communities represent similar Western counterparts of such BEC groups, again adapted to suit that culture, not only in name but also in the reduced emphasis they place on political or social action, given their more affluent context. However, community action through serving is encouraged as part of SCC meetings, which also revolve around sharing life's struggles and joys, Bible study and prayer (O'Halloran, 2002). RENEW, an idea for parish renewal developed in 1976 by Archbishop Peter Gerety of Newark, New Jersey, and launched in that diocese between 1978-1980, under the leadership of Thomas Kleissler and Thomas Ivory, is considered to be 'one of the most

important reasons for the spread of SCCs'. Estimates suggest forty thousand Catholics participated in Newark diocese SCCs, and further that RENEW attracted approximately three million Catholics to its SGs since 1980 (Kleissler, LeBert & McGuinness., 2003; Lee, D'Antonio & Elizondo, 2000, p. 168; *RENEW International History*, 2017).

Research carried out between 1995 and1998 noted the recent proliferation of such Catholic SGs in America, again highlighting social loneliness, evidenced in 'successive sociological studies' on America over the previous forty years, as a factor behind this. These groups gather voluntarily, usually in members' homes, and are generally lay-led, albeit often with the support of clergy (Lee et al., 2000, pp. 2–8). They also see their role as instruments of evangelism, not only through proclamation but in providing a lived example of a community where the principles of the heard message of the gospel can also be experienced. Thus, 'announcing Christ (evangelism) ... explaining the faith (catechesis)' and 'the witness of the small Christian community' work together to promote a holistic encounter with Christ (Mallon, 2014; O'Halloran, 2002, pp. 17–18; SGN, 2010, par. 40, 69-73, 76-79). James Mallon, a priest from Nova Scotia, Canada, is among those emphasising moving the Church from maintenance to mission. A key element of his approach involves the use of small groups in the local parish (Mallon, 2014).

The Four W's

The discussion above has highlighted something of the variety of SGs, but also the similarities in their practical running. Elements that take place in such groups may be summed up from a popular cell-group format, the four W's: welcome, worship, word and witness/works. Explanations, examples for and even recommended times for each section are found in many cell books, with the welcome section often including icebreakers, and the second section using creative worship approaches. The allocation of time for the word is usually the most extended, possibly forty out of a ninety-minute meeting. It usually involves more applicational type of group sharing as distinct from the Sunday message, which may be more didactic in style. Some groups consider the Sunday message again in the midweek meeting, possibly after a brief re-cap is presented for anyone who missed the main service. Everyone is allowed to share, encouraged by a leader, using a facilitation leadership approach, who often poses both closed and open-ended questions to the group. The fourth 'W' is where the cell looks outward, to witness through planning evangelism or 'works' of the kingdom. The latter is where some social care can be expressed (Comiskey, 2001). Howard Astin, from the UK, adds a fifth 'W', representing the wind of the Spirit. This 'W' emphasises reliance on God and not being 'structure-bound', recognising that the Spirit leads groups, and sometimes to focus more on one aspect of the meeting than the other (Astin, 2002). Whether the structure is more or less formal, most SGs combine the elements noted earlier of building community and encouraging one another often through sharing, prayer and Bible study. Many also emphasise an outward focus of ministering God's kingdom through evangelism or service.

Responding to the Criticisms of Small Groups

The survey of examples of SGs engaged with here positions us to offer a more considered answer to the critiques concerning people's involvement in SGs, noted at the beginning of this chapter.

Firstly, do people grow in biblical knowledge? Part of answering this question may depend on how narrow one defines such growth. For example, Henderson contends that Wesley's different groups each developed varying aspects of the believer's faith: the society, the cognitive aspect; the band, the affective aspect; and the class, the behavioural aspect (Henderson, 2016) – sometimes referred to elsewhere as head, heart and hands (Shaw, 2014). Small groups can do teaching or Bible study but are particularly strong with regard to the affective and behavioural domains of growth by focusing on the application of teaching (SGN, 2010). After all, the best theology not only cultivates correct thinking but proper living (McGrath, 2019). Facts need to be processed and applied, and educationalists have long highlighted the benefits of SG interaction for such procedures (Knowles, Holton & Swanson, 2005; Shaw, 2014). Indeed, the communal aspect of learning that takes place in SGs engenders a highly sophisticated form of education (Pring, 2018; SGN, 2010).

Secondly, that SGs induce a low-level self-gratifying commitment among their members. The research above, however, indicates a strong vision within the SG movement to not only serve one another, but look outside themselves to witness to, and serve others. Naturally, the commitment to any voluntary organisation will vary. As noted, regular attendance at Wesley's class meetings was compulsory for acceptance into the society. Even today some groups ask attendees to sign a covenant form, indicating one's commitment to carry out the tasks of the group for a required period (Ogden, 2018). Other groups, while less formal, may nonetheless attract very faithful members. Generally speaking, a strong communal rather than individualist attitude is suggested in SG literature (Arnold, 2004).

Finally, the question of some SGs separating themselves from the wider Church has been addressed above. Despite this tendency among some groups, the vision of the SG combining with the larger gathered Church, to offer a more holistic religious experience, is the predominant model advanced (SGN, 2010; Vandenakker, 1994). Kleissler, LeBert and McGuinness outline this process as a three-stage 'dynamic life cycle', in which the Catholic weekly SG meetings combined with the celebration of the Mass mutually 'complement' each other and strengthen parishioners to seek to live and witness to their Christian faith (2003, pp. 47–49; see also, SGN, 2010, par. 73).

Small Groups in Ireland Today

The historical review of SGs would not be complete without a brief mention concerning their popularity in Ireland today. Within the Reformed Tradition churches SGs of various kinds are well established (Evangelical Alliance Ireland, 2018; Presbyterian Church Ireland, 2016). The Catholic Church has also developed a wide variety of such groups ('Church Organisations', 2018; SGN, 2010). The Alpha course is an example of a popular SG approach represented across many Christian denominations. Like various western countries, Ireland is engaging with a postmodern culture, and the Church is encountering people at various points on their spiritual journey. Some who have experienced the Christian faith at an earlier point in their lives have lost their sense of commitment to Christ or to the Christian community. Others who have no familiarity with Christ and may be open to a relationship with him for the first time. Still others who are believers, and are in the Church, require teaching or catechesis to grow in their intimacy with Jesus, their life within the Church and society, and their witness to the world (SGN, 2010). Considering their continuous developing presence in Church one might posit that SGs represent a possible basis for a renewed Christian, and possibly ecumenical, witness in Ireland today (SGN, 2010). Such witness would give example, not only by using new language to invite others to meet Jesus but would be posited upon a renewed community, inculturating the message in a lived word that speaks to people's head, heart and hands (SGN, 2010).

Paul F. Perry

References

Aldhouse-Green, M.J. (ed), *The Celtic World*, London/New York: Routledge, 1995.

Anderson, B., Byrne, G. & Cullen, S., 'Religious Pluralism, Education, and Citizenship in Ireland', in E. Aslan, R. Ebrahim, &. M Hermansen (eds), *Islam, Religions, and Pluralism in Europe*, Dordecht: Springer, 2016, pp. 161–172.

Arnold, J., *The Big Book on Small Groups*, rev. edition, Downers Grove, IL: InterVarsity Press, 2004.

Astin, H., *Body and Cell: Making the Transition to Cell Church, a First-hand Account*, London: Monarch Books, 2002.

Atkinson, H.T., *The Power of Small Groups in Christian Formation*, Eugene, OR: Resource Publications, 2018.

Beckham, W.A., *The Second Reformation: Reshaping the Church for the Twenty-First Century*, Houston, TX: TOUCH Publications, 2005.

Bradley, I., *Pilgrimage A Spiritual and Cultural History*, Oxford: Lion Hudson Pub. Plc., 2009.

Bradley, I., *Celtic Christianity: Making Myths and Chasing Dreams*, Edinburgh: Edinburgh University Press, 1999.

Brondos, D.A., *Jesus' Death in New Testament Thought*, San Angel, México: Comunidad Teológica de México, 2018.

Buchanan, M.T., 'Pedagogical Drift: The Evolution of New Approaches and Paradigms in Religious Education', *Religious Education; Decatur*, 100/1, (2005), pp. 20–37.

Byrne, G. & Kieran P. (eds), *Toward Mutual Ground: Pluralism, Religious Education and Diversity in Irish Schools*, Dublin: Columba, 2013, pp. 147–155.

Byrne, G., 'Lifelong Faith Development in the Home, Parish and Other Educational Environments', in P. Kieran, & A. Hession (eds), *Exploring Religious Education: Catholic Religious Education in an Intercultural Europe*, Dublin: Veritas, 2008, pp. 35–41.

Carter, J.A., 'Preaching in the Global South', in Mark P. Hutchinson (ed), *The Oxford History of Protestant Dissenting Traditions, Volume V: The Twentieth Century, Themes and Variations in a Global Context*, Oxford: Oxford University Press, 2018.

Cavendish, J.C., 'Christian Base Communities and the Building of Democracy: Brazil and Chile', in *Sociology of Religion*, 55/2, (1994), pp. 179–195.

Cho, Y. & Hostetler, H., *Successful Home Cell Groups*, Plainfield, NJ: Logos International, 1981.

'Church Organisations', Catholicireland.net. Available at: https://www.catholicireland.net/organisations/

Clarke, R., *A Whisper of God: Essays on Post-Catholic Ireland and the Christian Future*, Dublin: Columba, 2006.

Comiskey, J., *Reap the Harvest: How a Small Group System Can Grow Your Church*, Moreno Valley, CA: CCS Publishing, 2015.

Comiskey, J., *2000 Years of Small Groups: A History of Cell Ministry in the Church*, Moreno Valley, CA: CCS Publishing, 2014.

Comiskey, J., *How to Lead a Great Cell Group Meeting So People Want to Come Back*, Houston, TX: Cell Group Resources, 2001

Comiskey, J., *Home Cell Group Explosion: How Your Small Group Can Grow and Multiply*, Houston, TX: Touch Publications, 1998.

Davies, O. & O'Loughlin, T., *Celtic Spirituality*, New York: Paulist Press, 1999.

De C. Azevedo, M., 'Basic Ecclesial Communities: A Meeting Point of Ecclesiologies', in *Theological Studies*, 46/4, (1985), pp. 601–620.

Donahue, B. & Gowler, C., 'Small Groups: The Same Yesterday, Today, and Forever?', in *Christian Education Journal*, 11/1, (2014), pp. 118–133.

Donahue, B. & Robinson, R., *Building a Church of Small Groups: A Place Where Nobody Stands Alone*, Grand Rapids, MI: Zondervan, 2001. Evangelical Alliance Ireland, *Growing & Vibrant: A Census and Survey of Christian Churches beyond the Traditional Four Main Denominations*, Evangelical Alliance Ireland, 2018.

Edwards, N., 'The Archaeology of Early Medieval Ireland, c.400-1169', in Dáibhí Ó Cróinín (ed), *A New History of Ireland 1: Prehistoric and Early Ireland*, Oxford: Oxford University Press, 2008.

Finney, J., *Recovering the Past: Celtic and Roman Mission*, London: Darton, Longman & Todd, 1996.

Ford-Grabowsky, M., 'Flaws in Faith Development Theory', in *Religious Education*, 82/1, (1987), pp. 80-93.

Fowler, J.W., *Becoming Adult, Becoming Christian: Adult Development and Christian faith*, 1st edition, San Francisco: Harper & Row, 1984.

Fuller, L., *Irish Catholicism since 1950: The Undoing of a Culture*, Dublin: Gill & Macmillan, 2004.

Gallagher, S.K. & Newton, C., 'Defining Spiritual Growth: Congregations, Community, and Connectedness', in *Sociology of Religion*, 70/3, (2009), pp. 232-261.

George, C.F., *Prepare Your Church for the Future*, Grand Rapids: F.H. Revell, 1991.

George, C.F. & Bird, W., *The Coming Church Revolution: Empowering Leaders for the Future*, Grand Rapids, MI: F.H. Revell, 1994.

Harrington, B., *Discipleship That Fits: The Five Kinds of Relationships God Uses to Help Us Grow*, Grand Rapids, MI: Zondervan, 2016.

Harris, M., *Fashion Me a People: Curriculum in the Church*, 1st edition, Louisville, KY: Westminster/John Knox Press, 1989.

Henderson, M.D., *John Wesley's Class Meeting: A Model for Making Disciples*, Wilmore KY: Rafiki Books, 2016.

Huebner, D.E., 'Christian Growth in Faith', in *Religious Education*, 81/4, (1986), pp. 511-521.

Hunter III, G.G., *The Celtic Way of Evangelism: How Christianity Can Reach the West … Again*, Nashville, TN: Abingdon Press, 2000.

Icenogle, G.W., *Biblical Foundations for Small Group Ministry: An Integrative Approach*, Downers Grove, Il: InterVarsity Press, 1994.

Inglis, T., *Moral Monopoly: The Rise and Fall of the Catholic Church in Modern Ireland*, 2nd edition, Dublin: University College Dublin Press, 1998.

Irish Episcopal Conference, *Share the Good News: National Directory for Catechesis in Ireland* [SGN], Dublin: Veritas, 2010.

Kleissler, T.A., LeBert, M.A. & McGuinness, M.C., *Small Christian Communities: A Vision of Hope for the 21st Century*, rev. and updated edition, New York: Paulist Press, 2003.

Knabb, J.J. & Pelletier, J., '"A Cord of Three Strands Is Not Easily Broken": An Empirical Investigation of Attachment-based Small Group Functioning in the Christian Church', in *Journal of Psychology & Theology*, 42/4, (2014), pp. 343-358.

Knowles, M.S., Holton III, E.F. & Swanson, R.A., *The Adult Learner: The Definitive Classic in Adult Education and Human Resource Development*, Burlington, VT: Routledge, 2005.

Lee, B.J., D'Antonio, W.V. & Elizondo, V.P., *The Catholic Experience of Small Christian Communities*, New York: Paulist Press, 2000.

Mac Donald, S., 'Irish Parishes Involved in Milan Parish Cells Seminar', *Catholicireland.net*, 2014. Available at: https://www.catholicireland.net/international-seminar-parish-cells-milan/

Mallon, J., *Divine Renovation: Bringing Your Parish from Maintenance to Mission*, New London, CT: Twenty-Third Publications, 2014.

McGrath, A., 'Navigating Towards Renewal: Lay Pastoral Ministry in the Church', *Studies: An Irish Quarterly Review*, 101/404, (2012), pp. 449-458.

McGrath, A., *Mere Discipleship: Growing in Wisdom and Hope*, Grand Rapids, MI: Baker Books, 2019.

Murray, D.B., *In a Landscape Redrawn*, Dublin: Veritas, 2017.

Ogden, G., *Discipleship Essentials: A Guide to Building Your Life in Christ*, revised and expanded ed., Downers Grove, Il: InterVarsity Press, 2018.

Ogden, G., *Transforming Discipleship: Making Disciples a Few at a Time*, revised and expanded edition, Downers Grove, Il: InterVarsity Press, 2016.

O'Halloran, J., *Small Christian Communities: Vision and Practicalities*, Dublin: Columba, 2002.

Oman, D. & Thoresen, C.E., 'Spiritual Modeling: A Key to Spiritual and Religious Growth?', in *The International Journal for the Psychology of Religion*, 13/ 3, (2003), pp. 149-165.

Otero, L.M. & Cottrell, M.J., 'Pioneering New Paths for Adult Religious Education in the Roman Catholic Community: The Promise of Communities of Practice', in *Journal of Adult Theological Education*, 10/1, (2013), pp. 50–63.

Pope Francis, *Evangelii Gaudium: Apostolic Exhortation on the Proclamation of the Gospel in Today's World*, 2013. Available at: http://w2.vatican.va/content/francesco/en/apost_exhortations/documents/papa-francesco_esortazione-ap_20131124_evangelii-gaudium.html

Pope John Paul II, *Redemptoris Missio: On the Permanent Validity of the Church's Missionary Mandate*, 1990. Available at: https://w2.vatican.va/content/john-paul-ii/en/encyclicals/documents/hf_jp-ii_enc_07121990_redemptoris-missio.html#-2C

Pope Paul VI, *Evangelii Nuntiandi*, 1975. Available at: http://www.vatican.va/content/paul-vi/en/apost_exhortations/documents/hf_p-vi_exh_19751208_evangelii-nuntiandi.html

Presbyterian Church Ireland, *Quick Start Guides for Working with Small Groups*, 2016. Available at: http://www.presbyterianireland.org/Resources/Training-Resources/Small-Groups/Quick-Start-Guides-for-Working-with-Small-Groups.aspx

Pring, R., *The Future of Publicly Funded Faith Schools: A Critical Perspective*, London/New York: Routledge, 2018.

Radcliffe, T., *Why Go to Church? The Drama of the Eucharist*, London/New York: Continuum, 2008.

Radcliffe, T., *I Call You Friends*, New York: Continuum, 2001.
RENEW International History, 2019. Available at: http://www.renewintl.org/RENEW/index.nsf/GO/History?OpenDocument

Robbins, J., 'The Globalization of Pentecostal and Charismatic Christianity', in *Annual Review of Anthropology*, 33/1, (2004), pp. 117–143.

Shaw, P., *Transforming Theological Education: A Practical Handbook for Integrative Learning*, Carlisle: Langham Global Library, 2014.

Sheldrake, P., *Living between Worlds: Place and Journey in Celtic Spirituality*, London: Darton, Longman & Todd, 1995.

Stancliffe, C., 'Religion and Society in Ireland', in P. Fouracre (ed), *The New Cambridge Medieval History: Volume 1: C.500-c.700*, Cambridge: Cambridge University Press, 2015.

Turner, V.W. & Turner, E.L.B., *Image and Pilgrimage in Christian Culture: Anthropological Perspectives*, Lectures on the History of Religions, New York: Columbia University Press, 1978.

Vandenakker, J.P., *Small Christian Communities and the Parish: An Ecclesiological Analysis of the North American Experience*, Kansas City, MO: Sheed & Ward, 1994.

Vatican II, *Lumen Gentium: Dogmatic Constitution on the Church*. Available at: https://www.vatican.va/archive/hist_councils/ii_vatican_council/ documents/vat-ii_const_19641121_lumen-gentium_en.html

Walton, R., Disciples Together: The Small Group as a Vehicle for Discipleship Formation', in *Journal of Adult Theological Education*, 8/2, (2011), pp. 99-114.

Wilkinson, L., 'Going Deeper: Books on Celtic Christian Spirituality', in *Christianity Today*, 44/5, (2000), p. 82.

Williams, J., 'Experiential Learning in Local Ministry Training: Insights from a "Four Villages" Framework', in *Journal of Adult Theological Education*, 4/1, (2007), pp. 63-73.

Wuthnow, R., *'I Come Away Stronger': How Small Groups Are Shaping American Religion*, Grand Rapids: Eerdmans, 1994.

Part III:

~~~~~~~~~~

Presence, Accompaniment, Transformation

Chapter 8

~~~~~~~~~~~~~~~~

To Be or Not to Be a Pastoral Presence: The Role of the Chaplain in Catholic Education and Beyond

Thomas G. Grenham

'*May You Awaken to the mystery of being here*
And enter the quiet immensity of your own presence.'
(O'Donohue, 2000, p. 99)

Introduction

I am currently chair of a chaplaincy Master's programme at Dublin City University (DCU). I also teach a module on loss and bereavement as well as a module on family systems on the programme. These are important areas when it comes to helping chaplains learn skills of presence in difficult circumstances. My background, as well as being an educator and theologian, is in hospital chaplaincy and parish ministry. These encounters have brought me into contact mostly with the Catholic Christian tradition. Ecumenical experiences, however, and interactions with people of other religious traditions and secular beliefs have been significant for me too, in Ireland and in other countries including the United States and Kenya. Ten years working in Kenya as a missionary forged a mindset for the need of chaplaincy without frontiers – beyond one's own religious and cultural tradition.

I have come to understand that chaplaincy is not just for Christians. Nor is the service only identified in the context of Catholic education. It is a service that extends to others who adhere to diverse beliefs both religious and secular in many different contexts. The word 'Catholic' means universal. James Walters writing about chaplaincy in the twenty-first century offers an insightful observation:

Catholicity may be the Church's greatest gift to public institutions in our age. A recognition of the contribution of different groups as a celebration of diversity needs to evolve into a more New Testament vision of interdependence and mutual flourishing. (Walters, 2018, p. 56)

Chaplaincy may have emanated from within the Christian tradition but it is universal in its reach to the whole world.[1] Traditionally, it was the role of the clergy to be chaplains. However, chaplaincy has moved beyond that in many contexts with people besides clergy becoming qualified and accredited chaplains. The contexts for chaplaincy have widened, too, beyond the traditional role in schools, hospitals, and prisons. Chaplaincy has extended into other workplaces and various caring organisations, such as nursing homes, police and defence forces and sporting organisations, and become associated too with parish ministry. Some also talk of chaplaincy for issues such as climate change and the environment. Indeed, chaplaincy takes on a new significance, too, in a time of pandemic. The Covid-19 pandemic is an example of where the service of chaplaincy can offer a non-anxious and reassuring presence for those experiencing stress and anxiety. In many contexts a chaplaincy service can be accessed virtually on various social platforms available on the internet.

The challenge for an effective chaplain is learning to be a supportive and life-giving presence to all they encounter within diverse contexts. Having the opportunity to participate in a programme that sets out to teach the necessary skills and knowledge not just for one's own tradition, but that also engages with the traditions, beliefs and worldviews of others, is significant. This chapter is an attempt to outline the necessary ingredients for a Catholic chaplaincy, one which is grounded in its own tradition but actively engaged in being a compassionate and life-giving presence to others of various worldviews, religious or secular. Although the challenge of creating a chaplaincy programme that achieves this is demanding, it is an important priority given the need for chaplains in a growing range of settings and circumstances. Sophie Gilliat-Ray and Mohammed Arshad in writing about multifaith chaplaincy maintain that,

The challenges and opportunities of multifaith chaplaincy have been severely tested in relation to the political contests that have surrounded chaplaincy since 9/11, and the increasing scrutiny placed upon chaplains to 'prevent violent extremism' and to promote 'community cohesion' (Gilliat-Ray & Arshad, 2016, pp. 117–118).

What is Presence? A Model for Chaplaincy

The first and most important area to begin with in chaplaincy is to explore what we mean by 'presence'. The chaplain is the person who brings all that they are, including their vulnerabilities, fragilities, weaknesses and limitations, into being an empathic presence to others who have similarly questioning, fragile and broken lives.

The philosopher John O Donohue writes about presence in much of his writing. He sees presence as a fundamental element in connecting to the deepest part of being human (O'Donohue, 2000). The heart's core is where the deepest desires and needs for love, belonging and value reside. In connecting to our deepest desire to belong, we can touch and belong to the transcendent presence. Such a presence is at the heart of effective pastoral care that is present to both the learner and teacher. Some scholars like Winnifred Fallers Sullivan writing from an American and evangelical perspective suggest that the 'ministry of presence' reduces religious traditions to bare basics. She writes:

> A ministry of presence has become commonplace in a breathtakingly short space of time. It has moved well beyond its Christian roots; the phrase, a ministry of presence, is used by chaplains from a wide spectrum of religious traditions in a range of institutional settings to denominate the work. The language of presence is also the language that the government and other institutions often use to describe what chaplains do. (Fallers Sullivan, 2019, p. 174)

In a pluralist world, I would suggest, such a model of presence has the capacity for inclusion of people with both religious and secular needs for chaplaincy without reducing the integrity of religious traditions. For example, within the education context and on a practical level, the chaplain has the role of reflecting a non-anxious, non-judgemental presence with both those who embrace a religious tradition and with those who live with a secular worldview. The chaplain, grounded and authentically faithful to their own religious or secular worldview, who 'loiters with intent' enables the discovery of a meaningful and life-giving presence for every learner, both formally and informally. I would maintain that the artful skill of 'presence' is an overarching model for chaplaincy in a pluralist and diverse society such as contemporary Ireland. Swift, Cobb and Todd (2016) suggest that,

> Chaplaincy is a practical discipline in the same way that psychiatry
> or the practice of the law is a practical discipline based upon a body
> of knowledge and involving skilled actions, reasoning and judgements
> about a set of particular circumstances with a degree of uncertainty.
> (p. 3)

Being an empowering pastoral presence is a life-long pilgrim journey in becoming more mindful of self, others, God and the created world. Pastoral presence is not something unique and pertinent to any one culture or religious context. Rather, to be present in a meaningful way implies the inner capacity to self-emptying – letting go of one's own biases, judgements, status, privilege and sense of position, so as to be free to 'be with' the other person's cultural and religious experience (Grenham, 2009, p. 40). An effective quality presence in a very conflicted and contested world can be the key ingredient to foster caring and inclusive relational communities everywhere. All cultures seem to experience and hold a sense of joy and happiness as well as a sense of woundedness, loss and bereavement. The skilful pastoral agent is open to learning and understanding the ways in which people feel joy and fulfilment as well as pain, loss and suffering within the specific cultural and religious reality of their lived experience (Grenham, 2009).

A quality pastoral presence is characterised by the skill to interpret one's own theology and spirituality through the lens of our own losses, as a bridge to enter the space of others' disappointments, betrayals and hurts. Such an interpretation can help to appropriately and authentically enter the space of the other and help them make sense of their suffering or indeed share their joy (Grenham, 2009). People are in need of finding life-giving meaning in both their joy and in their grief. The lens of the chaplain's theological vision, or perhaps a secular vision, can be a source of comfort to those who experience a vulnerability that causes them to despair and be anxious about the uncertainties of life. For Christians, the Bible story of Jesus' birth in a manger reveals God entering human affairs as a vulnerable human person, sharing in the joys and griefs of people. The power of God is in the meekness of the Bethlehem manger and not in the ostentation, wealth, privilege and status of the world around Jesus. Such a theological lens can help Christian believers to grasp the insight that being vulnerable, fragile, and limited can be a strength. The skill is to appropriately learn to use our fragilities and limitations as a means to gain life-giving insight into ourselves and others. Those who are non-Christian may find in their traditions, religious or secular, stories of faith and hope which help them to understand the human condition or human desire to meaningfully belong and be accepted. Chaplains can be very effective in accompanying others in that journey because they themselves have gone on that inner journey and discovered or rediscovered who they are and how they belong. For example, the school chaplain can be that powerful and effective presence to young people who are setting out on a journey of discovery in education. In that process, they learn something of who they are and how they want to belong.

Presence and Belonging

In that process of young people discovering who they are and how they belong, the school chaplain in the school context has a specific role, including spiritual leadership, and represents the life of faith, seeking to nourish those of faith and indeed those whose faith may be of a different belief or world view. There may be many beliefs represented in the school and chaplains need to be versatile and flexible in their approach to address the needs of all the students. This is a challenge in a multi-belief environment but not beyond the imagination to organise appropriate inclusive spaces for reflection and inclusive spiritual events. My assumption is that every person has an innate spirituality. What is needed from the chaplain are ways in which that spirituality can be discovered through a creative approach to spiritual events, using both secular and religious symbols and rituals for example. According to John Caperon, 'School chaplains speak of a "ministry of presence", where being is more significant than doing, where incarnation or embodiment is what counts' (2016, p. 320). Upon this understanding, Caperon, in quoting Martyn Percy, notes that chaplains 'occupy that strange hinterland between the sacred and the secular, the temporal and the eternal, acting as interpreters and mediators, embodying and signifying faith, hope and love' (pp. 320–321).

A quality chaplaincy presence is at the core of chaplaincy because it can enhance and indeed support learners in their discovery of themselves, their relationship with others and their interaction with an ultimate reality of meaning and purpose. Not only does learning involve the cognitive, but most learning also includes an appreciation and integration of emotional, moral, spiritual and faith intelligences, evoked in the realm of mystery, feelings and deep desires. Consequent upon this understanding of education, the chaplain has an important place in assisting, accompanying, supporting and empathising with learners in their ongoing development for a more holistic and life-giving journey, towards the mystery of presence for themselves, others, the environment and God. Swift, et. al., note that,

> In the case of chaplaincy the practice is intended to be conscientiously caring and supportive of the particular interests of those cared for. The practice of care is relational and depends upon the capacity to understand the needs of those being cared for and accepting a responsibility for meeting some or all of those needs. (2016, p. 3)

Chaplaincy encounters vulnerability in others and this can be disturbing as well for the professional chaplain.[1] What is it that gets disturbed in a chaplain when he or she meets vulnerability and fragility in others? For example, what is triggered in a chaplain when he or she engages with a family member, friend, or a close acquaintance who is dying? Can the chaplain hold the sacred dying space or the vulnerable space with them appropriately and just simply be present to their agony and despair, to their anguish, to their terrible fear of death, to their loneliness, and to their dying dreams? It is not an easy or comfortable presence for any chaplain or pastoral worker. I have discovered that there is no distinct and definitive point when I can say I have arrived at being fully present and attentive. I am always reminded of my own suffering and vulnerability and fear of dying as well – fear that was overcome by addressing the inevitable prospect of my own mortality. This was very helpful for my work as a hospital chaplain meeting everyday people dealing with loss and grief.

One of the experiences that helped me deal with my own sense of loss and grief was an assignment in the training and formation as a chaplain in the CPE programme (Clinical Pastoral Education). Disturbing as it may seem to the unconscious eye, to write one's own obituary and discuss it in the small supervision group was most enlightening and informative. There was the initial shock of being required to do this assignment, but it was well explained what the purpose of the assignment was – to be present and help us think and reflect on loss and grief not only for ourselves, but also to understand what it might be like for others going through such emotional trauma as death and dying. The idea or vision for this assignment was to help us trainee chaplains come to terms with our own mortality and have the capacity to be present to others who are dying and close to death. I found it a great exercise in coming to terms with my own dying and inevitable death, something which accompanies every one of us. Death is a shadow that does not go away but we might find ourselves ignoring it and putting it aside, though we know it will come one day. However, having said how helpful writing the obituary was, the thought of dying is still nerve racking and I wonder can chaplains really have this fully integrated into the ebb and flow of life. Perhaps some have and the rest are still working on it! Death and dying is certainly a powerful dynamic in the provision of a quality presence. It is so much easier to be present to those who experience joy, happiness, fulfilment and personal success. Being present to those who are joyous and fulfilled is part of chaplaincy too and rejoicing when people are in a good space is important for the wellbeing of everyone. Celebration is part of the Chaplain's repertoire of life-giving presence.

Dynamics and Principles of a Quality Presence

John Patton states that:

> The pastoral carer, whether laity or clergy, is present to the person cared for in a particular kind of relationship – one that 're-presents' the presence of God through relationship to the person cared for. Pastoral carers 're-present' or remind persons of God by remembering and hearing, and affirm by their action that God continues to hear and remember them. (2005, p. 22).

Patton's idea of presence is linked to his faith in God. He sees pastoral carers/chaplains as, in some way, by the quality of their presence, really making the presence of God felt in their encounters with students, prisoners, the lonely, the lost and so on. In exploring the dynamics and principles of how the school chaplain can be an authentic and relevant presence for both teachers and students, either in formal or informal education, one discovers that being or journeying with learners creates a space for new insights into what seems a daunting task. Walking with learners, listening to their worries and concerns, as well as their hopes and dreams, will allow time and space for learners to come to an understanding of their story of despair or worry for themselves, others and the environment around them. Celebrating the learners' achievements and their joy at succeeding is very important. Organising celebratory rituals to mark those joyous and successful milestones is the work of the effective chaplain in any school context. The response from learners sometimes is thanks for listening, thanks for celebrating, thanks for being on the journey with us; the journey ahead does not seem so bad! The exam is not so much of a concern, and so on. Or the suffering makes sense; there is a sense of hope at the end of the conversation. There is a connection to something more than themselves. Swift et al. offer a convincing analysis that the distinctiveness of chaplaincy is

> found in its attentiveness to the sacred, a term that itself could easily be the subject of a whole book. The adoption of the term sacred is a carefully chosen signifier of those fundamental qualities of life that go beyond the material and mundane by which people orientate and make sense of their lives. The sacred can be expressed in all aspects of human thought and behaviour including beliefs, values and practices, and in artefacts, symbols, places and environments. (2016, p. 3)

Biblical Foundation for Chaplaincy Presence (Emmaus): To Teach as Jesus Did or To Accompany as Jesus Did

The Christian scriptures reflects in many of the parables and stories on the historical Jesus and on his continuing presence to Christians as the Christ of faith. As such they illustrate a presence of love, compassion, advocacy, hospitality and empathy. One such powerful biblical foundation for chaplaincy is the Emmaus story (Lk 24:13–15).I am always fascinated by this resurrection story. I am particularly fascinated by the risen Jesus who appears to the two disciples on their way to Emmaus. I wonder why Jesus never says to them, 'I have risen; it is I.' I often wonder if any of us rose from the dead would we be so disciplined and not tell someone immediately. And even without such a dramatic experience as rising from the dead, we have a tendency to jump in and tell people the answer, fix the problem or suggest solutions that seem obvious to us. Still, one would imagine that rising from the dead is not the sort of thing you would be quiet about! It is an extraordinary boundary that Jesus holds as he walks with the two very disillusioned disciples. It is an amazing boundary that, when kept, allows the two disciples to express their hurt, anger, expectations and feelings of concern for themselves and others who had hoped that Jesus was the Messiah. And interestingly, the two disciples eventually discover for themselves the 'solution' to their despair and despondency.

Later in the story, it might seem that Jesus is giving out to the two disciples for being slow to *see* the meaning and purpose of their despair and great loss. A good chaplain or a good teacher waits and waits and waits for the answer, but like Jesus, might need to encourage them to find the answer, perhaps challenge them, just as Jesus did saying, 'You foolish men! So slow to believe the full message of the prophets!' Jesus at this point almost lets it go. However, he goes on: 'Was it not ordained that the Christ should suffer and so enter his glory?' (Lk 24: 25–27). And Jesus explains to them the story beginning with Moses and so on. All through this Jesus holds the boundary between himself and his puzzled and misunderstanding disciples. Jesus is trying to get them to understand the meaning and purpose that the suffering Messiah went through. He wants them to grasp the significance and indeed the 'solution' for themselves. He still does not tell them the answer or offer them a 'solution'. Jesus does not 'fix it' or 'rescue' them from their troubles. He explains some more to them on the journey as they walk together. And, finally, their eyes were opened. They begin to understand. They have insight. They found joy and hope and purpose once again in his presence to them. They were excited and returned to Jerusalem.

How their hearts burned within them when Jesus explained the scriptures! Jesus was an attentive listener. He did not 'fix' his companions, but he was there for them. He allowed them to talk and express their despair and bewilderment at what had happened in Jerusalem three days earlier. He was an attentive listener in his life-giving presence to them. Jesus, in this narrative, illustrates what developing the whole human person entails. He promoted respect for the dignity of each individual person no matter what the context. Jesus is compassionate in his understanding of those in despair and who have lost hope. Being an attentive, compassionate listener, he does not 'fix' those he was accompanying. He explains the scriptures, explains their religious tradition for them and they discover the hope that they need to move on in their own lives. Of course, we also see in this story the role of hospitality in chaplaincy. Jesus was invited to stay the night, rest and eat. And as soon as the bread is broken, their eyes are opened. Similarly, an effective chaplain will offer hospitality. A nice cup of tea or coffee never goes amiss or even a pizza to share can sometimes 'open eyes' and allow people to talk freely about important issues and concerns for them. This sort of hospitality can help create a safe space within which to have a healing conversation as well as encourage and foster appropriate boundaries in the welcoming context.

Boundaries

Much has been written about the need for boundaries in the area of pastoral care. Richard Gula's work, particularly, comes to mind (Gula, 2010, pp. 129–143). Boundaries are necessary not only for the protection of the person being accompanied but also to enable the chaplain to be meaningfully present and active in a supportive manner. Gula explains that

> boundaries are the way we set limits that create a hospitable space wherein others can come in and feel safe with someone who makes room for them and accepts them. In the safe space created by clear boundaries those seeking pastoral service can trust that we will not take advantage of their vulnerability. Then they can be free to focus on their own needs and experiences without having to deal with ours. (2010, p. 130)

The Emmaus story underlines some of these necessary boundaries. Jesus kept his own 'stuff' to himself, particularly the astonishing part that it was he who had risen from the dead. This story of Emmaus tells a lot about how appropriate boundaries are contained. I imagine Jesus might have felt like telling them that he had risen in order to save them the pain of telling their stories of despair and to rescue them from their suffering. There was no rescue. Jesus did not dilute or shrug off their despair and hopelessness. He allowed them to articulate their anxiety and fears. There is an enormous learning here for chaplains not to start with their own stories of hope, joy and excitement at coming out the other end of a painful experience. Rather, the chaplain has to park their own stuff and let the person speak their troubles. People need the opportunity to tell their stories of pain and need someone like a chaplain to have the necessary skill to attentively listen and receive that story without judgement. It is because Jesus' keeps the boundary between himself and the two disciples that wonderful things happen for these two disillusioned people. Their hearts are burning within them as they listen to Jesus, whom they do not yet recognise. Their despondency is transformed at the breaking of the bread. They return to Jerusalem so that they can tell the story of their life-giving experiences to those in Jerusalem, where they find they are not alone. The risen Jesus has made himself present to Simon Peter as well. The man accompanying them on the road could have told them who he was, but he did not, and he allowed them to speak out of their story of despair at the awful things that had happened in Jerusalem. This is an astonishing boundary and piece of knowledge that Jesus kept to himself until the disciples on the road were able to discover for themselves that he had risen. He was a life-giving presence for them and compassionately accompanied them on the road. Jesus was a powerful, unobtrusive presence and, in that presence, he assisted the two disciples to make sense of their life experiences. The risen Jesus can provide the same possibilities for chaplains today and for the young people in schools that they accompany, as well as for others. He helped the two disciples to struggle to find meaning and value in the events of the previous three days in Jerusalem. He can help us too to open our eyes to what is happening all around us.

Jesus' presence was non-intrusive and it was non-anxious. No anxiety was created by this person accompanying them on the road. Their despair and disappointment was not increased by the apparent gentle presence of this stranger. The stranger among them was the risen Jesus. Jesus explained to them what the scriptures meant and he listened to them and yet they did not recognise him. In other words the presence of Jesus as a care-giver did not interfere with the healing taking place along the road. The healing was not about Jesus and his rising from the dead, but it was about the two disciples coming to know a different reality for themselves. It was about transforming their own suffering and despair into hope and joy. Such a transformation took place in the moment of hospitality in the sharing of a meal and the sharing of bread. It was in this eucharistic meal that the transformation of their lives took place. The two disciples made a 'heart-burning' discovery in the hospitality encountered between them and Jesus.

The Power of Hospitality

As noted earlier, effective chaplains are aware of the importance of good hospitality. It was not different in Jesus' time. Hospitality was significant in the Emmaus story. A hospitable chaplain is a very approachable person. Interestingly, it was the invitation by the two disciples for Jesus to stay with them for the night that the real significance of hospitality emerges. It was only in the breaking of the bread at the end of journey that the two disciples realised who Jesus was and then he seemed to vanish from their sight. Where did he go? Jesus became present in a different way. He vanished into themselves as they recognised him in the bread.

The vanishing of Jesus is intriguing for it teaches chaplains that there is an appropriate time to leave the scene. Knowing when to leave the person or patient or student during the visit is important. There may be a more positive or life-giving impact upon the person by the chaplain's presence in a shorter stay. The chaplain can always come back again at another time or at the invitation of the person. It is significant to note that once the disciples recognised him that Jesus departed, for that moment at least. Interestingly, Jesus was still present to the disciples in a different way because he was now present in their hearts. A boundary is uncovered here. The chaplain needs to know during a visit to a student, a patient, or a prisoner, that they can be tired, sick, vulnerable and not always in good spirits. A brief visit might be sufficient. Chaplains, like Jesus in the Emmaus story, learn to recognise when their presence is no longer required, as the person they have been accompanying might need to be alone to discover for themselves the hope and meaning in their suffering situation.

Quality Presence as a Model for Chaplaincy

To conclude, key ideas for developing and fostering an effective chaplaincy built around presence can be identified. First, a quality presence, as a model for chaplaincy, is the living core of being an effective chaplain. Second, chaplaincy, while grounded in the Christian tradition, can go beyond that religious tradition in order to be present to others of no particular religious faith and to those who hold a secular worldview. Third, the chaplain is uniquely placed to serve the spiritual needs of a society that is unfamiliar with formal religion. Fourth, the intercultural and multi-faith reality of much of our world creates the space for a pastoral presence that is dynamic in its provision. Finally, reading the signs of our age, such as climate change, pandemics, the environment, and the threat of extinction of life on the planet, and interpreting them for significance and new life, puts the role of chaplain into a special context of 'presence' in order to hear and listen to these signs for new hope, meaning and purpose.

ENDNOTES

1   Notwithstanding the origins and interpretation of chaplaincy in the New Testament, the history of the term itself goes back to the fourth century AD with the story of St Martin of Tours (316?-397). See David O'Malley 'The Origins of Chaplaincy', 2015.

References

Caperon, J., 'Case Study', in C. Swift, M. Cobb & A. Todd (eds), *A Handbook of Chaplaincy: Understanding Spiritual Care in Public Places*, London and New York, Routledge, 2016, pp. 315–325.

Fallers Sullivan, W., *A Ministry of Presence: Chaplaincy, Spiritual Care and the Law*, reprint edition, Chicago: The University of Chicago Press, 2019.

Gilliat-Ray, S. & Arshad, M., 'Multifaith Working', in C. Swift, M. Cobb & A. Todd (eds), *A Handbook of Chaplaincy Studies: Understanding Spiritual Care in Public Places*, London and New York: Routledge, 2016, p. 109–122.

Grenham, T.G. (ed), *Pastoral Ministry for Today: 'Who Do You Say That I Am?' Conference Papers 2008*, Dublin: Veritas, 2009.

Gula, R.M., *Just Ministry: Professional Ethics for Pastoral Ministers*, New York/ Mahwah, NJ: Paulist Press, 2010.

O'Donohue, J., *Eternal Echoes: Exploring Our Hunger to Belong*, New York: Harper Perennial, 2000.

O'Malley, D., 'The Origins of Chaplaincy', 2015. Available at: www. catholicyouthwork.com/the-origins-of-chaplaincy-from-fr-david-omalley-sdb/#

Patton, J., *Pastoral Care: An Essential Guide*, Nashville, TN: Abingdon Press, 2005.

Swift, C. Cobb, M. & Todd, A. (eds), 'Introduction to Chaplaincy Studies' in *A Handbook of Chaplaincy Studies: Understanding Spiritual Care in Public Places*, London and New York: Routledge, 2016, pp. 1-9.

Walters, J., 'Twenty-First Century Chaplaincy: Finding the Church in the Post-Secular', in J. Caperon, A. Todd & J. Walters (eds), *A Christian Theology of Chaplaincy*, London and Philadelphia: Kingsley Publishers, 2018, p. 43–58.

Chapter 9

~~~~~~~~~~~~

Salesian Accompaniment in Formal and Non-formal Settings

John J. Lydon and James G. Briody

Introduction

In a Catholic Christian context, accompaniment is rooted in the way in which Jesus accompanied his disciples at every stage of their journey. This is encapsulated best in the episode in scripture recalling the encounter between Jesus and the two disciples on the road to Emmaus (Lk 24:13–35). There are several striking features in this passage, not least the reciprocity and mutuality captured in the dialogue between Jesus and the two disciples. Michael T. Winstanley highlights in particular the way in which Jesus allows the disciples to take the initiative in inviting him to stay with them:

> The disciples thus take the initiative in responding to Jesus and his words. It is not without significance that Jesus waits to be asked, for he never imposes himself, never forces his friendship; with remarkable sensitivity he reverences our freedom. But once the offer of hospitality is extended, he accepts it promptly. (Winstanley, 2017, p. 351)

'Never imposing himself' reflects the classical 'offer not impose' perspective which permeates the documents of the Second Vatican Council:

Catholic education is offered not imposed. One phrase can recapture its impetus: 'Proposing faith in modern society'. A very similar form of this expression occurs in the opening homily of the Second Vatican Council by Pope John XXIII. It involves thinking simultaneously and jointly of the mission of Catholic teaching in Church and in society. (Derycke, 2007, p. 335)

Derycke, addressing faith formation in a contemporary context and the movement in France from 'a sociological to an evangelical' anchor in the context of formation in the faith, is reflecting upon the seminal statement of the Congregation for Catholic Education (CCE) which insisted that a Catholic school 'cannot relinquish its own freedom to proclaim the Gospel and to offer a formation based on the values to be found in a Christian education' (CCE, 1988, par. 6). This notion of 'offer rather than impose', in essence a dialogical concept, is also central to the underpinning methodology of many religious education programmes following the Second Vatican Council.

The Emmaus Paradigm and Religious Education

Thomas Groome, in his classic and foundational text *Christian Religious Education* (1980), points out that the Emmaus story has become paradigmatic for people committed to what he describes as a shared praxis approach to religious education. The term shared praxis emphasises that growth in Christian faith in essence takes the form of a journey. The term also highlights Groome's conviction that dialogue between teacher and student must form a central component of all religious education.

By adopting this approach Groome (1980) sought to ensure that all religious education programmes maintained a balance between the faith tradition of the Catholic Church on the one hand and the experience of students on the other. Groome, while reflecting Winstanley's (2017) point referenced earlier that Jesus demonstrated his commitment to personal presence in accepting the disciples' hospitality, suggests that Jesus takes the initiative in pronouncing his blessing over the bread and distributing it to them (Lk 24: 30). Groome (1998) writes that 'in this simple but profound act of service – feeding others – they came to recognise "the stranger" for themselves' (p. 307).

Groome (1998) goes on to insist that the verb translated as 'recognise' is the Greek '*epignoskein*', meaning conversion, a recognition that leads to discipleship.

The five-stage process outlined below underpins many Catholic religious education programmes and is equally significant in the context of the educational approach of St John Bosco (1815–1888) who emphasised the importance of meeting students at their stage of the faith journey.

The Emmaus Story – Luke 24:13–35	Five Stages
Verses 13–17	Jesus joins the disciples on their journey.
Verses 18–24	Jesus encourages the disciples to talk about what they have experienced and how they feel.
Verses 25–27	Jesus reminds the disciples of the scriptures and the faithful Saviour God portrayed in their tradition.
Verses 28–32	The disciples find joy and encouragement in Jesus' company. He shares their meal and, in the blessing and breaking of bread, they recognise him.
Verses 33–35	They run back to share the news with the other disciples.

Each of the five stages is integral to the notion of presence and accompaniment underpinning Salesian accompaniment, encompassing taking the initiative in engaging young people in dialogue through allowing them to share their story and creating the space for purposeful dialogue on the journey to becoming 'honest citizens and good Christians', the central aim of the Salesian educative project (Bosco, 1884, cited in Lemoyne (ed), *Memorie Biografiche* [MB], 1989, p. 46).[1]

'Go to the Pump'

Reflecting the initiative of Jesus in inviting the two disciples to share their story, St John Bosco's advice to one of his key early collaborators, Vespignani, was to 'go to the pump' (Vespignani, 1930). At the water pump in Valdocco, Turin, near the site of Bosco's first oratory, boys often came together. Bosco expected his educators to be where the boys were. Such encounters in a non-formal context have the effect of building up trust which forms the basis of every educational practice or encounter. As Carlo Loots suggests 'this practice teaches that it is best to follow first to be allowed to guide later' (2018, p. 5).

Bosco's idea was that the boys would be inspired, through these initial invitational encounters of 'going to the pump', to join his oratory, a name which reflects the influence of St Philip Neri (1515–95), the founder of the Oratorians. Don Bosco took over the basic features of the Oratory including catechism lessons and opportunities for recreation. He would often make the point that oratories without some element of religious instruction were simply games rooms. Luciano Pazzaglia (1993) is insistent on the latter point, cautioning against a reductionist view of the first oratory as a playground or a meeting place for children: 'what Don Bosco had in mind was a school ... where ... religion was practised and youngsters were inspired to live a Christian life' (p. 282).

Bosco (1989) was undoubtedly affected deeply by his experience of visiting the Turin prison, the Generala, a prison where he saw large numbers of boys aged between 12 and 18. In the *Memoirs of the Oratory* (1989) he recalls that the experience of seeing them idle, without food for body and soul, left him with a deep sense of concern:

> What shocked me most was to see that many of them were released full of good resolutions to go straight, and yet in a short time they landed back in prison, within a few days of their release. (Bosco, 1989, p. 182)

This was undoubtedly a foundational experience for Don Bosco, together with a deeply rooted conviction that developing meaningful relationships with young people was the key to educational progress. Avallone notes that in the period of history in which Bosco lived: 'there was a great psychological barrier between teacher and pupil. The distance was a tool for stern discipline'. He goes on to point out that Bosco bridged the divide by emphasising the necessity of 'rapport and kindness, so vital for security and warmth and closeness in the maturing process' (1979, p. 8).

St John Bosco's Educative Project

In the context of Bosco's (1884) educative project, his initial aim was to break down this barrier between educator and teacher, encapsulated in his 'Letter from Rome' (1884, cited in Braido, 2005) to Salesians, constituting an evaluation of the extent to which the original inspiration of the project was being maintained:

The teacher who is seen only behind his lectern is a teacher and no more. But when he spends recreation time with the boys, he will become like a brother. When someone sees a priest preaching from the pulpit, one will say that the man does no more neither less than his duty. But if he speaks words during recreation time, that will be the words of someone who loves. (p. 384)

Spending recreation time with the boys was, therefore, seminal in terms of Bosco's educational vision. Presence in the form of constructive engagement by educators was the key to gaining the trust of the young people. For St John Bosco, the first principle of pastoral care was presence. Like the picture painted of the Good Shepherd, the Salesian educator knows his pupils, goes before them and, like the father in the story of the Prodigal Son (Lk 15), is prepared to make the first move. Far from being simply passive watchfulness, the presence-assistance advocated by St John Bosco reflected the optimistic humanism both of himself and that of Frances de Sales. As Bosco's biographer John Lemoyne (1989) puts it:

Just as there is no barren land which cannot be made fertile through patient effort, so it is with a person's heart. No matter how barren or restive it may be at first, it will sooner or later bring forth good fruit ... The first duty of the animator is to find that responsive chord in the young person's heart. (MB, Vol. III, pp. 236-237)

The use of the word 'animator' (from the Latin '*anima*' meaning 'soul') here is significant since it reminds us of the Greek word for soul, '*psuche*' – the soul or breath of life, the dynamic principle or life-force within every human being. Salesian presence, therefore, should be dynamic, breathing life into situations, making things happen. The Salesian animator should be involved with the young people in their activities, arousing their interest and leading them to constructive engagement. In the writings of Don Bosco there is often reference to the importance of informal presence among young people. In a book entitled *Life in the Recreation Ground*, with reference to Don Bosco, Albert Caviglia (1943) states:

He considered it a sacred duty to be familiarly present among young people ... it is in the Salesian's informal contacts with young people that true education of character is more than anywhere made possible. (p. 16)

It is clear, then, that contact with young people in the classroom and other formal situations alone does not suffice. The educator must establish an abiding presence with young people. He must seek to be in touch with young people in all possible situations of the school day and beyond, especially in activities that allow the educator to associate with young people not simply in the role of a teacher but as a brother or friend. In the 'Letter from Rome', cited in a volume published by the Salesians of Don Bosco, Don Bosco writes:

> By being loved in the things they like, through their teachers taking part in their youthful interests, they are led to those things too which they find less attractive, such as discipline, study and self-denial. In this way they will learn to do these things also with love. (1972, p. 271)

Such active, dynamic presence, of its nature, takes its inspiration from the Gospel in terms of the self-sacrifice involved, reminding us again of the Good Shepherd who 'lays down his life for his sheep' (Jn 10:11) The tireless zeal demanded by such an abiding presence among young people also echoes Jesus' three-fold criteria for discipleship: 'if anyone would come after me, he must deny himself and take up his cross and follow me' (Mk 8:34). Don Bosco's reference to Jesus 'making himself little with the little ones' indicates a further, perhaps deeper, way in which presence is an imitation of Christ.

Reminding us of Francis de Sales' reference to God disregarding himself (cited in McPake, 1981), Bosco's 'becoming little with the little ones' (p. 137) involved the animator, by definition, in divesting himself of the vestiges of authoritarianism which marked the traditional standpoint of the teacher of the day. At a human level, 'meeting the students on their own turf' (Lenti, 1989, p. 7) involves taking a risk by letting go of the 'safety valve' inherent in the traditional teacher-student relationship. By being familiarly present to young people, as opposed to maintaining an institutional superior-inferior style of imposition, the assistant reflects the *ekenosen*, the self-emptying, of Christ himself. Bosco, then, interprets the entry into young people's recreation as an act of loving condescension, going beyond mere utilitarianism or paternalism. It involved adults leaving the lofty heights of their 'power over' or even 'power on behalf of' positions in order to engage in a genuine sharing of the bread of life. This engaging familiarity reflects the 'I-Thou' relationship spoken of by Martin Buber (1974):

... every human person looks bashfully yet longingly in the eyes of another for the yes that allows him to be. It is from one human person to another that the heavenly bread of self-being is passed. (p. 75)

Such a relationship, according to a recent major study from a psychoanalytical angle by Xavier Thévenot (1988), is developed primarily in the encounter between educator and pupils 'when they are relaxing together in recreation' (p. 710). These encounters constitute the kernel of the 'Preventive System', summed up by Pope St John Paul II (1988) in the following terms:

> The Salesian educators who participate in the lives of young people are interested in their problems, become aware of how the young see things, take part in their sporting and cultural activities and in their conversations as a mature and responsible friend. Furthermore, prospects, itineraries and good aims help to intervene to clarify problems, to indicate criteria, to correct with prudence and loving firmness ... (p. 12)

Creating a family spirit is central to the Salesian educative project. According to Lenti (1989), one of the principal advantages of the involvement of animators in recreation lay in its fostering of family spirit. Recreation contributed to the building up of an atmosphere of happiness and joy, which for Bosco was a fundamental prerequisite for education. Informal, uninhibited self-expression in recreation offered the educator an opportunity to learn about the youngster and his character. The presence of educators, *almost as equals*, enhanced the morale of young people, fostering the family spirit and mutual confidence. Summed up by Giuseppe Dacquino (1988):

> Don Bosco's didactic method was not predominantly cerebral in approach, something that could be completed sitting at a desk; it was an educational method based essentially on an affective relationship that spanned the entire day ... (p. 135).

Sodalities: A Family within the Salesian Family

'Going to the pump', involving relationships that are clearly non-authoritarian, helped sow the seeds of empowerment which, like recreation itself, became an integral part of the Salesian style of atmosphere, giving it an unmistakable character of solidarity and participation.

Sodalities, derived from the Latin '*soliditatem*', were seminal to the Catholic ecclesial tradition and emerged strongly following the founding of major religious orders such as the Dominicans in the thirteenth century. In Bosco's time, the formation of sodalities, referred to by him as '*compagnia*', was a key expression of empowerment, regarded by him as fundamental to the Salesian family. The terms 'sodality' and 'confraternity' are sometimes used interchangeably, connoting a concept of solidarity around a common mission. Joseph Hilgers describes such sodalities as:

> From the era of the Middle Ages very many of these pious associations placed themselves under the special protection of the Blessed Virgin, and chose her for patron under the title of some sacred mystery with which she was associated. The main object and duty of these societies were, above all, the practice of piety and works of charity ... in the course of the sixteenth century and the appearance of the new religious congregations and associations, once more there sprang up numerous confraternities and sodalities which laboured with great success and, in many cases, are still effective. (1912, p. 142)

Lemoyne (1989) describes the founding of several sodalities around 1859 which combined spiritual exercises with charitable activities. The boys themselves were responsible for the running of the sodalities, under the guidance of one of the Salesians who acted as a spiritual director (MB, Vol. VI, p. 103). Such an organisational structure promoted the building up of energetic and integrated Christian characters who gained confidence through the delegation of responsibility. Sodalities were an essential, indispensable factor in Don Bosco's educational organisation, and they grew along with the maturing of his experience. They were an instrument for the practical realisation of those educative collaborations between pupils and educators, without which it would be idle to speak of a family spirit.

Initially the charitable activities were focused on the members of the school community. Louis Grech (2019, p. 96) refers to the Sodality of Mary Immaculate to which the schoolboy Saint Dominic Savio belonged and makes the point that 'being of service to others was a very useful means which Bosco used to empower the young people to mature in responsibility and spirituality'. Lemoyne points out, however, that the work of the sodalities was extended to include service to others beyond the confines of the school community. Collaboration with the Society of St Vincent de Paul was significant in this context. This accompaniment in the service of others has been described by Miguel Morcuende as an experience of compassion which promotes service and love for what is essential:

> Compassion is the criterion by which one's inner life is judged to be authentic. Compassion is not a feeling. It is something much deeper, its roots in the depths of the heart. From a soul that is open to what is essential in life are born genuine Gospel experiences, missionary hearts and actions with a social outreach and generous solidarity benefitting the poor. (p. 200)

Spiritual Accompaniment

Sodalities represent a significant bridge between the building of trust gained in non-formal contexts and accompaniment at a more deeply spiritual level. This is made possible by the maturing of relationships between Salesians and young people through the media of recreation and participation in sodalities. Jack Finnegan encapsulates this bridge when suggesting that:

> Salesian spirituality develops in spaces where intense interior energy and social solidarity converge. Through the art of friendly conversation, Salesian spiritual accompaniment encourages and supports dynamic convergence. Through gentle dialogue it seeks, identifies and promotes wise and reasonable ways to harmonise interior and social practices with the abilities and understanding of those accompanied. Salesian spirituality seeks God in ordinary ways in the ordinary activities of life, ways centred in and driven by the heart, a heart that is open and generous, humble, gentle and committed. (2018, p. 144)

An Integral Concept of the Human with Space for Spiritual Meaning and Religion

It is important, in any discussion of aspects of Salesian pedagogy and methodology, to place emphasis on the spiritual and religious dimensions of meaning. A holistic view of being human avoids accepting the human person as the only active creator of meaning. The Salesian pedagogical perspective transcends such a narrow anthropocentric image of the human and emphasises human openness to the transcendent. This openness allows a movement from focusing on the self towards focusing on the other. It can take the form of a 'radical otherness' (Burggraeve, 2016, p. 1) and might be described as the capacity to transcend the physical, the empirical and even the inner worldly. Such underpinning allows human beings a way of coming to terms with experiences of suffering, disaster, guilt, failure and death in the sense that these do not have the final word on the human condition.

Denying this openness for transcendence and the encompassing meaning of human existence, which it could be argued is one consequence of a dominant post-modern secular narrative, does not do full justice to the essential dimension of being human. For Burggraeve (2016), the Salesian pedagogical project in the spirit of Don Bosco rejects such a closed image of the human. In contrast it 'honours an integral or holistic view of the human whereby the existentially spiritual openness to transcendent meaning is not shied away from but actually takes centre stage' (Burggraeve, 2016, p. 2).

Towards Maturity, Holiness and Wholeness

The human person's quest for understanding life's mystery is an ongoing journey. Spirituality, if explored with appropriate care and support, can assist in seeking further truth. It attempts to offer insights about the transcendental, life in God, life in the universe. Spirituality can therefore be identified with a particular anthropological approach. 'Spiritual' refers to something beyond the material. Engaging in spiritual accompaniment is engaging in a desire to work towards human maturity, holiness and wholeness. These ideas are reinforced in the *Final Document of the Synod of Bishops on Young People, Faith and Vocational Discernment*:

> Spiritual accompaniment is intended to help people integrate step by step the various dimensions of their lives so as to follow the Lord Jesus. In this process three elements can be identified: listening to life, encounter with Jesus and mystical dialogue between God's freedom and that of the individual. (2018, par. 97)

This necessarily involves engaging with others and with the spirit of God. At the same time, young people need to be heard first and foremost, through their own experiences, i.e. *where they are*. Having said this, the word 'spiritual' deals, not only with external actions, but with the inner life. It concerns matters of the heart, that is, the personal core of being from which emerges the good and the bad that people think or do. It also concerns the head, which is about using reason to decide whether something is good or bad. This is acknowledged in the exhortation: 'in personal spiritual accompaniment one learns to recognise, interpret and choose from the perspective of faith, listening to the Spirit's promptings within the life of every day' (Synod of Bishops, 2018, par. 97).

The Salesian pedagogical project takes seriously the dimensions of meaning, spirituality and religion as an anthropological constant. Don Bosco is concerned not only with the material, affective, intellectual, professional and social well-being of his young people but also and especially in their spiritual development. At the same time the educator strives for and develops those other dimensions highlighted in being faithful to the Christian view of integral meaning and wholeness through the pastoral care which is part of the Church's mission.

Building Relationships, Journeying Together

Accompanying contains in itself the element of participation in another's personal life and the element of journeying. Some use the word 'guidance', others 'mentoring', others 'accompaniment' to express these elements. For Bosco accompanying the young was integral to the daily life of his students. The programme he set out was holistic in nature with the spiritual life integrated into each day. Bosco accompanied young people in order to integrate the realm of the spiritual with actual living. He saw accompaniment as a relationship of complete spiritual and emotional assistance which helped a person grow and mature in awareness, responsibility and freedom. It also enabled the individual to discover the will of God. For Bosco the ultimate goal of pastoral care was to help people to centre their lives in the mystery we call God.

Accompanying therefore contains two critical elements:

- the first is building a relationship,
- the second is the idea of journeying together through life.

Accompaniment can be assimilated with the great biblical journeys, such as the journey of Abraham, giving it a biblical foundation. We are told in the Old Testament that all initiatives come from God and that he accompanied his own people. Biblical journeys and itineraries all have a beginning, a development stage and a completion-fulfilment stage. God asked individuals, and others, to be attentive to his Word. This same Word transforms the heart and inclines it towards God.

Accompaniment as Christocentric

In a Christian context, central to the journey undertaken in accompaniment is the person of Jesus Christ. The accompaniment is Christocentric. It is impossible to specify a precise route that Abraham was asked to undertake; likewise, it is impossible to map the route of the soul. We must however follow the person of Jesus, as the Synod of Bishops reminds us: 'Jesus accompanied his group of disciples, sharing his daily life with them' (2018, par. 96).

To guide the soul, to clear doubts, and to be resolute in the face of the daily call to conversion that Christ extends to each of us is the goal. In spiritual accompaniment one is accompanied by others; but one does not simply follow them. We might ask 'Where does the journey lead?' It is not simply to heaven nor is it to an external physical place. Instead it is a journey to discover uniqueness. In a Salesian context this is generally accomplished, not individually, but in the company of others. The Synod of Bishops makes clear that as well as following Jesus fellow pilgrims are involved in accompaniment:

> Community experience highlights the qualities and the limits of every person and helps us to recognise humbly that unless we share the gifts we have received for the common good, it is not possible to follow the Lord. (2018, par. 96)

Within this it is essential that each person undertake their own journey according to their own route. Ultimately for Bosco, the journey is the search to do God's will in Christ; the destination is the same; all must arrive at God. This thought resonates with one of the defining moments of Vatican II, which centres on its assertion in *Lumen Gentium: Dogmatic Constitution on the Church* (1965, par. 7), that the Christian vocation is a call to holiness and fullness of life itself. This is the end point of the biblical quest 'to see the face of God and live' (Ex 33:18–23; see also Ps 105:4, and Jn 11: 40). For the follower of Christ this fundamental vocation is sealed in baptism. The waters of baptism symbolise that heritage of abundant life given by God in Christ.

Conclusion: Returning to Emmaus

The Synod of Bishops sets out for us the efficacy of the Emmaus model:

> As the account of the Emmaus disciples shows us, accompanying requires availability to walk a stretch of road together, establishing a

significant relationship. The origin of the term 'accompany' points to bread broken and shared (*cum pane*), with all the symbolic human and sacramental richness of this reference. (2018, par. 92)

In returning to the Emmaus story it is worth reminding ourselves, following Winstanley's assertion quoted earlier, that Jesus is prepared to make himself present to the disciples on the road and to take the initiative in helping them understand the significance of the events they have experienced. He also identifies himself in the breaking of bread.

Bosco's recognition that the accompanier of the young, in any situation, is prepared to walk alongside, making the first move to offer a listening ear or the hand of friendship, follows the Emmaus paradigm in that the teacher/pastoral worker makes themselves available where there is a situation of need. It is this point of giving which can prove transformative both for the accompanied and the one accompanying.

Again the Synod of Bishops is clear that the invitation to accompany goes out to all of those who are stakeholders in the education of young people:

As well as family members, those called to exercise a role of accompaniment include all the significant persons in the various spheres of young people's lives, such as teachers, animators, trainers, and other figures of reference, including professional ones. (2018, par. 93)

They are also clear that accompaniment does not stop simply with the spiritual but must have a wider holistic impact:

Accompaniment cannot limit itself to the path of spiritual growth and to the practices of the Christian life. Equally fruitful is accompaniment along the path of gradual assumption of responsibilities within society, for example in the professional sphere or in socio-political engagement. (2018, par. 94)

This sentiment fits well with the maxim of Salesian education to form 'good Christians and honest citizens'.

ENDNOTES

1 This seminal aim of the Salesian educational system permeates the primary and secondary Salesian sources. The phrase first appeared in St John Bosco's 'Plan for the Regulation of the Oratory' in 1854, and cited in Lemoyne, J., (ed.), *The Biographical Memoirs of St John Bosco: Memorie Biografiche di don Giovanni Bosco* [MB], New Rochelle, NY, Salesian Publications, 1989.

John J. Lydon and James G. Briody

References

Avallone P., *Reason, Religion and Loving Kindness*, New Rochelle, NY: Salesian Publications, 1979.

Bosco, J., *Memoirs of the Oratory*, Memoirs of the Oratory of St. Francis de Sales from 1815 to 1855 (1815-1855), The Autobiography of Saint John Bosco, trans. by D. Lyons, with notes and commentary by E. Ceria, L. Castelvecchi, and M. Mendl, New Rochelle, NY: Salesian Publications, 1989.

Bosco, J., 'A Letter from Rome' (1884), in P. Braido, *Don Bosco Writings and Testimonies*, Rome: LAS, 2005.

Bosco J., 'Plan for the Regulation of the Oratory' (1854), in J. Lemoyne (ed) *The Biographical Memoirs of St John Bosco*, trans. from Italian, *Memorie Biografiche di don Giovanni Bosco* (MB), Volume II, New Rochelle, NY: Salesian Publications, 1989.

Buber M., *To Hallow This Life: An Anthology*, Westport, CT: Greenwood Publishing Group, 1974.

Burggraeve R., 'The Soul of Integral Education Orientations for a Contemporary Interpretation of "Religione"', *The Salesian Pedagogical Project*, KU Leuven: 2016.

Caviglia, A., *Life in the Recreation Ground*, Turin: LDC, 1943.

Congregation for Catholic Education [CCE], *The Religious Dimension of Education in a Catholic School*, London: Catholic Truth Society, 1988.

Dacquino, G. *Psicologia di Don Bosco*, trans. from Italian, *Psychology of Don Bosco*, Turin: SEI, 1988.

Derycke, H., 'Catholic Schooling in France: Understanding La Guerre Scolaire', in G. Grace & J. O'Keefe (eds), *International Handbook of Catholic Education: Challenges for School Systems in the 21st Century*, Part 1, Dordrecht: Springer, 2007, pp. 329–345.

Finnegan, J., 'Spiritual Accompaniment: The Challenge of the Postmodern and the Postsecular in the Contemporary West', in F. Attard & M. Garcia (eds), *Salesian Accompaniment*, Part 3, Bolton: Don Bosco Publications, 2018, pp, 131–152.

Grech, L., *Accompanying Youth in a Quest for Meaning*, Bolton: Don Bosco Publications, 2019.

Groome, T., *Christian Religious Education*, San Francisco: Jossey-Bass, 1980.

Groome, T., *Christian Ministry: An Overview*, San Francisco: Wipft & Stock, 1998.

Hilgers, J., 'Sodality', in C.G. Herbermann (ed), *The Catholic Encyclopaedia: An International Work of Reference on the Constitution, Doctrine, Discipline, and History of the Catholic Church Vol. 14*, New York: Robert Appleton Company, 1912.

Lemoyne, J. (ed), *Memorie Biografiche di don Giovanni Bosco* [MB], trans. from Italian, *The Biographical Memoirs of St John Bosco*, Volumes 1-XVIIII, New Rochelle, NY: Salesian Publications, 1989.

Lenti A., *Don Bosco's Educational Method*, New Rochell, NY: Salesian Publications, 1989.

McPake, M., *The Constitutions: A Simple Commentary*, Madras: The Citadel, 1981.

Morcuende, M., 'Personal Accompaniment in the Salesian Educative-Pastoral Plan', in F. Attard & M. Garcia (eds), *Salesian Accompaniment*, Part 3, Bolton: Don Bosco Publications, 2018, pp.187-200.

Pazzaglia, L., 'Don Bosco's Option for Youth and his Educational Approach', in P. Egan & M. Midali (eds), *Don Bosco's Place in History*, Rome: LAS, 1993, pp. 267-296.

Pope John Paul II, *Iuvenum Patris: Father of Youth: Apostolic Letter written on the first centenary of the death of Don Bosco*, Rome: Libreria Editrice Vaticana, 1988.

Salesians of Don Bosco, *The Constitutions and Regulations of the Society of St Francis of Sales*, Rome: LAS, 1972.

Synod of Bishops, *Final Document of the Synod of Bishops on Young People, Faith and Vocational Discernment*, Rome: Libreria Editrice Vaticana, 2018.

Vatican II, *Lumen Gentium: Dogmatic Constitution on the Church*, Rome: Libreria Editrice Vaticana, 1964.

Vespignani, G., *A Year at the School of Blessed Don Bosco (1886-87)*, San Benigno Canavese: Salesian Publications, 1930.

Winstanley, M.T., *Walking with Luke*, Bolton: Don Bosco Publications, 2017.

Chapter 10

∿∿∿∿∿∿∿∿

See-Judge-Act:
A Proposal to Adopt the Pastoral Cycle Promoted at Vatican II as a Basis for a Distinctively Catholic Pedagogy in School and as the Basis for Lifelong Formation in the Faith

Raymond Friel

Introduction

The pastoral cycle See-Judge-Act was endorsed by Pope John XXIII in *Mater et Magistra*, his encyclical published in 1961 to mark the seventieth anniversary of the first of the social encyclicals, *Rerum Novarum* (1891). The cycle had been developed, in its modern form, by Joseph Cardijn, a Belgian priest who founded the Young Christian Workers at the beginning of the twentieth century. His starting point was that in any engagement with another person or community one had to 'see' the other as fully as possible, to immerse oneself in their reality, more so if they were oppressed. In this way an outsider to the community will not take as normative their own perspective or bring a pre-determined 'solution' to the situation of the oppressed.

Cardijn's central concern, writing in 1951, was the 'transformation of life' through individual and collective action by lay people. The aim was to 'replace human vision and judgement with the vision and judgement of God' (Cardijn, 1964, p. 97). The discernment required to do this was matured by the See-Judge-Act process, which he developed with the Young Christian Workers as an 'apostolic dialectic' by which lay people would bridge the gap between what God willed to be the case and what was the case, between the kingdom of God and the kingdom of the World. 'Lay people are formed first of all by the discovery of facts, followed by a Christian judgement, resulting in the actions they plan, the plans they carry into effect' (Cardijn, 1964, p. 98).

In *Mater et Magistra* John XXIII adopted Cardijn's approach as the exemplary way to apply the Church's social doctrine. He said that the approach 'should be taught as part of the daily curriculum in Catholic schools, particularly seminaries' (Pope John XXIII, 1961, par. 223). Not only was the content of social doctrine to be taught but See-Judge-Act was to be used as the preferred pedagogical method: 'It is important for our young people to grasp this method and to practice it' (Pope John XXIII, 1961, par. 237). The desire that this approach should be part of the curriculum in Catholic schools was not realised, at least not in Europe and North America, apart from a small number of stand-alone examples. It was in the soil of South America that See-Judge-Act took root in the post-Vatican II era and the next phase of its evolution unfolded. The papacy of John Paul II did not hold out much encouragement for this approach, perhaps because of its association with liberation theology and the lingering suspicion of proximity to Marxism.

Adaptation of the Method in South America

Leonardo and Clodovis Boff describe how liberation theologians adopted what they call the three traditional stages involved in pastoral work and re-cast them as the three main mediations of socio-analytical mediation, hermeneutical mediation and practical mediation. In the first stage, Cardijn's search for 'objective facts' is taken a stage further as the theologian asks the question, '*Why* is there oppression and what are its causes' (Boff & Boff, 1978, p. 24). Of the three explanations of poverty in liberation theology – the empirical, the functional and the dialectical – the dialectical explanation, poverty as oppression, sees poverty as the result of economic organisation, a contrivance, not a natural or spontaneous phenomenon, by which many are exploited (workers) and others are excluded (unemployed, marginal). Unlike the approaches of aid and reform, this approach argues that poverty can only be overcome by replacing the present system with an alternative system. In this, it is very close to the vision for Catholic education described by the Congregation for Catholic Education (CCE) in the 1982 document, *Lay Catholics in Schools*, when it states:

> The vocation of every Catholic educator includes the work of ongoing social development: to form men and women who will be ready to take their place in society, preparing them in such a way that they will make

the kind of social commitment which will enable them to work for the improvement of social structures, making these structures more conformed to the principles of the Gospel. (par. 19)

This in turn is in line with Vatican II's teaching on the 'special vocation' of the laity which was to 'seek the kingdom of God by engaging in temporal affairs and ordering these in accordance with the will of God' (Vatican II, *Lumen Gentium*, 1964, par. 31). The apostolic dialectic developed by Cardijn, (a formation in the process of recognising the incompleteness of social reality from a Gospel perspective) can be understood as being a key point in the Church's teaching on education.

See

In the context of a Catholic school, this methodology provides an approach to the curriculum. Any body of knowledge can be regarded as a way of 'seeing' the world, but the See-Judge-Act methodology, especially as matured in South America, invites us to ask questions relevant to an analysis of the power equations at work: essentially, who 'runs' this seeing? Who has 'permitted' this seeing and why not others? Who is not 'seen' in this account of reality? Whose dignity are we oblivious to? Whose story is unheard? Beyond these striking questions, we also need to apply suspicion to our own point of view: do I understand or 'own' my own prejudice? Am I in danger of regarding the poverty I see as functional, to be reformed, with the poor as passive objects of my benign intervention?

In educational terms, this 'seeing' translates into the design of the curriculum, what the teacher means to propose to and achieve with the students. What scope of 'seeing' do we intend to put before our pupils, what reality will we expose them to? Whose history? Whose literature? In the apparently 'neutral' school subjects such as languages or mathematics, the examples or applications we choose are part of our 'seeing'. In languages are all our examples drawn from commercial exchanges (buying food, arranging travel)? In mathematics, in the teaching of percentages, say, consider the difference between using the example of calculating the interest rates on mortgage payments and the example of the interest rates on a pay-day loan taken out by a single parent on a zero-hours contract.

Judge

When we have assembled and interrogated the 'primary data' of the situation or event with as much self-awareness as possible, then we may be in a position to 'judge' or interpret the event 'in the light of faith'. This pedagogical approach is favoured by the documents of the CCE from 1977 onwards. In *The Catholic School* (1977), the document which some refer to as the 'foundation charter' of Catholic education, it states that all teachers should be trained in 'the art of teaching in accordance with the principles of the Gospel' (par. 37). Like many of the Congregation's documents, the ideal is held up but is unsupported by any suggestions for implementation, perhaps an understandable approach when the teaching is received in so many jurisdictions. Boff and Boff's approach to this part of the cycle, judge, what they call liberative hermeneutics, is concerned not with the meaning-in-itself of the text but 'interpreting life according to the scriptures' (1987, p. 34). This begs the question of how we arrive at a 'correct' reading of an event or situation in the light of scripture. A 'proof texting' approach to scripture is insufficient. Gadamer's approach is more instructive: that 'the whole of scripture guides the understanding of individual passages' (Gadamer, 2013, p. 182). Without doubt, this pre-supposes a high level of formation in the teacher, theological as well as educational.

James Alison offers us a way out of regarding the teacher as one who needs to be well versed in scripture to teach in the light of faith. He offers Luke's story of the encounter on the road to Emmaus as the definitive account of the dynamics of Christian interpretation. Alison notes that the two disciples are more than just 'talking' on the road. The Greek word *antiballete* is stronger and implies that they are having a heated disagreement. They cannot agree on the significance of the events they have just experienced, they have all the fragments but don't know how to read them yet. They are at odds. Jesus 'came near and went with them' (Lk 24:15). His accent reveals him to be a 'stranger in Jerusalem' (sojourner). Having given them a chance to demonstrate the incoherence of their account, he 'interpreted to them the things about himself in all the scriptures' (Lk 24: 13-35).

Luke presents Jesus here as their interpretative principle – and as a crucified and risen rabbi he is their *living interpretative principle*. The same point is made by Matthew when he described Jesus as our 'one teacher' (Mt 23:8). We are all his students. The two disciples take part in the greatest seminar of all time, being inducted into salvation history by the hermeneutical key himself. If only they had taken notes, our lives might have been so much simpler. But as Alison points out, that would have just left us with 'yet more text to interpret and there is no end of interpreting texts' (2013, p. 66). In biblical theophany YHWH is only grasped as he passes by and so it proved here. YHWH cannot be grasped fully in any text or experience.

But nevertheless, we have an account of an experience which the disciples know to be genuine: 'Did not our hearts burn within us.' They *know* it's genuine before they report back (no longer at odds with each other) to what Alison calls the 'Apostolic A-team' (Peter and the ten) in Jerusalem. What is remarkable to note is that this, the definitive account of Christian interpretation, happens away from the gaze of authority. When they go to Jerusalem, their story is *confirmed.* This is the shape of ecclesial authority and will help us in our application of this part of the cycle for schools. The experience of God is not received from Church authority, as Peter discovered when the Spirit descended on Cornelius and his household before he had a chance to fret about the correct ritual. If it is real, we will know it as we share it. If we share it and it turns out to be eccentric, we have a Church to support us which is 'authentically interpreting the word of God' and although that Church itself has not and cannot have arrived at the fullness of knowledge but is undergoing an 'ever deepening understanding of revelation' (Vatican II, *Dei Verbum*, 1965, par. 10).

The ordinary Christian experience according to Luke, is in Alison's reading, 'to have your text, your story, your very self, interrupted by, re-interpreted by a crucified and risen Lord' (Alison, 2013, p. 72). This is our interpretative principle. It is in as much as the Spirit of the forgiving loving Christ grows in us that we will be able to judge (interpret) our own story, our cultural heritage and our present reality in the light of faith. This approach, from the perspective of the one who offers all he has, gives us a hermeneutical key and a view of social reality, which does not require expert knowledge of the entire canon of scripture or the deposit of faith, although both are available to confirm and guide our work of interpretation. Boff and Boff adopt what they call the 'viewpoint of the oppressed'. They acknowledge that it is not the only possible and legitimate reading of the Bible, but they claim that for their community it has become the "hermeneutics of our times" (Boff & Boff, 1987, p. 32). It was not the dominant hermeneutics in the west until quite recently. Pope Francis, who himself was formed in See-Judge-Act methodology, has insisted on his vision of a poor church for the poor since his election in 2013.

In a school or parish setting, when we are engaged in a process of discerning the signs of the times, trying to judge a text, event or situation in the light of faith, we are invited to consider the perspective of the servant, the poor, the oppressed, the view from the bottom, from the margins. We are guided by the social doctrine of the Church, with its emphasis on human dignity and the nature of social structures which enhance or diminish human flourishing. We are guided by our own conscience through which we reflect on circumstances. A much-debated formulation in the *Declaration on Religious Freedom* states that the faithful 'ought to carefully *attend to* [my italics, note: not 'conform to'] the doctrine of the Church' (Vatican II, *Dignitatis Humanae*, 1965, par. 14) when exercising conscience.

Act

The final step is to act, to discern the best course of action to build the kingdom, to make the world a little more conformed to the will of God. In this step, Boff and Boff highlight the importance of strategy and tactics such as non-violent methods, dialogue, persuasion, moral pressure, passive resistance and other courses of action sanctioned by the ethic of the gospel (1987, p. 40). In Aristotle's terms, this is the application of practical wisdom, the virtue or excellence in deliberation, which involves 'rightness with regards to end, manner and time' (Aristotle, 2009, p. 112). Without such wisdom, seeing can become addictive voyeurism, judging can become paralysing reflection and action can become thoughtless intervention. Schools are invited to form their students in the habit of virtuous deliberation, seeing as fully as possible, judging what the plan of God is for the most vulnerable and acting to enhance human dignity and diminish human suffering.

The application of the methodology in a school setting can be illustrated by two examples which are currently testing the discernment of educators: the migrant crisis and digital literacy. When considering a boat full of migrants making their way to European shores, we invite our pupils to consider what they see, whose stories remain muted, who 'runs' the seeing of this story, *why* is this happening. We judge the situation from the point of view of the oppressed, the intervention of YHWH in the suffering of his people in exile in Egypt, the desire of Jesus to liberate the poor from their states of bondage and exclusion. Our action could be to understand more fully the status of migrants, their numbers in our community, to meet them, to hear their stories, to improve their physical condition in a benefit system which is hostile to their well-being. Likewise, with digital literacy, we can guide our children through the virtual environment, helping them how to see and to judge what is 'real' or 'fake' – i.e. that which bears no relation to any factual basis – and how to act in this space, how to interact safely, respectfully and creatively with other humans.

The methodology as outlined above is primarily a moral, or even political concern and for some in the Church this is limiting. It can, however, be applied in a spiritual, or personal way. In this approach, the individual is encouraged to 'see' into his or her interior life, to understand motivations and actions, to observe the gap between the actual life and the transformed life (the gap between nature and grace), to discern the promptings of the Holy Spirit towards the good. In this way the person can then act, under the influence of grace, to 'reform' the inner life and its motivations, which will lead to actions more conformed to the Gospel. If it is conformed to the Gospel, in the terms outlined by Alison and Boff and Boff, then a focus on the most precarious and fragile will not be lost.

In the Jesuit tradition, inspired by St Ignatius of Loyola, the method used for this reflective personal practice is the *Examen*. Mark Thibodeaux SJ comments that 'in the *Examen*, we review our recent past to find God and God's blessings in daily life' (Thibodeaux, 2015, p. x). The *Examen* does not use the language of See-Judge-Act but the elements are similar. Thibodeaux identifies five stages (the five Rs) in the *Examen* as follows: Relish the gifts in life and what has gone well; Request the Spirit to lead a review of the day; Review the day; Repent of any mistakes or failures; Resolve, in concrete ways, to live well tomorrow.

The review of the day is a way to see the day under the guidance of the Spirit and to judge or discern the aspects of the day which fell short of God's plan. This includes repentance for failures or shortcomings. The final part, the resolve, is the engagement of the will, again under the direction of the Holy Spirit, to resolve to live better, to act in the world in a more gospel-inspired way.

The two approaches, the moral and the spiritual, are intrinsically linked. They both work towards acting in the world in a way which will enhance the kingdom of God, bringing justice and peace where it is absent. The moral approach encourages group discernment, seeing a concrete situation as fully as possible, with a view to an examination of the power dynamics at work, interpreting the situation in the light of the gospel and then discerning the appropriate course of gospel-inspired action. This is well suited for use in schools and would, as Pope St John XXIII envisaged, provide an underpinning pedagogical approach to the curriculum. The moral approach can of course be applied by individuals formed in the practice. Hence its suitability into adulthood. Likewise, the spiritual approach is an ongoing lifelong journey, which works to the same end, the common good, aimed at an inner discipline which encourages the participant to grow in the practice of discerning past patterns of behaviour so that future behaviour can be more Spirit-filled.

Conclusion

The adoption of See-Judge-Act as the basis for lifelong learning is explicitly endorsed and encouraged by Vatican II. The *Decree on the Apostolate of the Laity* states that, 'Since formation for the apostolate cannot consist in merely theoretical instruction, from the beginning of their formation the laity should gradually and prudently learn how to view, judge and do all things in the light of faith' (Vatican II, *Apostolicam Actuositatem*, 1965, par. 29). This definition in fact could be applied either to the moral or the spiritual approach.

The Second Vatican Council's promotion of this methodology was part of the remarkable shift from a *deductive* approach, characterised by a teaching Church in which the laity was regarded as passive recipients of revealed truth from the magisterium, to an *inductive* approach, characterised by a learning Church which honours the faith encounter between the person and God. It honours conscience and understands that commitment to the faith, commitment to the gospel and the transformation of the world is not likely to be sustained by blind obedience to a body of teaching. Rather the Christian is one who experiences a lifelong induction into generous self-giving, loving forgiveness, into another story, told by the one who loves the poor in all their humanity, no matter what. He invites us to see the world otherwise than it first appears, and act in solidarity with the marginalised and oppressed. It is there, with him, that we will find ourselves.

References

Alison, J., *Jesus the Forgiving Victim*, Book I, Glenview, Il: Doers Publishing, 2013.

Aristotle, *The Nicomachean Ethics*, Oxford: Oxford University Press, 2009.

Boff, L. & Boff, C., *Introducing Liberation Theology*, New York: Orbis, 1987.

Cardijn, J., *Laypeople into Action*, Adelaide: ATF Theology, 1964.

Congregation for Catholic Education, *The Catholic School*, London: Catholic Truth Society, 1977.

Congregation for Catholic Education, *Lay Catholics in Schools: Witnesses to Faith*, London: Catholic Truth Society, 1982.

Gadamer, H.-G., *Truth and Method*, London: Bloomsbury, 2013.

Pope John XXIII, *Mater et Magistra*, 1961. Available at: http://www.vatican.va

Thibodeaux, M., *Reimagining the Ignatian Examen*, Chicago: Loyola Press, 2015.

Vatican II, *Lumen Gentium: Dogmatic Constitution of the Church*, 1964, in Abbott W. (ed), *The Documents of Vatican II*, New York: Herder and Herder, 1966.

Vatican II, *Apostolicam Actuositatem: Decree on the Apostolate of Lay People*, 1965, in Abbott W. (ed), *The Documents of Vatican II*, New York: Herder and Herder, 1966.

Vatican II, *Dei Verbum: Dogmatic Constitution on Divine Revelation*, 1965, in Abbott W. (ed), *The Documents of Vatican II*, New York: Herder and Herder, 1966.

Vatican II, *Dignitatis Humanae: Declaration on Religious Freedom*, 1965, in Abbott W. (ed), *The Documents of Vatican II*, New York: Herder and Herder, 1966.

Part IV:

Religious Education and
Faith Formation

Chapter 11

∿∿∿∿∿∿∿∿

Faith-talk and Reflection Spaces: An Empirical Study of Catholic Primary School Pupil Accounts of the Exploration of Faith at Home

Ann Casson

Introduction

In the Catholic faith tradition, the home is seen as the primal space for the child's religious socialisation, supported by the Catholic school and parish. There is however, a paucity of research on how the three work together to facilitate a child's exploration of faith. This chapter considers Catholic primary school pupils' descriptions of their explorations of faith at home, and investigates the stimulus for this activity. The focus is on the child's perspective, recognising that the child is an active agent, not a passive recipient in the faith transmission process. It employs the lens of French sociologist Danièle Hervieu-Léger's (2000) concept of 'religion as a chain of memory' to illuminate the changing patterns of influence of the three pillars of home, school, and parish church. The data is drawn from three Catholic primary schools, part of a wider empirical research study, 'Faith in the Nexus', which investigated how twenty Church primary schools facilitated children's exploration of faith in the home. A consideration of two aspects described by pupils in all three Catholic schools, reveals that children are often the initiators of faith-talk in the home and seek out time and space to reflect and pray. The chapter concludes with a reflection on the changing importance of home, school, and the parish church in the process of transmission of the Catholic faith tradition to the next generation.

Religion as a Chain of Memory

All three pillars involved in a Catholic child's faith education are being challenged and changing in an increasingly fragmented and secular society. The changes can be seen as a decline in transmission of faith in the home, a waning influence of the Church, and a weakening of Catholic identity in schools; 'the decline and fall narrative in Catholic education since Vatican II' (McDonough, 2019). Another interpretation, and the approach adopted by this chapter, is to accept that a religious tradition is always in flux as each generation adapts. Faith is lived out by individuals influenced by the perceptions and attitudes of the age in which they live. Hervieu-Léger (2000), in *Religion as a Chain of Memory* interprets religion as a form of believing, a commitment to a chain of beliefs, which involves invoking the religious tradition. In a modern society characterised by fragmentation, the transmission of faith is problematic and yet essential; it is the process by which religion constitutes itself as religion across time (Hervieu-Léger, 1998). Nevertheless, despite this fragmentation, individuals still express a need to believe and belong, albeit in different forms; connecting the act of believing to the authority of the tradition acts as a means of social identification. Hervieu-Léger argues the religious tradition is not disappearing, although there is a move to de-institutionalisation; the chain's form is continually adapting and changing. There is a creative dynamic in the transmission: it adapts to modernity, and thus religion persists, albeit in different ways (Hervieu-Léger, 2000). A fruitful investigation of faith transmission focuses on the process rather than whether elements of the tradition are transmitted the right or wrong way.

Three recent studies have applied Hervieu-Léger's concept of religion as a chain of memory to quite different scenarios. Arweck and Nesbitt (2010) explored to what extent and in what way religious values are transmitted from generation to generation in mixed-faith families in the UK. The study revealed the variety of ways mixed-faith families connected or disconnected from the chain of memory. Marianne Holm Pederson (2017) investigated how Muslim parents in Denmark transmitted their faith tradition in a society very different from the one in which they learned about faith. Hazel O'Brien (2020) recently highlighted how the connection to the faith tradition was evolving as digital religion flourished in Ireland at the time of Covid-19. All three studies highlighted how external factors influenced the nature of the transmission and a changing need to connect with the faith tradition.

The Changing Role of Home, School, and Parish

Individuals connect to the faith tradition differently; they express a sense of belonging to different religious dimensions. An individual's religious identity involves combining one or more of the four dimensions – communal, ethical, cultural, and emotional – of religious identification (Hervieu-Léger, 1998). For example, a sense of belonging is often expressed through a communal dimension – a sense of belonging to the Catholic faith through the sacraments of initiation and church attendance. For many individuals, the sense of connection is expressed primarily in the ethical dimension, a connection with the tradition's values. The cultural is often expressed in the sense of belonging through family heritage. The emotional dimension is associated, for example, with the connection experienced by young people at World Youth Day or on diocesan pilgrimages to Lourdes. Each of the three pillars, home, school, and parish, offer different pathways to connect to each of or a combination of these different dimensions of the faith tradition.

Transmission of Faith in the Home

In the Catholic tradition, parents are seen as the child's primary educators (Vatican II, *Gaudium et Spes*, par. 48). The family's importance was stressed at the Second Vatican Council (Vatican II, *Lumen Gentium*, par. 11), where the Council portrayed the family like a domestic church (Atkinson, 2005). The family's fundamental role in the children's education in faith has recently been re-emphasised by Pope Francis (2015; 2016). Empirical research also stresses the importance of the family in faith transmission. Conversations about faith in the home make a significant contribution to shaping young people's religiosity, beliefs, church attendance, and prayer (Boyatzis & Janicki, 2003; Francis, Ap Siôn, Lankshear, & Eccles, 2019). An analysis of fifty-four published studies (Mark, 2016) spotlighted that parents' beliefs, practices, and relationships have an important influence on whether children become believing adults.

This focus on the family as the space for the child's religious socialisation is challenged in a twenty-first-century society characterised by pluralisation, de-institutionalisation and individualisation (Boeve, 2012). These changes are visible in the different interpretations of Catholic identity and parental attitudes to the transmission of faith. Within Catholic schools, there are a diversity of expressions of family life in England and Wales today; a plurality of interpretations of

Catholic identity reflects the variety of ways individuals connect to the faith tradition's dimensions. Individuals acquire the beliefs and practices that are of relevance to them. They are bricoleurs; that is to say, they construct their religious identity from materials available to them (Hervieu-Léger, 1998). Previous research (Casson, 2013) illuminated how young Catholic secondary schools pupils operated as bricoleurs, often expressing their identity only through a connection to their cultural heritage or Catholic values' ethical dimension. Secondly, research has highlighted many parents' reluctance to transmit the faith to their children. Boyatzis & Janicki, in research on Christian parent-child faith conversations, concluded that often parents 'had only modest conviction in their comments' about faith (2003, p. 264). These parents were either consciously avoiding imposing their own beliefs on the children or were not clear or well informed about their beliefs. Mark (2016) noted evidence of Christian parents' lack of concern with regard to passing their faith on to the next generation. With fragmented identities and an apparent reluctance to pass on a religious identity, this does not seem a fruitful environment for children's exploration of faith.

The Influence of the Parish Church

The Catholic parish church has a crucial role as collaborators with the family in the faith formation of their children (Frabutt, Holter, Nuzzi, Rocha & Cassel, 2010). This responsibility is increasingly challenged when the traditional means of contact with families disappear, with the decline in church attendance and lack of family engagement with parish activities. Although research (Francis & Casson, 2019) has shown that parental attendance at church influences children's practice in later life, Catholics in England and Wales are less frequently transmitting a sense of belonging to the faith's communal dimension attendance at Sunday Mass. The general decline in Sunday church attendance in England and Wales is well documented (Bullivant, 2016):

> Of those who currently identify as Catholic, 27.5% say they attend church services at least once a week. 39.2%, however, say they never attend or practically never. Furthermore, 59.6% of all cradle Catholics say they never or practically never attend church. (Bullivant, 2016b, p. 3)

However, this well-known narrative of decline is more complicated. Bullivant (2016) notes that secularising trends are expressed differently within different denominations. While the Church of England church returns reveal that 38% of Church of England churches have no 0-to 16-year-olds and 68% of them have five or fewer 0- to 16-year-olds (General Synod 2161, 2019), Ben Clements' (2017) analysis of the trends among Roman Catholics found that those with children in the household were more likely to attend. However, there is little research on how children connect with faith, apart from church attendance figures' analysis and to what extent church attendance is an indicator of religiosity is disputed. Evidence that religiosity persists is harder to measure; interestingly, Bullivant (2016) notes tentatively that many of the disaffiliated have continuing connections to certain religious beliefs and practices. Nevertheless, the decline in attendance does mean that the parish church's role in the transmission of faith to children is limited when there is little or no contact with the Church, except through the Catholic school.

The Catholic School

The Catholic school offers a point of contact with a large percentage of Catholic young people in England. In 2019, there were 439,530 pupils in England and Wales in 1,714 Catholic primary schools (Catholic Education Service, 2019). The Catholic school was originally set up to provide a Catholic education for Catholic children to assist the Church in its mission to preserve the faithful (McLaughlin, O'Keefe & O'Keefe, 1996). However, there is a steady decline in the number of Catholic teachers and pupils in Catholic primary schools, 68.5 % of pupils are described as Catholic, and 59.5 % of teaching staff are Catholic (Catholic Education Service, 2019), a reflection of the changing nature of the Catholic community in England. For many pupils, the Catholic school is their first encounter with the Catholic faith tradition; the school is the primary place of religious socialisation (Rossiter, 2018). For others who identify as Catholic, there are varied interpretations of what it means to be Catholic. There is no longer clear-cut unitary habitus within Catholic faith schools, (Grace, 2002). The Catholic identity of schools is changing.

Byrne & Devine (2018), in their research study in Ireland, spoke of a continuum of Catholicity, identifying three types of Catholic schools. Faith-Visible schools expressed a strong sense of a religious community, with more religious activity and iconography; Faith-Transition schools were identified as having a looser traditional Catholic identity, characterised by low rates of practice, tending towards an individualistic practice of faith and focused on the ethical dimension of religion; and Faith-Residual schools, where the school had moved away from a distinctly Catholic identity. The question is to what extent schools moved through the continuum towards only expressing a residue of Catholicity. A perception of a weakening of the Catholic identity has led to calls for the renewal of spiritual capital (Grace, 2010) and Catholic identity to be re-animated in schools (Rymarz, 2013). However, to look at this through the lens of the chain of memory rather than a continuum, Faith-Transition schools could be interpreted as transforming the school's Catholic identity, reflecting the plurality of interpretation of Catholic identities within the school community. Rather than looking at the Catholic identity as moving from strong to weak; Catholic schools should be actively engaging with the contemporary secular spirituality of young people (Rossiter, 2018) and cultivating an 'intra-ecclesial plurality of identities' to enable Catholicity to flourish in Catholic schools (McDonough, 2019). How does a changing interpretation of Catholic identity in schools affect the Catholic school's role in the transmission of the faith tradition to pupils?

The Child as an Active Agent

Religious socialisation connects children with the religious tradition's beliefs and practices and contributes to the formation of a child's religious identity. It is only in the last thirty years (Ridgely, 2012) that research has begun to consider religious socialisation from the child's viewpoint. A fruitful investigation of this process must start with 'the beliefs and behaviours or religious preferences that young people hold, and then attempt to understand the social sources for these preferences' (Klingenberg & Sofia, 2019, p.168). Boyatzis and Janicki (2003), in their child-centred research on the nature of faith conversations within Christian families, argued that children are active participants in religious socialisation; they are not passive recipients of parental influences.

Recognising children's active agency requires acknowledging that their perspective, experience of, and engagement with the faith tradition are different. Susan Ridgely (2017, p.142) argues viewing children as the future, as 'placeholders ... obscures children's influence' in the here and now. It fails to recognise that 'children engage in often unseen processes of co-creation'. Ridgely suggests using the term of 'parallel congregations' (developed by Paul Numrich in his study of Buddhist communities in the USA) to understand children's engagement with the faith tradition.

Children's expressions of faith are not a watered-down version; their experience of the lived faith tradition is different. This is not to say they are unconnected with adult experience. A child's engagement with faith holds the potential to develop into a mature spirituality and a lifelong connection to the faith tradition. The next section of the chapter considers evidence from the 'Faith in the Nexus' research of the faith activity in the home as described by Catholic pupils. It looks at how these examples illuminated children's faith expression in the home and then seeks to identify the sources of the faith transmission.

The Research Methods

This chapter draws on an empirical mixed-methods research project undertaken by the National Institute for Christian Education Research (NICER) investigating how Church primary schools in England collaborate with the local Church and parachurch organisations and facilitate opportunities to explore faith spiritual life in the home. The wider project involved 1456 participants. The research data employed in this chapter is drawn from seven focus-group interviews with thirty-seven pupils and twelve parents and 335 participants an online survey in three English Catholic primary schools. The data forms part of a more extensive empirical research project, with twenty Church primary schools (Casson Hulbert, Woolley & Bowie, 2020). The research visits were undertaken from June 2018 to January 2019. Each followed a similar format of semi-structured focus group interviews with pupils, parents, staff, local clergy (where possible), and other interested stakeholders. Pupil interviews usually consisted of selecting students from years 5 and 6 (aged 10–11 years). The engagement of parents in the process varied from school to school. Analysis of the interviews was aided by NVivo 12 software; transcriptions were coded, and themes identified as they emerged. A quantitative online survey (2019) designed by Dr Sabina Hulbert, was informed by the qualitative data and aimed to capture the views of a more significant number of parents and pupils. The key focus of the research was to as much as possible capture the perspective of the child. The interview questions were open-ended such as: What happens in school/home, which helps you explore faith or spiritual things? Definitions were left vague for the children and parents to interpret as they saw fit. So, for example, parents might interpret faith activities at home to include talking about the values of the school; on the other hand, children focused on asking questions about faith or times of reflection. This study's apparent limitation is that the interviews were undertaken in the Catholic primary school and in focus groups rather than individually. This means responses are, to some extent, coloured or viewed through the lens of their role as a pupil or parent in a Catholic primary school.

Catholic Primary Case Study Schools

The three Catholic primary schools have been anonymised; all participants in the study gave consent to involvement and were assured of confidentiality when sharing their views. The three schools are referred to in-text by the numbers assigned to them in the original study, thus School-1, 7 & 12. All three schools are urban 4–11 years Catholic primary schools, with a faith-based admissions policy; they follow the Catholic Education Service's guidance. The schools have a varying percentage of pupils eligible for Free School Meals (FSM). FSM is, in fact, widely used as the closest proxy for deprivation. Two of the schools have less than 10% of pupils eligible for FSM; the third school is situated in multiple deprivation areas with just under 40% of pupils eligible for FSM.

The families in English Catholic primary schools are increasingly diverse; in many schools, there are increasing numbers of non-Catholic families and those of mixed faith, that is to say, one parent is from a different denominational, faith or non-faith background. However, the majority of parents and pupils in these schools defined themselves as Christian or Catholic. In response to an open text question on religious affiliation in the online survey, of the 221 pupils who responded, 93% identified themselves as Christian or Catholic, 18% included a reference to going to church; for example, 'we are Catholic, and we go to church every week'. Others qualified this; for example, 'we go to church mainly every two weeks', 'we are Catholics and try to go to church as often as we can'. A few included references to not going to church, 'we believe in God, but we don't attend church', 'we have beliefs, but we do not attend church'. A small minority, 7%, described themselves as not Catholic or not religious.

Research Findings

The 'Faith in the Nexus' research project (Casson et al., 2020) identified many ways pupils explored faith in the home. This chapter focuses on the findings highlighting the child's role and the key sources of influence in faith transmission. It draws on two examples found in all the three Catholic primary schools: faith-talk and reflection/prayer time and spaces. An analysis of these examples illuminates the differing influences on a child's encounters with faith.

Talking about Faith

One of the key findings to emerge from this research was children's desire to talk about or ask questions about faith-related matters at home, exploring existential questions such as: Is God real? Was the world created in seven days? Why does God let people starve to death? (Casson, Hulbert, Woolley & Bowie, 2020).

> 'You know the other one that died on the cross, one of them went to heaven didn't he and one of them didn't why' (School-1)
> 'How do you get to heaven, and what if I want to go to heaven' (School-1)
> 'I want to know why Jesus wants me to be like that.' (School-12)

The questions asked reflected issues the children considered they had to think deeply about, the relationship between God and Jesus, the puzzle of scientific and biblical accounts of Creation, or questions about death. The latter questions parents found particularly challenging, but as Year 6 pupils in School-12 pointed out, they asked questions about death precisely because they were not given satisfactory answers. In an analysis of the pupil and parent responses, it was clear that the child instigated faith-talk; parents often assumed this was in response to something that the child had done in school. The link to the faith tradition in these conversations was shaped by school experiences, rather than home or parish. The questions were often sparked by topics discussed in Religious Education, such as stories from the Bible or questions about God. However, for faith conversations to be meaningful, there needs to be two sides, and what is of interest here is how parents' responded to these questions. There was some evidence that grandparents were less reluctant to engage in faith conversations with the child. For example, 'my grandparents are Eucharist Ministers, and I find that they are often people to explore my faith with asking questions about God' (Pupil-1).

Different ways parents responded could be identified in an analysis of pupils' and parents' descriptions of faith-talk at home. In some households, there was an apparent absence of conversations. A parent in School-12 explained talking about faith was done in school or parish church but not at home. A parent in School-1 explained that they focused on actions rather than sitting down talking about faith. On the other hand, some parents and pupils explained how they relished engaging questions about God or Creation; when the child raised a question, parents and children would explore the issue together. Other parents encouraged their child to ask the questions at school or the priest, who were more likely to know the 'right' answer. There was evidence of a lack of confidence on the parents' part, a deference to the knowledge and authority of leaders in the school or the parish church. An interesting finding was the reluctance of some parents to engage because they did not want to impose their views but instead would let the child choose freely, encouraging them to come to their own conclusions. Occasionally there was a hint of embarrassment to talking about faith in the home. The findings echoed Boyatzis & Janicki (2003) research with parent-child conversations that parents are tentative in engaging in conversations about faith.

Reflect and Pray

When asked how they explored faith at home, the most common response from pupils was to speak of times of reflection or prayer. Pupils used the terms reflection and prayer interchangeably, although parents referred to prayers often meaning formal prayer and only used reflection about children's practice. Pupils spoke of making reflection spaces at home and seeking time to reflect. A pupil in School-7 explained she had made a table in her bedroom into 'a prayer focus', 'I've got a cross and some candles and then I've put little candles on it as well. And they're all in the shape of a love heart'. A parent in School-12 had been surprised by the reflection corner her son had made in his bedroom, a dynamic space, with objects added and taken away regularly. Often pupils spoke of reflection time outdoors, on a walk, or in the park; 'when you're out playing, and you just want to relax, then you can hear the birds and all of the nature that God created' (Pupil-7). When pupils were questioned why they wanted or needed to reflect, they spoke of worries about their or others' wellbeing; for some, these were also times when they 'talked to God'. It was apparent that the child was seeking out these times and making the spaces for reflection at home.

The descriptions of reflection space and time at home were often modelled on spaces or prayers in school. The three Catholic primary schools all had reflection spaces in the school; often, there was a prayer corner in each classroom and a spiritual garden on the school grounds.

Pupils in School-1 spoke of the many spaces in their school, where they could go and think about refugees' problems, people who had died, or those who had no friends. The links with the Catholic faith tradition were clear; pupils in School-1 spoke of reflecting at the Stations of the Cross; in School-7, the pupils spoke of meditation time in school as being like saying the Rosary.

The Child as an Initiator

What, then, do these findings tell us about the changing roles of the child and each of the three pillars, home, school, and parish church? An analysis of pupils' description of faith-talk and times of reflection revealed that it is the child that is often the initiator of faith-talk in the home, and, secondly, that a key element of the Catholic tradition that children are choosing to explore at home is time for prayer or reflection. In this study, Catholic pupils actively explored faith in school and at home, asking questions and seeking spaces to reflect or pray. These reveal two of the wider study's key findings, namely that the child is often the initiator of faith activity in the home, and secondly that children are actively seeking to explore faith in the home through reflection and prayer. The child is not a passive recipient but rather an active agent in their exploration of faith; there is a suggestion of what Ridgely (2012) has called the co-creation of the tradition. Further research is needed to establish whether children were becoming co-creators of religious traditions, particularly with whom were they co-creators; the evidence did not strongly suggest that it was with the parents. This is not necessarily, however, a new phenomenon, just not previously researched. Children's voices, like those of women, are not often found in the historical record (Ridgely, 2012).

Interestingly, the element of the faith tradition children are choosing to explore in the home is reflection and prayer. O'Brien (2020) found that in the Covid-19 lockdown period, individuals were expressing a need to connect or re-connect to the faith tradition through accessing Mass and prayers online. This expression of a need to pray at a time of crisis is perhaps also part of why the children focus on reflection. This time was needed for their spiritual wellbeing. Stern and Shillitoe's (2018) report on prayer spaces in school highlighted how such spaces had value in reducing pupil stress and 'fulfilling pupil wishes for more opportunities for solitude in school' (p. 39). For the pupils in this study, the prime way they were choosing to connect was through seeking out space and time for reflection. This practice connected to the Catholic faith tradition through the choice of elements provided by the Catholic school. At home, however, it was an individual rather than communal activity; pupils rarely spoke of praying with their family.

Both parents and teachers inevitably influence children, and children use many elements to construct their religious world. Two critical questions arise from this: firstly, how family, school, and parish church influenced the aspects of faith pupils in this study were chosen to explore; and secondly, to what extent parents, teachers and clergy were aware of the elements of faith children chose to explore to make sense of their world.

The Home

The analysis suggests that parents' role as primary educators, the traditional trajectory of transmission from parent to child, is challenged. Who is passing on faith traditions? Many parents appeared reluctant to engage in faith-talk with their children. There was little evidence that parents provided the time and space for reflection; more often, it appeared tolerated as an activity for the child. The investigation did not focus on parents' views, but hints of their responses were apparent when discussing children's exploration of faith in the home. In previous studies that have applied the concept of the chain of memory, there was differing evidence of parents' attitudes to transmission. Pedersen (2017) found that the Muslim parents in Denmark were adapting the transmission of the faith to fit in with the new situation in which they found themselves. Arweck and Nesbitt (2010) identified that some parents were choosing elements of the chain to connect with, such as the cultural dimension of religion. One area which emerged in this study is worthy of further exploration: many of the parents did connect with the faith tradition through what Hervieu-Léger (1998) termed the ethical dimension. Parents' response to how they explored faith at home was often to refer to conversations about the school values. An open-text question in the online survey asked parents their expectations of the school for their child's future. The overwhelming focus was on inculcating moral values; the parents were seeking education in values; sometimes, they described them as Christian or Catholic values. There was also evidence of a connection with a cultural heritage dimension, in so much that many choose a Catholic primary school to give their child the same experience as they had as a child.

There was evidence of an absence of transmission in many of these Catholic pupils' homes. As Arweck and Nesbitt (2010) found, some parents were content to leave it to the children as to whether they became part of the chain or 'forged their own chain' (p. 84). A key concern raised then is to what extent transmission in the home is in flux and to what extent it is absent.

The Parish

The parish church's role in facilitating children's encounters with faith in the home was mediated through the school. The pupils did not directly mention the church's influence on the exploration of their faith at home; the primary stimulus was activity in school. It was striking that pupils did not mention the church building as a place for reflection. The extent of contact between the parish church and school families varied. Some families were regular churchgoers and active in a variety of church activities. The absence or limited reference to Mass attendance in this study is a result perhaps of the questions being focused on an exploration of faith in the home and that, as the school and parish church leaders suggested, many of their school families did not contact the church. For example, one head stated, 'a lot of them don't necessarily go to church'; a priest suggested he tried to be on the school playground as much as possible, as that was the place he would meet the families. The absence of attendance at Sunday Mass is not necessarily a measure of religiosity; the children in this study expressed a sense of belonging to the parish through the connection with the school. Parents spoke of encountering the priest in the school playground or school services in the church at festival time. There was a perception of a strong connection between the parish church and school, but the findings suggest that the parish church's role in transmitting the faith was through the school rather than directly to the families.

The Catholic Primary School

The prime influence on the pupils' exploration of faith at home was undoubtedly the Catholic primary school. In both examples considered, talking about faith and reflection times, the child was the main initiator of the activity, but the stimulus for the activity could often be traced back to activities within the school. The spark for faith-talk, for the questions, was often discussions in Religious Education lessons and collective worship. The reflection spaces at home were modelled on those in school. The school is a crucial place for contact with the memory of the faith tradition. Three of the factors in the Catholic primary schools that facilitated this activity in the home were a prioritisation of the Catholic ethos in the school, an emphasis on developing the children as young leaders in faith, and, thirdly, school leader's prioritisation of a connection with the local Church or parachurch community.

The three Catholic primary schools in this study visibly expressed a strong Catholic ethos. The first question asked of participants was how a visitor would know this is a Catholic school. Pupils and parents described the environment, the displays and reflection spaces, and the activities such as worship and Religious Education. Parents remarked in particular on displays in the foyer and the school hall and the faith-talk in school, how it was customary to talk about faith in school. The schools had provided a range of reflection spaces in the school, in classrooms and outside as spiritual gardens, responding to children's need for prayer and solitude. For pupils and parents, there was a sense of the school being in a Catholic space.

Secondly, there was a focus on developing children as leaders in spiritual activities. Opportunities were built-in to the Religious Education curriculum for children to ask questions and share their opinions. Many Catholic primary schools have pupil-led worship committees, prayer groups, or spiritual councils. In these schools, these were more than a group of pupils responsible for setting at the chairs for worship; pupils met and discussed how to improve reflection spaces around the school or organised liturgies for the younger children or the whole school. Although not all pupils were on these committees, all knew of them and accepted the idea that children could take responsibility for worship. There was recognition here that children were active agents and potential co-constructors of the faith tradition.

The third factor contributing to the facilitation of faith activity in the home was school leaders' determination to strengthen these connections between school and parish church and school and home. Often the school leaders function as the animator of spiritual capital (Friel, 2018); they were driving the faith agenda in school. This was in part through necessity with the increasing workload of the parish priest. The schools in this study were not seeking to replace the parish but instead actively encourage the local parish to collaborate to facilitate children's exploration of faith in the home.

Conclusion: Is the Chain of Memory Being Re-forged?

The Catholic pupils in the 'Faith in the Nexus' study were often initiators of faith activity in the home. Children appeared to be seeking to connect to the faith tradition in the home, through times for reflection and their questions about faith. There remains the question of the strength of these connections to the Catholic faith tradition. The evidence from this study suggests that children are selecting elements of the faith tradition that they explore at home, influenced by their experience in school. Employing the concept of religion as a chain of memory highlighted the ways children connect to the faith tradition, the elements selected. It also revealed that the influence of the family and the parish church on the choice of elements appears only as a faint echo. It could often be suggested that both of these spheres appear indifferent or ignorant of how children are choosing to connect with the faith tradition. The findings suggest that Catholic primary school is a crucial source of faith transmission. It is a space for religious socialisation; as Rossiter (2018) argues, for some it might be the only space for religious socialisation. This has the potential to engender a connection to the faith tradition which stays rooted while in primary school but is not sustained beyond the school experience. Although evidence reveals that the school is the primary contact with the Catholic faith tradition, the findings suggest the local Church's role through its connection with school is not negligible. To conclude, then, the 'Faith in the Nexus' research findings highlight the child's active agency in religious socialisation; they also suggest that more attention needs to be paid to the transmission of faith through of strengthening the connections between school, parish church, and home.

References

Arweck, E. & Nesbitt. E., 'Young People's Identity Formation in Mixed-Faith Families: Continuity or Discontinuity of Religious Traditions?', in *Journal of Contemporary Religion* 25/1 (2010), pp. 67–87.

Atkinson, J.C., 'Family as Domestic Church: Developmental Trajectory, Legitimacy, and Problems of Appropriation', in *Theological Studies* 66/3 (2005), pp. 592–604.

Boeve, L., 'Religious Education in a Post-Secular and Post-Christian Context', in *Journal of Beliefs & Values* 33/2 (2012), pp. 143–156.

Boyatzis, C.J. & Janicki. D.L., 'Parent-child Communication about Religion: Survey and Diary Data on Unilateral Transmission and Bi-directional Reciprocity Styles', in *Review of Religious Research* 44/3 (2003), pp. 252–270.

Bullivant, S., 'Catholic Disaffiliation in Britain: A Quantitative Overview', in *Journal of Contemporary Religion*, 31/2 (2016), pp. 181–197.

Bullivant, S., *'Contemporary Catholicism in England and Wales: A Statistical Report Based on Recent British Social Attitudes Survey Data'*, St Mary's College, Twickenham: Benedict XVI Centre for Religion and Society, 2016b.

Byrne, R. & Devine, D., '"Catholic Schooling with a Twist?", A Study of Faith Schooling in the Republic of Ireland during a Period of Detraditionalisation', in *Cambridge Journal of Education* 48/4 (2018), pp. 461–477.

Casson, A.E., *Fragmented Catholicity and Social Cohesion: Faith Schools in a Plural Society*, Bern: Peter Lang, 2013.

Casson, A.E., Hulbert, S., Wooley, M. & Bowie, R., *Faith in the Nexus: Church Schools and Children's Exploration of Faith in the Home: A NICER Research Study of Twenty Church Primary Schools in England*, Canterbury Christ Church University, 2020.

Catholic Education Service, *Census Digest*, 2019. Available at: https://www.catholiceducation.org.uk/images/CensusDigestEngland2019.pdf.

Clements, B., 'Weekly Churchgoing amongst Roman Catholics in Britain: Long-term Trends and Contemporary Analysis', in *Journal of Beliefs & Values* 38/1 (2017), pp. 32–44.

Frabutt, J.M., Holter, A.C., Nuzzi, R.J., Rocha, H. & Cassel, L., 'Pastors' Views of Parents and the Parental Role in Catholic Schools', in *Journal of Catholic Education*, 14/1 (2010), pp. 24–46.

Francis, L.J., Ap Siôn, T., Lankshear, D.W. & Eccles, E.L., 'Factors Shaping Prayer Frequency among 9- to 11-Year-Olds', in *Greek Journal of Religious Education*, 2/1 (2019), pp. 39–52.

Francis, L.J., & Casson, A., 'Retaining Young Catholics in the Church: Assessing the Importance of Parental Example', in *Journal of Religious Education*, 67/1 (2019), pp. 1–16.

Friel, R., 'Renewing Spiritual Capital: The National Retreat for Catholic Head Teachers and the National School of Formation: The Impact on Catholic Head Teachers in the UK', in *International Studies in Catholic Education*, 10/1 (2018), pp. 81–96.

General Synod of the Church of England, Children and Youth Ministry GS2161, 2019. Available at: www.churchofengland.org/sites/default/files/2020-01/GS%202161%20Children%20and%20Youth%20Ministry%20Full%20with%20Appendix%20-%20Final.pdf

Grace, G., *Catholic Schools: Mission, Markets, and Morality*, London: Routledge, 2002.

Grace, G., 'Renewing Spiritual Capital: An Urgent Priority for the Future of Catholic Education Internationally', in *International Studies in Catholic Education* 2/2 (2010), pp. 117–128.

Hervieu-Léger, D., 'The Transmission and Formation of Socio-religious Identities in Modernity: An Analytical Essay on the Trajectories of Identification', in *International Sociology* 13/2 (1998), pp. 213–228.

Hervieu-Léger, D., *Religion as a Chain of Memory*, New Brunswick, NJ: Rutgers University Press, 2000.

Klingenberg, M. & Sofia, S., 'Theorizing Religious Socialization: A Critical Assessment', in *Religion* 49/2 (2019), pp. 163–178.

Mark, O., *Passing on Faith*, London: Theos, 2016.

McLaughlin, T, O'Keefe, J. & O'Keeffe, B. (eds), *The Contemporary Catholic School: Context, Identity, and Diversity*, Hove, East Sussex: Psychology Press, 1996.

McDonough, G.P., 'Pluralizing Catholic Identity', in *Religious Education* 114/2 (2019), pp. 168–180.

O'Brien, H., 'What Does the Rise of Digital Religion during Covid-19 Tell Us about Religion's Capacity to Adapt?', in *Irish Journal of Sociology* 28/2 (2020), pp. 242–246.

Pedersen, M.H., 'Becoming Muslim in a Danish Provincial Town', in *The Bloomsbury Reader in Religion and Childhood*, London: Bloomsbury, 2017, pp. 131–138.

Pope Francis, *Amoris Laetitia: On Love in the Family*, 2016. Available online at http://www.vatican.va/content/dam/francesco/pdf/apost_exhortations/documents/papa-francesco_esortazione-ap_20160319_amoris-laetitia_en.pdf

Pope Francis, 'General Audience, September 9, 2015: The Family - 26, Community'. Available at: www.vatican.va/content/francesco/en/audiences/2015/documents/papa-francesco_20150909_udienza-generale.html

Ridgely, S., 'Children and Religion', in *Religion Compass* 6/4 (2012), pp. 236–248.

Ridgely, S., 'Faith Co-creation in US Catholic Churches: How First Communicants and Faith Formation Teachers Shape Catholic Identity', in A. Strhan, S.G. Parker & S. Ridgely, (eds), *The Bloomsbury Reader in Religion and Childhood*, London: Bloomsbury Publishing, 2017, pp. 139–146.

Rossiter, G., *Life to the Full: The Changing Landscape of Contemporary Spirituality: Implications for Catholic School Religious Education*, Kensington, NSW: ASMRE, 2018.

Rymarz, R., 'Permeation of Catholic Identity: Some Challenges for Canadian Catholic Schools, Part 1', in *Journal of Religious Education* 61/1, (2013), pp. 14–22.

Stern, J. & Shillitoe, R., *Evaluation of Prayer Spaces in Schools: The Contribution of Prayer Spaces to Spiritual Development*, 2018.

Vatican II, *Lumen Gentium: Dogmatic Constitution on the Church*, 1964. Available at: http://www.vatican.va/archive/hist_councils/ii_vatican_council/documents/vat-ii_const_19641121_lumen-gentium_en.html

Vatican II, *Gaudium et Spes: Pastoral Constitution on the Church in the Modern World*, 1965, in Abbott W. (ed), *The Documents of Vatican II*, New York: Herder and Herder, 1966.

Chapter 12

~~~~~~~~~~~~~~~

Religious Education in English Catholic Schools: Reflections on Formal and Informal Catholic Education

Sean Whittle

Introduction

Change is on the horizon for Religious Education in English Catholic schools. Since the autumn of 2018, planning has been under way for a whole scale revision and reframing of Religious Education in Catholic schools. This change is being led and overseen by the Catholic Education Service (CES) of England and Wales. This is an agency of the Bishop's Conference of England and Wales, representing the collective interests about matters of education of all twenty-two dioceses. Despite the effects of the Covid-19 pandemic, the hope is to begin implementing the revised *Religious Education Curriculum Directory* from September 2022. These impending changes to the Religious Education curriculum provide an apt opportunity to reflect on some challenging questions about what ought to be the nature and scope of this part of the curriculum within the context of Catholic education taken as a whole. The reflections in this chapter will approach these questions from the lens of both formal and informal Catholic education. Moreover, these reflections will be deeply rooted in the authors experience as a serving Religious Education teacher with over twenty-five years working exclusively in Catholic second-level schools and colleges in London.

What is Changing?

Since 1996, Religious Education teachers in Catholic schools in England and Wales have had the benefit of a document which gives guidance on the content of Religious Education lessons and across primary and second-level schools, known as the *Curriculum Directory for Religious Education* (RECD). One of the key strengths of the first version of the *RECD* in 1996 was that it was theologically framed around the four central documents of Vatican II. This was a symbolic way of demonstrating that Religious Education in Catholic schools coheres with the modern magisterium as summed up in the Council. At the practical level, the *RECD* became a very important component in the development of a benign system of formal inspection that was implemented to complement the government's Office for Standards in Education (OFSTED) inspections, known as Section 48 Inspections. Back in 1989, the English and Welsh education system was swept up in far reaching changes that came with the introduction of a national curriculum, new style public examinations (GCSEs) and a reinvigorated school inspection system. The CES and the Anglican Church (Church of England) successfully negotiated an inspection system that allowed for a separate inspection framework for schools of religious character that focused on the school ethos and the provision of classroom Religious Education. This led to the development of Section 48 Inspections for Catholic schools, paid for by the state. The inspectors (appointed by the bishops to represent them in this role) were able to judge how well a Catholic school was delivering the *RECD* and other aspects of Catholic ethos and values. It is important to emphasise that the *RECD* was instrumental in allowing the Section 48 process become a fundamentally positive and supportive process (see Whittle 2020a for a fuller discussion of this). The *RECD* was revised and enlarged in 2012, in order to include an expanded presentation of the aims of Religious Education in Catholic schools and to supply an extensive listing of information from the *Catechism of the Catholic Church* that needs to be covered as young people progress through their primary and second level Catholic schools. Although criticism can be readily raised about the 2012 *RECD* (see Whittle 2018c), it is deeply intriguing that a process of revision was drawn up just five years later. It is perhaps an indicator that these days there can be major education shifts in just a handful of years.

Since 2018, the CES has been involved in a wide-ranging consultation process, in particular with academics working on Religious Education in both Catholic and non-Catholic settings. There have also been consultative questionnaires surveying the opinions of serving Religious Education teachers and a number of meetings to update and allow for feedback. This commendable level of consultation should allow for a positive buy-in from serving Religious Education teachers, even if there is considerable change to the nature of the *RECD*. The early indications are that everything will be approved and ready for implementation from September 2022, providing that the Covid-19 pandemic does not interrupt plans too much. A new way of framing the nature and content of Religious Education in English Catholic schools is clearly on the horizon. This time of impending change is an apt moment to step back in order to reconsider some of the big questions about Religious Education in relation to the wider project of Catholic education.

How are Religious Education and Catholic Education Aligned?

It is not uncommon to hear advocates of Catholic education refer to 'Catholic Religious Education' when discussing this part of the curriculum. Presumably the insertion of 'Catholic' is to serve as an identity marker which is asserting that Religious Education in a Catholic school is distinctively different to the sort of Religious Education that happens in other schools. The issues here quickly become complex because they are embroiled in assumptions about the centrality of Religious Education within the whole project of Catholic education. Clarifying what is the relationship between Religious Education and Catholic education continues to be surprisingly difficult to achieve (Whittle 2021).

Moreover, in referring to Catholic Religious Education, it is a moot point as to whether or not it is merely referring to differences in content (perhaps with less world religions and a far greater focus on Catholic doctrines) or to it being a confessional activity, ultimately aimed at nurturing students *in the faith* in the hope that they will embrace Catholic Christianity throughout their adult lives. Of course, both these senses of Catholic Religious Education emphasise that this sort of Religious Education is different. However, it is instructive to recognise the oddness of referring to Religious Education in terms of being Catholic Religious Education as opposed to Religious Education in Catholic schools. No other part of the curriculum in a Catholic school is described as 'Catholic' in this way, in that we do not routinely refer to *Catholic* English, *Catholic* science, or *Catholic* Gaeilge lessons.

There are of course aspects of science or Irish studies in which Catholic Christianity has played a pivotal role. A Catholic worldview permeates the various disciplines which underpin the entire curriculum, however this is different from recasting every subject as Catholic. We readily recognise that the curriculum as a whole is not well served by demarcating every subject as Catholic or not. Just as there is not a Catholic version of the entire curriculum, there is something strange in designating one part of it as a Catholic version of the subject. Perhaps the repeated use of the phrase Catholic Religious Education has blunted our ability to recognise just how odd this way of framing the subject is.

Christian Education as a Right Flowing from Baptism

The issue here over framing the subject as Religious Education in Catholic schools or as Catholic Religious Education is one that reflects the nebulous relationship between the entire project of Catholic education and what happens in Religious Education lessons in Catholic schools. When the bishops at Vatican II issued the declaration on the 'Extreme Importance of Education' (Vatican II's *Gravissimum Educationis*, 1965), the focus was on reaffirming the rights and prerogatives of the Catholic Church to be involved in the delivery of state education in order to support the parents of Catholic children. The declaration was about Christian education generally, rather than about the specifics of Religious Education. The Council firmly anchored Christian education as a right which flowed from baptism. A baptised person has a right to be educated about what it means to be a Christian. At the same time *Gravissimum Educationis* does not simply equate Christian education with a Catholic schooling. Indeed the bishops at Vatican II were very aware that in many parts of the world Catholic schools operate with very small numbers of Catholic children. In numerous so-called missionary contexts, Catholic schools exist as a service to the wider society rather than primarily serving the needs of just the Catholic community. Moreover, given the patchy provision of Catholic schools in many parts of the world, the Council recognised too that baptised young people will receive their post-baptism Christian education in a range of settings, besides their formal education – which may or may not be at a Catholic school. It is important to realise that *Gravissimum Educationis* is inviting us to operate with a broader vision of Catholic education, something more akin to a lifelong endeavour, one that flows as a right from having been baptised. Crucially, this Vatican II declaration does not either make Religious Education central to the curriculum nor does it conflate Christian education with Religious Education. In effect

Gravissimum Educationis does not tightly align Religious Education and Catholic education.

At the Service of Catholic Families and Wider Society

The tricky challenge after Vatican II has been about how best to explain the alignment, clarifying how both the Catholic school and Religious Education fit into this broader vision of Catholic education. Two post-conciliar documents produced by the Congregation for Catholic Education have sought to offer guidance on this – the 1977 presentation on the *Catholic School* and the 1988 discussion of the *Religious Dimension of Education in a Catholic School*. In the former, the nature and purpose of the Catholic school is explored in some detail. It is a unique educational environment because in providing State education, it is offering a service for the benefit of the children of Catholic parents *and* for the wider society. There is no presumption that these schools exist exclusively for Catholics. Indeed, the document is forthright in asserting that Catholic schools are primarily offered to educate the poor (Congregation for Catholic Education, 1977 par. 46; Grace, 2002, p. 4). Moreover, these schools are for the poor generally and not merely poor Catholics. A Catholic school strives to deliver the curriculum to the highest standards and in a way that is informed by values of the gospel (thus with a heavy emphasis on pastoral care and attentiveness to the needs of each student).

The Religious Dimension: A Shared Endeavour across the School

In the second guidance document published in 1988, the attention shifts to the way that the entire curriculum and life of the school has what can be described as a religious dimension. In large part the religious dimension of Catholic education is a way of bringing in spirituality and religiously grounded values to frame what happens in Catholic schools. Crucially the religious dimension of education is a shared endeavour across the life of the entire school and is more than what goes on in Religious Education lessons. Moreover, this document is also aware that not all students at a Catholic school will be baptised Catholics, let alone practicing their faith. It demonstrates this through its attempt to give a nuanced account of the different ways the same Religious Education lessons might be received by students. In paragraphs 66–8 the guidance explains that for some students the Religious Education lesson will be received as a catechesis which nurtures and deepens already existing faith commitment. For others in the same class it might be received as pre-evangelisation, or a ground-clearing that will allow the student to receive the gospel message at some future point in life. A third alternative is that for some in the same lesson it will be received as a topic within Religious Education and have no catechetical or pre-evangelical dimension. The 1988 guidance document is intriguing because it appears to offer a way of understanding Religious Education in a Catholic school being simultaneously catechetical and non-catechetical, depending on how an individual student receives these lessons. However, an ambiguity with this approach concerns the intention behind this teaching. The 1988 guidance document is intriguing because it appears to offer a way of understanding Religious Education in a Catholic school being simultaneously catechetical and non-catechetical, depending on how an individual student receives these lessons. However, it can be argued that there is an ambiguity with this approach, triggered by the possible intentions behind the teaching of Religious Education. This is because it is one thing recognise and appreciate that the same lesson content and teaching might be received in very different ways by different students even in the same class in the same Catholic school; it is another thing to establish that the teacher's intention is differentiated in a corresponding way. As I have argued elsewhere (Whittle 2018a), the question of intention is important for a number of reasons. First, it is possible that the teacher's intention could be primarily catechetical, in that their desire would actually be to catechise the whole class. In this case it would be what is wanted or intended, but in practice it is not actually achievable. Of course, if the intention is to catechise the whole class this raises concerns over indoctrination. Even if in practice indoctrination does not take place (because of the differing ways different students receive it) this is not enough to sidestep these concerns. A second but closely related issue is to do with the rapidly changing composition of Catholic schools, even in countries like Ireland and the UK. The ever-increasing percentages of students who are not baptised raises again concerns over attempted indoctrination. It could be argued that any sort of intention to catechise or evangelise all, including non-Catholic children being taught, reflects a deeply confessional stance, and this is normally taken to be a morally suspect way of teaching Religious Education today because of diversity in the classroom. Drilling down to establish what the intentions of the Religious Education teacher might be is tricky and it is this which makes the distinction drawn in paragraphs 66–8 ambiguous.

Formal and Informal?

The relationships between the Catholic school, Religious Education in Catholic schools and Catholic education is complex. The conciliar and post-conciliar Church documents on education referred to above challenge us not to treat these as synonymous themes or concepts. One helpful way of taking the issues further is by framing the issues at play in terms of the formal and informal dimensions of Catholic education.

Perhaps because Catholic education is broader than what happens in the formal confines of the Catholic school, it might be helpful to draw on the relationship between the formal and the informal Catholic education. Here, rather than classifying a strict separation and divide between what constitutes formal and informal Catholic education (in terms of Religious Education), it will be assumed that the relationship is something akin to a spectrum. At one end of this spectrum Catholic education is intimately aligned to the formal education that takes place in the setting of the Catholic school. In countries like England this would be state-funded educational settings that fall under the policy and oversight of the government's Department for Education. Thus it is in the formal delivery of the curriculum, individual lessons over time, that Catholic education takes place, spanning from primary school to the school-leaving age of 18. Given that all parts of the curriculum have the shared religious dimension described in the 1988 document, alongside the particular role of Religious Education, it is this formal education which is delivering Catholic education. In contrast, at the other end of the spectrum, Catholic education occurs in a wide range of informal settings, such as in a parish small group or within the home or in the context of Church-based voluntary work.

The idea of there being a spectrum like relationship between formal and informal education is helpful in not drawing too heavy a separation between the two. This is important because informal Catholic education can also take place within the formal setting of school, because in schools there are less formal parts of the curriculum. This tends to be described in a number of ways, including the 'pastoral curriculum', 'extended curriculum' or even 'co-curriculum'. In Personal, Social and Health Education lessons or in Human Development programmes a range of important but less formal sets of ideas are offered to the students, without the spectre of needing to complete examinations about what is learnt in these lessons. In addition, in many Catholic second-level schools retreat days are often blended into the school year. In this less formal part of schools lie the pastoral care structures and the ethos of the school. These guide and inform the quality of the relationships, such as how pupils and teachers engage with each other. In a similar way, at the informal end of the spectrum, which might include family life, parish sacramental programmes (for First Communion and Confirmation preparation) and small group initiatives within parishes, there can be many of the trappings of formal education. Within parish sacramental programmes there would frequently be studious and disciplined engagement with scripture and study of Catholic doctrines. Within informal settings serious and theologically rich ideas will naturally crop up and be part-and-parcel of the Catholic education taking place. It is important not to conflate informal Catholic education settings with low-level learning and teaching.

At one level the differences between the formal and informal settings for Catholic education are very striking. Children attend Catholic schools on the basis of choices made by their parents, and there is a compulsory legal element to their participation in school. Almost inevitably, when being compelled to attend and participate in formal education over many years of childhood and adolescence, this can negatively impact on how students feel about their education. In contrast, in informal settings amongst adults, the participants are not legally compelled to attend. They freely do so for their own reasons. Another key difference is around the intention or goal of the Catholic education that takes place in the formal and informal settings. In informal settings there is typically an openness to the primary intention being the nurturing of faith and an explicit desire to foster faith development. As such the framing language is more catechetical.

One of the paradoxical features of Catholic education, at least in England, is that at the formal end of the spectrum, in Catholic schools generally and in Religious Education lessons in particular, there has emerged over recent decades a growing reticence about using such catechetical language. This is not merely a semantic issue, but rather a strengthening conviction that in the formal or school setting the emphasis is on making academic goals and achievements the overriding priority. The emphasis is on framing Religious Education as an academic endeavour, rather than something which is intentionally catechetical.

The Emerging Dominance of Public Examinations in Religious Education Lessons in Catholic Schools

On a number of occasions I have argued that Religious Education in Catholic second-level schools in England has changed dramatically over the past four decades, particularly in relation to public examination (see Whittle 2018a, 2018b, 2018c). During the early part of the 1980s many Catholic second-level schools did not compel all students to take public examinations in the examination subject Religious Studies. At this time Religious Education was typically referred to as Religious Instruction, and it was assumed to be a catechetical endeavour. Moreover, there was a consensus that faith (religion) is something that is 'caught not taught'. This old saying, emphasising action, refers to the widely acknowledged truism that handing on the Christian faith is not a transmission of creedal statements, but rather fostering a living relationship with God through Jesus Christ. It was assumed that it is the power of witness (actions) over words which teaches most powerfully to modern people (see Paul VI, *Evangelii Nuntiandi*, 1974, par. 41). In contrast, now all students in Catholic second-level schools in England take a public examination in Religious Studies at age of 16. It is the academic credentials of the Religious Education provision which are most often recognised and celebrated.

It is important to appreciate that the reasons for this changed situation lie primarily in the education policy shifts championed by the Conservative government of Margaret Thatcher (during the 1980s) which culminated with the introduction of a national curriculum and a public examination qualification that replaced the Ordinary Level and Certificate of Secondary Education qualifications (through the *Education Reform Act 1988*). A new qualification called the General Certificate of Secondary Education (GCSE) was established. In preceding decades, students took a handful of O Levels. With the advent of the GCSE examinations it became common for students to take ten or more GCSEs at age 16, before specialising to take three or four A Levels. After 1988, in Catholic schools, it became routine to enter all students for the GCSE Religious Studies examination. This brought about many positive consequences for Religious Education. For example, it helped to raise the status of the subject alongside many other parts of the curriculum, because it too was a route to gaining formal qualifications. There was also a significant expansion of personnel in Religious Education departments, as increased numbers of teachers were needed to deliver the Religious Studies GCSE course. The examination boards devised specifications (and supporting textbooks were published) that were geared to Catholic schools. Religious Education in English Catholic schools had been transformed into a serious examination subject. These positive consequences need to be counterbalanced by a recognition of the negative ones.

Sean Whittle

The Impact of the Dominance of the Examination System on Religious Education

At the general level, it has become almost acceptable to characterise second-level schools in England as 'examination factories'. This is because preparing students for GCSE examinations dominates so much of the school's work. For example, it is not uncommon for second-level schools to devote three entire school years to completing the GCSE specifications, starting when the students are just 13 years old. This means students are making decisions about their subject options, with potential implications for their subsequent careers, during their second year at high school. In effect it is only the first year of second-level school which is free from the long shadow cast by GCSE work and examinations. Thus preparing for GCSEs too easily becomes the *raison d'être* of school life. The same dominance of the GCSE examinations across the school is found to be infecting Religious Education in the Catholic school. What can be referred to as the 'trickle-down effect' (Whittle 2018a) means that the changes to the Religious Studies GCSE specification spill over into the way Religious Education is taught in younger years. There are many instances of Catholic schools setting GCSE exam style questions to the pupils in the youngest years. Although this might be rooted in a good intention of providing exam practice, it could easily be misconstrued as making achievement in the Religious Studies GCSE the most important priority in Religious Education. It can also be seen as fostering a sinister utilitarianism, in which Religious Education's importance is intrinsically linked to achieving a high level in this GCSE. This subject will give the student an all-important qualification, and perhaps this is why it primarily matters to the students, and maybe even to the school. If GCSE Religious Studies exam questions dominate the vast majority of Religious Education lessons in English Catholic second-level schools, it might mean that achieving this qualification has become just too important. The break with the situation just four decades ago is profound.

Another negative consequence for Religious Education in Catholic schools is the inherent problems found within the Religious Studies GCSE specification (implemented from 2016). In particular the style of questioning and responses required for higher levels are triggering a skewed understanding of Catholic theology. Bowie (2020) has cogently demonstrated that there is an adversarial stance deliberately built into the way the GCSE exam questions are set. This inevitably forces students to respond in terms of binaries that are seeking to resolve theological dilemmas as they are evaluated in their answers. This is linked to a hermeneutical approach in which scripture or Church teachings are used as mere 'proof texts' that can *defeat* competing theological claims. The problem with this is that it develops the false assumption that there are indeed theological arguments that are there to be won or lost. As I have argued elsewhere (Whittle 2020b), this does not resemble in any adequate way Catholic theology as it is currently framed. It is at best a throw-back to the disputations of the scholastic theologians of the Middle Ages. More seriously, the current GCSE specifications for Religious Studies used in Catholic schools reveal that theology is actually in a precarious place in Religious Education lessons in English Catholic schools (see Whittle 2020b for a fuller discussion of these issues).

On balance, the negative consequences demonstrate that there is now an overemphasis on public examinations in Religious Education in Catholic schools in England. As a result of this, formal Catholic education in relation to Religious Education is intrinsically bound up with the Religious Studies GCSE. Inevitably a danger of this is that Religious Education becomes synonymous with passing this GCSE. The richer senses of Religious Education aligned with the broader project of Catholic education can easily become lost or misunderstood.

Moreover, once the GCSE in Religious Studies is completed the formal part of Religious Education has been achieved – potentially for life.

A Way Forward?

It would be naive to even begin an argument in favour of uncoupling Religious Education in Catholic schools from the public examination system that it has become embroiled with over recent decades. Fundamentally this is because of the political influence now generated by matters of education across the whole of society. Schooling and education policy are now profoundly important parts of government and even day-to-day party politics. As a result, the process of generating certification/exam qualifications now dominates the later years of second-level education in England. The entire curriculum in second-level schools is built around GCSE examinations at age 16 and A Level examinations at age 18. Inevitably Religious Education, particularly in Catholic schools, is part-and-parcel of this. Even the Covid-19 pandemic of 2020-21 and the great lockdown did no more than interrupt the process of generating GCSE and A Level certificates. Given that there is unlikely to be a whole-scale reappraisal of education policy and the place of public examinations in school settings, the current set-up is likely to continue into the foreseeable future. This triggers questions about what might be the best way forward and it is here that attention needs to return to the revision of the *RECD*.

One way forward for the *RECD* revision would be to return to the broader vision called for in *Gravissimum Educationis*, where Christian education (which is inclusive of Religious Education) is best understood as a life-long endeavour, because it is a right or prerogative that is rooted within baptism. A Catholic education will enable children and young people to make sense of what it means to live as a baptised Catholic Christian. It is important to note this is distinct from nurturing them in overtly catechetical terms to be baptised or accept their baptism. The focus of Religious Education lessons would be on grasping the ways in which baptism frames the worldview and day-to-day life of Catholic Christians. Moreover, the focus of Religious Education in Catholic schools – borrowing terms inspired by Biesta and Hannam (2020) – would be upon the teacher helping children and young people to make sense of what it is to live out well the baptised life. Naturally this would involve exploring in Religious Education lessons how central the place of faith is in life as a baptised Catholic Christian. Inevitably, this would involve devoting significant lesson time to exploring how a living baptismal faith involves a loyalty to and relationship of trust in God, through Christ. Fundamentally, living the baptised life well involves what Kierkegaard described as the 'leap *into* faith'. The emphasis, here, is on a relationship of trust and openness to God. As Kierkegaard's metaphor draws out, this relationship is not something one investigates with an academic interest and perhaps emotional neutrality, rather it is something that is leaped into. The role of Religious Education in a Catholic school could become an ongoing exploration of what it means to live a life as a baptised Catholic Christian, where making a leap into faith makes sense throughout every stage of life.[1] This is to set Religious Education on a very different trajectory, one that possibly subverts and challenges the excessive examination focus. Not least because exploring faith in this way is something far harder to assess in written examinations.

However, it is clear that revision of the *RECD* will not be setting out on this alternative trajectory. The early indications are that there will be a heavy emphasis on core knowledge and framing Religious Education along firmly disciplinary lines, in which (Catholic) theology is the central underpinning of the subject.[2] As such a key goal for Religious Education is to deliver 'school level theology'. On first impressions this is an appealing metaphor, emphasising an integral relationship between the academic discipline of theology and the Religious Education that takes place in Catholic schools. There is an intuitive appeal to the idea that (Catholic) theology could be packaged and delivered in an age appropriate way at both primary- and second-level schools. There are well researched examples developed by Carswell (see for example 2018), in which scripture is taught in Religious Education in Catholic schools using a hermeneutical model. This approach employs the same hermeneutic principles that underpin contemporary biblical scholarship. Moreover it is tempting to draw a comparison with those who are advocates for 'philosophy in schools'. Perhaps just as the Philosophy for Children (P4C) movement has mushroomed since the pioneering early days of Lipman (1977), there is the potential of a flowering of a 'theology for children movement within Religious Education lessons in Catholic schools. Moreover, aligning Religious Education in Catholic schools with (Catholic) theology can readily draw on the arguments developed under the umbrella of 'powerful knowledge'. These arguments seek to draw a close connection between subjects taught in school and their disciplinary equivalents in academia. A working assumption built into using the powerful knowledge arguments is that through studying Religious Education (when understood as school-level theology), a student will encounter a challenging and academically rigorous discipline. There is a natural progression built into such school-level theology which ultimately leads onto pursuing the discipline further, eventually at university.

Going beyond 'School-level Theology'

However, on second impressions the intuitive appeal around the metaphor of 'school-level theology' can be seriously challenged and rejected as flawed in some significant respects. First, the relationship between individual subjects on the school curriculum and the wider academic disciplines researched at universities and amongst academics is actually very complex. Yet the metaphor of school-level theology suggests a simplistic relationship, where theology can be readily divided up into different levels. At the epistemological level it is not clear that the content within theology is like this. For example, the central theological issues surrounding the problem of evil defy being packaged up in terms of a school-level version of the problem and a university-level version. A student in the latter context ought to be able to engage with a wider range of sources which have attempted to respond to the problem of evil, however it is fundamentally the same theological issue whether it is examined in school or whilst at university. It has already been observed that Carswell's skill has been to use the same hermeneutical principles of contemporary biblical studies, rather than invent or create a school-level version of biblical theology. It is just not clear that any real distinction can be established between school-level and university-level theology.

Second, any attempt to emulate P4C by arguing for some sort of 'theology for children will quickly come across the differences in approach between philosophy and theology. Lipman (1977) recognised the potential of Socratic questioning and Platonic dialogue when working with even the youngest children. The process of scrutinising challenging questions and ideas is the starting point of philosophy and this is something that children in school settings have been able to quickly and successfully engage with. Although theology shares many affinities with philosophy, the primary focus is not on questioning the fundamental mysteries of life, but on offering responses and ways of making sense of them. The role of theology is, as Rahner explains, to begin by giving a name to the ultimate mystery and to draw attention to the significance of the word or concept of 'God' (1969; 1976). In theology the focus is on offering insights, drawn from scripture and tradition, about how to make sense of or even resolve challenging issues and questions. This means that theology in schools would not be built around a circle of enquiry (as promoted by P4C) where questions are critically engaged with, but rather are more likely to become what might be characterised as a 'circle for listening' in which the focus is on well-presented apologetics. This would put the emphasis on accepting and assenting to well-presented theological responses. It is the methodology of theology that would be the stumbling block in developing a theology for children movement that parallels P4C.

A third, perhaps more elementary, point is to question the cogency of treating subjects of the school curriculum as if they are roughly equivalents of the academic disciplines studied at university. Naturally, to depict school students as mini-theologians, mini-scientists, mathematicians-in-the-making or budding poets has an appeal particularly when motivating them to engage in classroom activities. However, if these ways of understanding school students is pushed even a little, it would result in school becoming an overly complex arena, akin to it being a scaled-down university. This is because in each of their subjects students would be expected to see themselves as on a trajectory (perhaps expressed in terms of a learning journey) which ultimately leads to them pursuing the subject at university. The idea that each student is effectively to study the eight or nine subjects of the school curriculum at university level lacks coherence. Not only does it ignore the educationally important idea of there being a common curriculum (the schooling or curriculum that *all* students ought to receive), but also places the students in an unenviable situation in relation to all of their lessons. They could never achieve the possibility of pursuing most, let alone all, of their school subjects to university level. Ultimately, the relationship between higher education and the school curriculum is far more ambiguous. This makes the notion of there being a school-level theology, in which students would be characterised as theologians-in-the-making, highly problematic.

A final more general challenge is around the desire to characterise Religious Education as an 'academic' subject in the school curriculum. It is important to recognise that designating a subject as 'academic' is a highly significant framing metaphor. Amongst subjects of the curriculum there is some jockeying for position between subjects. In terms of the English national curriculum there are three subject levels, with subjects listed in terms of priority. There are core subjects (English, mathematics and science), common subjects (history, geography, languages, design and technology, art and design, music, physical education, citizenship, computing), and the 'basic curriculum'. The latter includes Religious Education and Relationship and Sex Education. For advocates of Catholic education it has been an important priority to emphasise that Religious Education is an academically rigorous subject. In the earlier versions of the *RECD* there was a repeated emphasis on the academic status of Religious Education in Catholic schools. It is highly probable that the impending revision will reiterate the academic nature of Religious Education. However, there are negative connotations associated with the concept of being 'academic'. For example, 'academic debates' can often be dismissed as unimportant or ultimately of merely trivial significance. Similarly, an academic pursuit or discipline might be one which is largely irrelevant for day-to-day life or pursued for the sake of a personal whim. Perhaps an unintended danger that comes from emphasising the academic characteristic of Religious Education, is that it is the negative connotations that might begin to rise to the fore. There is an implicit danger that when fortifying Religious Education in Catholic schools as a challenging *academic* part of the curriculum, the subject might ultimately be misconstrued as irrelevant or an overly intellectual pursuit. As such it might have little relevance to the ordinary lives of those studying it, other than being a way of achieving an additional GCSE qualification.

Sean Whittle

Conclusion

This chapter has focused on Religious Education in English Catholic schools which is about to undergo considerable curriculum change. It has been argued that the public examination system now dominates both the style and substance of Religious Education, even in Catholic schools. This has a significant impact on both the formal and informal dimensions of Catholic education in England. The thrust of the analysis in this chapter has been on arguing that the impending changes to Religious Education in Catholic schools will not rectify this situation. Instead of returning to the broader vision offered in *Gravissimum Educationis*, rooting Religious Education in baptism, renewed emphasis will be given to this subject being a firmly academic pursuit. This will be a consequence of framing Religious Education in Catholic schools in terms of being school level theology.

ENDNOTES

1   Whilst this exploration *could* be for everyone, there is a risk that even this way of framing Religious Education might lead back to the catechetical intention question noted earlier and raise again concerns over the indoctrination of non-Catholic students.

2   See the presentation from the CES in February 2020: https://www.atcre.co.uk/videos/Robinson

References

Biesta, G. & Hannam, P. (eds), *Religion and Education: The Forgotten Dimensions of Religious Education*, Leiden: Brill, 2020.

Bowie, R., 'Implicit Knowledge Structures in English Religious Studies Public Exam Questions: How Exam Questions Frame Knowledge, the Experience of Learning, and Pedagogy', in G. Biesta & P. Hannam (eds), *Religion and Education: The Forgotten Dimensions of Religious Education*, Leiden: Brill, 2020.

Carswell, M., 'Teaching Scripture: Moving Towards a Hermeneutical Model for Religious Education in Australian Catholic Schools', in *Journal of Religious Education.* 66 (2018), pp. 213-223.

Catholic Education Service [CES], *Religious Education Curriculum Directory for Catholic Schools and Colleges in England and Wales*, London: Department for Catholic Education and Formation of the Catholic Bishops of England and Wales, 2012.

Congregation for Catholic Education, *The Catholic School*, London: Catholic Truth Society. 1977.

Congregation for Catholic Education, *The Religious Dimension of Education in a Catholic School*, London: Catholic Truth Society, 1988.

Grace, G., *Catholic Schools: Missions, Markets and Morality*, London: Routledge, 2002.

Lipman, M., Sharp, A. and Oscanyan, F., *Philosophy in the Classroom*, USA: Universal Diversified Service, 1977.

Pope Paul VI, *Evangelii Nuntiandi,* 1974. Available at: http://www.vatican.va

Rahner, K., 'The Concept of Mystery in Catholic Theology', in *Theological Investigations Volume IV*, New York: Crossroads, 1969, pp. 36-73.

Rahner, K., *Foundations of Christian Faith: An Introduction to the Idea of Christianity*, (trans. W. Dych), New York: Crossroads Publishing, 1976.

Vatican II, *Gravissimum Educationis*, 1965, in Abbott W. (ed.), *The Documents of Vatican II*, New York: Herder and Herder, 1966.

Whittle, S., 'Contemporary Perspectives on Religious Education in English Catholic Schools', in J. Lydon (ed), *Contemporary Perspectives on Catholic Education*, Gracewing: Leominster, 2018a.

Whittle, S., *Researching Catholic Education*, Singapore: Springer, 2018b.

Whittle, S., *Religious Education in Catholic Schools: Perspectives from Britain and Ireland*, Bern: Peter Lang, 2018c.

Whittle, S., 'An Evaluation of the Catholic Response to the Final Report from the Commission on Religious Education', in *Journal of Religious Education*, 68 (2020a), pp. 359-369.

Whittle, S., 'On the Precarious Role of Theology in Religious Education', in G. Biesta & P. Hannam (eds), *Religion and Education: The Forgotten Dimensions of Religious Education*, Leiden: Brill, 2020b.

Whittle, S., *Irish and British Reflections on Catholic Education*, Singapore: Springer, 2021.

Chapter 13

~~~~~~~~~~~~~~~

Critical Issues in State Assessment of Religious Education in Ireland, 2000–2020: Participation, Attainment, Gender, Biblical Studies

Philomena Clare

Introduction

The lives of those who have navigated the educational system in the Republic of Ireland have been tattooed by the memory of two major state assessments. Students have their first engagement with uniform national examinations at Junior Certificate level, known simply as Junior Cycle since 2017, undertaken by 15- to 16-year-olds after three years of second-level education. The Leaving Certificate is the terminal examination at second level. It is completed at the end of their schooling by 18- to 19-year-olds and has been considered as an achievement barometer for over a century. In the last two decades, one of the more recent additions to the list of possible state-assessed subjects at both levels is Religious Education. This chapter will look at the participation and attainment levels of students in this new Religious Education context. The data available does not address the religion of the students participating in the state-certified Religious Education examinations (as neither does the state) nor, for example, whether their education is at a Catholic school. The findings are important, however, for Catholic schools and their understanding of the contribution, visible and less so, that the Religious Education syllabuses can make in schools. Interestingly, while the data available on Religious Education identifies the educational achievement of students, a close analysis reveals who benefits most and who misses out. Succinctly, girls outperform boys. This chapter attempts to explore why. Mining deeper, this analysis also sheds light on how students' preference and attainment levels differ significantly between the various units of the state-sponsored Religious Education syllabuses at Junior Certificate and Leaving Certificate levels (Department of Education and Science, 2000, 2003). Bible-centred units were least positively engaged with by students. This raises questions about how scripture is engaged with in the Religious Education syllabuses and consequently within Religious Education classrooms in all schools. This, too, will be of particular interest in Catholic schools.

State Assessment of Religious Education: A Journey of over a Century

Religious Education has only been available as a standardised and state-assessed syllabus for a relatively short period. Shortly after the establishment of the Irish Free State in 1922, approximately one thousand students sat the 1925 Leaving Certificate examination (Walsh & Dolan, 2009). Females accounted for 25% of the 1925 cohort (Ó Buachalla, 1987, p. 364). One subject which would not have featured in this cohort's results would have been Religious Education, or 'religious instruction' as it was then termed. Although this faith-based subject was taught in every second-level school at the time, no national assessment of Religious Education in the classroom in Ireland would be considered for over seventy-five years because a legal impediment blocked its evaluation at national level (Devitt, 2000; Byrne, 2013). This was removed in the *Education Act, 1998*, which allowed the historic introduction of state-certified Religious Education programmes. Throughout the 1990s, the introduction of state assessment of Religious Education raised many questions about what exactly was to be measured (Deenihan, 2002). The inaugural state Religious Education syllabuses, when it was unveiled, focused on the provision of religious literacy through a body of knowledge, skills and attitudes; a literacy that can, in fact, be assessed at national level in a way that makes it comparable to other subjects (Devitt, 2000; Byrne, 2013; Dillon, 2013). The assessment intention of the Religious Education programme was communicated as follows:

> The assessment and certification of the Religious Education syllabus at national level would provide student and society with certified statements of achievement based on knowledge, understanding, skills

and attitudes implicit in that syllabus. (Department of Education and Science, 2000, p. 4)

Currently, approximately forty-five subjects are assessed at state level and Religious Education has equivalent examination status to all other subject areas (Carmody, 2018).

While the *Education Act, 1998*, heralded the national assessment of Religious Education, it also witnessed the genesis of the State Examinations Commission (SEC), a statutory body established in 2003, whose responsibility is to oversee the operation of the state examinations provided for by the Department of Education. Structural reform which overarched this act also witnessed the establishment of the Teaching Council of Ireland, An Comhairle Mhúinteoireacha. The SEC is responsible for the development, assessment, accreditation and certifications of the second-level examinations of the Irish state: The Junior Certificate/Cycle and Leaving Certificate. Central to its work is the publication of the Chief Examiners' Reports. Produced intermittently, these provide statistical analysis on a random selection of subjects each year. They also contain feedback on students' performance and recommendations for teachers and students and include some exemplars of student response. Each report has to be read in conjunction with the examination papers for the year in question, the published marking schemes and the syllabus for the subject.

Ireland's Religious Education examinations have been administered by SEC since their commencement in 2003 in the case of the Junior Certificate and 2005 for the Leaving Certificate. Currently, state assessment in Ireland is in the throes of significant overhaul. Religious Education is not immune to the changing approach, characterised by a shifting the focus from summative to formative assessment at what is now termed the Junior Cycle level. Within the new framework for Junior Cycle, the *Junior Cycle Religious Education Specification* (National Council for Curriculum and Assessment [NCCA], 2019) embodies this change. For an initial period teachers have been teaching the old Junior Certificate and new Junior Cycle syllabuses simultaneously to different year groups.

Of further interest in setting up an understanding of educational development in the Republic of Ireland, and marking forty years of free second-level education, the Department of Education and Science provided a statistical report *Sé Sí* in 2007, exploring the impact of gender on educational attainment (Department of Education and Science, 2007). This research presented a subject-by-subject analysis from 1992 to 2002. Religious Education, however, is omitted because its first year of assessment (2003) fell outside date parameters of this report.

Junior Certificate Religious Education Syllabus, 2000 to the Present

While nationally there is one state-developed Religious Education curriculum, there is no compulsion on students to take the subject. Schools make localised decisions whether to provide an opportunity for their students to prepare for and to sit the Religious Education examination. SEC data from 2003 onwards spotlights broad trends in uptake. Initially 9.7% of the total possible Junior Certificate candidature sat the Religious Education examination in 2003. This rose to a high of almost 50% of total candidature sitting the examination by 2012. Since this high point, however, a pattern is revealed whereby, as the total number of Junior Certificate candidates continued to increase, the numbers presenting for Religious Education fell to just below 42% of the total cohort in 2019. Research is needed to comprehend the factors behind this trend. The level of participation, aligned with the evidence of decline, may in part be accounted for by Byrne's observation that many of those who teach Religious Education in Catholic schools 'find themselves dealing with their own crises of faith, crises of confidence, crises of relevance and even sometimes crises in connecting with the frantic pace of change dominating the lives of their young people' (Byrne, 2018, p. 207). Currently Religious Education is the tenth most popular subject with slightly more girls sitting it than boys.

Table 1: Numbers of students sitting the Junior Certificate (data provided by SEC, adapted by the writer)

Year	Total number who sat the Junior Cert exam	Number of students sitting Religious Education exam	% of the total sitting exam Religious Education
2003	59,637	5,787	9.7%
2004	57,074	14,918	26.1%
2005	56,792	21,251	37.2%
2006	57,944	23,997	41.5%
2007	57,395	24,605	42.9%
2008	54,940	24,508	44%
2009	55,557	25,016	45%

2010	56,086	25,930	46%
2011	56,930	26,845	47%
2012	58,798	28,605	49%
2013	59,822	28,850	48%
2014	60,327	28,598	47%
2015	59,522	27,408	46%
2016	60,248	27,328	45%
2017	61,654	27,437	44.5%
2018	62,587	27,170	43.4%
2019	64,330	26,913	41.8%

This Junior Certificate curriculum structure explores the following areas in six designated sections:

Part 1 (select any two of the following)
Section A: Communities of Faith
Section B: Foundations of Religion – Christianity
Section C: Foundations of Religion – Major World Religions
Part 2 (select all of the following)
Section D: The Question of Faith
Section E: The Celebration of Faith
Section F: The Moral Challenge

Between 2003 and 2019 at Junior Cycle there has been only one Chief Examiners' Report for the curriculum area of Religious Education giving feedback on candidate achievement at higher and ordinary level (SEC, 2008). Authored by the Chief Examiner of Religious Education, it was based on a random sample of 10.7% of student responses where a total of 24,508 candidates sat the examination (p. 10). Almost 23% of candidates took the ordinary level (OL) paper, with 77% taking the higher level (HL). For OL, the 2008 report states that students 'performed very well overall in the examination and journal components. Results overall were encouraging: 83.1% of OL candidates were awarded a grade C or higher while only 3.7% of candidates were awarded less than a grade D (SEC, 2008, p. 9). At HL, 86% obtained a C grade or higher with 14% receiving D grade or lower (SEC, 2008, p. 21).

Looking into the examination itself, this Religious Education report indicates that the section of greatest achievement in the examination was Section One. It comprised of twenty knowledge-based questions designed to briefly assess objectives from the syllabus's six sections (A, B, C, D, E, and F). The short questions utilised a variety of approaches such as multiple-choice, true/false questions, item-matching questions, completion questions and brief answer questions. They were intended 'to help candidates settle into the paper' (SEC, 2008, p. 8). The examination generally presented material in a student-friendly manner, using both colour and images. The report revealed high levels of student engagement with Section One of the examination with students awarded an average grade of 98% for HL candidates and 91% for OL candidates respectively (SEC, 2008, p. 22, p. 11). The subject area that was least successful and least popular at OL was Section C: 'Foundations of Religion – Major World Religions' (SEC, 2008, p. 12). The style of assessment here required literary dexterity, involving paragraph style responses. At HL, however, it was noted that 86.2% of candidates were awarded a grade C or higher and 1.7% of candidates were awarded less than a grade D for that section (SEC, 2008. P. 22).

An inter-subject comparison between Religious Education and its 'curriculum cousin', history, reveals interesting insights. The following table shows the examination performance of Junior Certificate OL Religious Education students relative to history. More Religious Education students achieved higher grades in Religious Education than in history, with 2% more at A level, 7% more at B level and 2% more at C level. This suggest that Religious Education teachers have a substantial and grounded understanding of curriculum outcomes that could be clearly communicated to their students. Twenty-three per cent of history students but only 12% of Religious Education students were awarded D and E grades.

Table 2: Spread of performance Junior Cert 2019 – Religious Education and history OL compared (SEC, 2019; adapted by the writer)

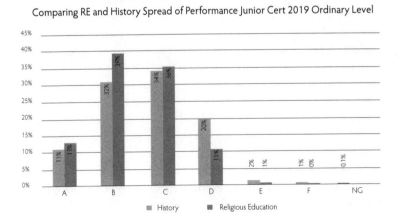

Interestingly, the SEC data highlighted gendered achievement in Religious Education. In 2019, for example, at Junior Certificate level, 17% of females obtained an A grade compared to 7.6% of males. At the lower grade spectrum 15.7% of boys obtained a D grade compared to 8.7% of females.

Table 3: Breakdown of results by gender 2019 results at OL Junior Cert (SEC, 2019)

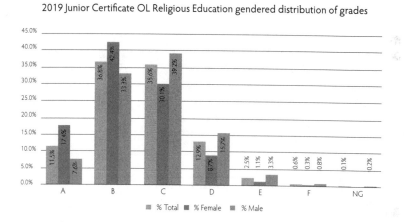

2019 Junior Certificate OL Religious Education gendered distribution of grades

Leaving Certificate Religious Education Syllabus, 2003 to the Present

The introduction of the Leaving Certificate Religious Education syllabus in 2003, as stated, led to its first state-certified assessment in 2005. The numbers sitting Leaving Certificate Religious Education has increased steadily but slowly from 0.1% of the cohort taking the Leaving Certificate in 2005 to approximately 2% (1,293 students) of the total in 2019 (56,071). This is quite miniscule, then, relative to the total number of Leaving Certificate candidates. Certainly, further research is called for to ascertain the factors that influence the poor student uptake of Religious Education at Leaving Certificate compared to Junior Certificate.

Table 4: Uptake of Religious Education examination at Leaving Certificate from 2005 to 2019 (data adapted from SEC)

Year	Total number of Leaving Certificate exam candidates	Number (and %) of total Leaving Certificate candidature taking Religious Education
2005	54,073	80 (0.1%)
2006	50,955	352 (0.7%)
2007	50,873	535 (1.1%)
2008	52,144	778 (1.5%)
2009	54,197	1,013 (1.87%)
2010	54,480	962 (1.77%)
2011	54,344	1,085 (2%)
2012	52,592	1,186 (2.26%)
2013	52,767	1,280 (2.4%)
2014	54,025	1,221 (2%)
2015	55,044	1,167 (2.1%)
2016	55,707	1,320 (2%)
2017	55,770	1,309 (2%)
2018	54,400	1,189 (2.18%)
2019	56,071	1,293 (2.3%)

To meet the aims of the Religious Education programme, the Leaving Certificate syllabus (Department of Education and Science, 2003) is structured around three broad units:

Unit One:
Section A: The search for meaning and values
This compulsory unit investigates ways in which humankind in the past and present have asked existential questions and attempted to make meaning in life.

Unit Two: (select two)
This curriculum unit ranges from the historical origins of Christianity to the voices of different world faiths, and to morality and its intersection with religion.

Section B: Christianity: origins and contemporary expressions
Section C: World religions
Section D: Moral decision-making

Unit Three: (select one)
Unit Three comprises of six optional topic areas of which one area is selected for the Leaving Certificate final examination and two others are chosen for project coursework.
Section E: Religion and gender
Section F: Issues of justice and peace
Section G: Worship, prayer, and ritual
Section H: The Bible: literature and sacred text
Section I: Religion: the Irish experience
Section J: Religion and science

At the subject macro level, Leaving Certificate Religious Education exhibits a relative gender balance in uptake. Statistics from the State Examinations Commission (SEC, 2019) relating to Religious Education at OL in 2018, for example, reveal that, with a small cohort of 108, a slightly higher percentage of males (52%) took the examination. At HL, for a cohort of 1,081, females accounted for 52%. The balance in gender uptake is comparable, then, with Junior Cycle Religious Education, with only a very slightly higher number of girls participating.

Table 5: Breakdown by candidates taking OL and HL Leaving Certificate Religious Education 2018 (SEC, 2019; adapted by the writer)

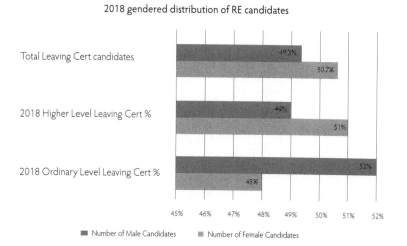

2018 gendered distribution of RE candidates

The current Leaving Certificate figures challenge perceptions elsewhere that Religious Education is a subject principally taken by females. O'Dell's research within the United Kingdom (2012) reveals that there were significant perceptions that Religious Education was a 'girl's subject' (p. 83). Francis and Byrne (2019) demonstrate a positive correlation between religiosity and the female gender. Sweetman (2016) acknowledges the role of the female in maintaining the tradition of family religious history. By way of clarification from a male student perspective, Engebretson's study of Australian boys spotlights their difficulty talking about issues related to their experience of God and beliefs (2007, p. 206). Further research in Ireland on the choices and experiences of girls and boys in this area would be very useful.

SEC data reveals an interesting pattern with respect to Leaving Certificate subject selection which reflects Ireland's changing demographic. Census data reveals an increased diversification of Ireland's population, leading to the introduction of newly assessed foreign languages. Acknowledging this demographic change, subjects such as Arabic, Russian and Polish have been added to the curriculum options for Leaving Certificate candidates, (SEC, 2019). Given Religious Education's longevity in the Irish curriculum context, albeit in multiple guises, it is interesting to note that the sum total of students studying Arabic, Russian, and Polish in 2018 equates, and in 2019 supersedes, the numbers sitting the Leaving Certificate Religious Education. Considering the heritage and role religion has played in Irish society historically and culturally, it is noteworthy that Leaving Certificate Religious Education has not established itself at a higher level. With a relatively low uptake, Religious Education faces challenges in the coming years, certainly at Senior Cycle, if students are to view it as a vibrant and suitable choice in a highly competitive field of optional subjects.

The Importance of Gender in Educational Achievement

Several studies have revealed that some curriculum areas have benefited from an analysis of student performance in subject areas (Elwood, Hopfenbeck & Baird, 2017; Kellaghan & Millar, 2003; Department of Education and Science, 2007). An NCCA study analysed student assessment achievement in Junior Certificate and Leaving Certificate English, Maths and Science in 2000 and 2001. This study focussed on the intersection of gender and academic achievement, revealing the tendency for boys to be overrepresented in lower grades (Elwood & Carlisle, 2003, p. 7).

Table 6: Summary of outcomes by gender for OL Leaving Certificate 2013 (SEC, 2013)

Grade awarded	E grade	F grade	NG	Total
Female	3.6%	0%	1.2%	4.8%
Male	11%	1.4%	1.4%	13.8%

Possible awarded grades for Leaving Certificate range from A (1/2/3), B (1/2/3), C (1/2/3), D (1/2/3), E, F, NG (no grade)

Table 7: Summary of 'A-grade' outcomes by gender for HL Leaving Certificate 2013 (SEC, 2013)

Grade	A1	A2	A3
Female	5.1%	9.9%	9.5%
Male	3.1%	3.7%	11.9%

Religious Education and Gender: A Call for Cultural Performance Data

Elwood (2006) states an evidential truth when she contends that we experience the world through our gendered bodies. The traditional understanding of learning has been framed in binary gender terms, leading to a belief that females and males, because of biological differences, experience learning differently in different subjects. SEC data is derived in female and male gendered format. Currently, with the exception of Gaelscoileanna (Irish language immersion schools where the student examination response is captured through indigenous Gaeilge), the SEC data does not capture statistics pertaining to other aspects of the cohort's culture. The SEC data itself warrants critique here as international studies show that such awareness could sponsor engagement with culturally responsive pedagogy, fostering a teaching methodology that is attentive to classroom gender and culture. New Zealand (NZ)'s equivalence of the SEC, the NZ Aotearoa Qualifications Authority (NZQA), captures student performance in state examinations data by ethnicity (NZQA, 2019). The harvesting of culturally nuanced achievement data (Maori, Pacifica, Asian and European) provides an ethnic dimension on its reporting of student performance and serves to inform Ministry of Education policy and educational practice. This leads to culturally targeted policy which provides for augmentation in the education outcomes of indigenous Maori learners, such as in *Ka Haikitia – Accelerating Success 2013–2017* (NZ Ministry of Education Te Tāhuhu o te Mātauranga, 2013) and the *Action Plan for Pacific Education 2020–2030* (NZ Ministry of Education, 2020).

While data generally reveals that boys experience less success, several studies ask the pertinent question, 'which boys?' Several NZ studies reveal that the cohort at greater risk of failure was gendered male as well as ethnically Maori and Pacifica (Praat, 1999; Ministry of Education, 2018). By so doing, they acknowledge that gender intersecting with culture plays a role in this underachievement (Smyth, 2016; Coolahan, Drudy, Hogan, Hyland & McGuinness, 2017). While in the Irish case students are recorded by gender, SEC data does not currently capture ethnic or cultural data relating to candidates, a situation commented on by Smyth (2016, p. 6). The question therefore is to focus less on the oppositional categories of female/male or what Elwoood names the 'circus of comparison' (2006, p. 265), and to focus more on the role which gender intersecting with culture plays, and the impact this has for indigenous and migrant females/males to Ireland. O'Dell (2012), however, asks a pertinent question: does the focus on boys' experience of Religious Education further marginalise girls?

The Religious Education Examination Paper

State assessment of Religious Education at Junior Certificate level, up to the changes announced in 2019, comprised of two compulsory components, a summative examination worth 80% and a journal component of 20% that was completed within class time. Both aspects were assessed externally by the SEC. The Junior Certificate Religious Education examination paper comprised of five sections ranging from multi-choice, closed-style questions (Section One), to free-style open response questions, to an essay style assessment (Section Five). Unlike the Leaving Certificate Religious Education examination paper, the Junior Certificate assessment was helped by the presence of coloured stimulus materials; visual tools which assist student achievement and question comprehension. Studies from the UK and Ireland have revealed that the form of examination papers is not socially or gender neutral. Gipps and Murphy (1994, p. 212) found that girls outperform boys in open questions/essay style assessment because of greater verbal skills. However, boys outperform girls in multi-choice, objective-style questions. A blended assessment form, which encompasses gender-friendly modes of testing, can be observed in the Junior Certificate examination's Section One. Unfortunately, this section represents only 8% of marks for the total marks awarded.

By way of direct contrast, the Leaving Certificate Religious Education paper demands that a student have a comfortable expertise with the construction of essay or paragraph responses. The following examples will give a clear indication of standard at HL and OL, as well as the conceptual level of response that is required from students. The 2018 HL example reads (SEC, 2019): '*Religion and science can exist in harmony with each other.* Discuss this statement making reference to the work of *either* Galileo *or* Newton.' Another example is taken from the 2011 OL examination paper: 'Outline **two** examples of how inculturation contributed to the development of Christianity in Ireland.'

In the Leaving Certificate paper there is a dominance of more academic essay style modes of assessment. The absence of provision of male friendly (Gipps and Murphy, 1994) multi-choice, objective-style questions, in fact, prioritises responses which more often favour girls. This academic assessment mode leans towards literacy, and can play a role in the underachievement of boys.

Measuring the 'Soul of Theology': Problems Working with Texts from the Bible

When the Religious Education syllabuses were being crafted, Devitt (2000) acknowledged the importance of the Bible in terms of Christianity in the Irish setting. Commenting on the draft range of topics in Leaving Certificate Religious Education, he wrote, 'the section on the Bible was to be welcomed' (p. 7). At Junior Certificate level, 'Foundations of Religion – Christianity' is one of the optional units which focuses on Jesus' context and teachings. Its link to the Bible is such that the learning objectives communicate that students 'have [to] read and be familiar with the Gospel accounts of the death of Jesus' (Department of Education and Science, 2000, p. 18). At Junior Certificate HL, this unit is almost the least preferred. In Section One of the Junior Certificate Religious Education examination, comprising twenty short questions, the least attempted and least successful question, as reported in 2008, came from this unit where students were asked to provide an example from the life of Jesus of table-fellowship. This curriculum topic rooted in the gospels 'if attempted, was frequently inaccurate' (SEC, 2008, p. 23).

The issue concerning the Bible is not limited to the Junior Certificate only. The Leaving Certificate Religious Education syllabus contains an overt Bible-centric topic. Section H, 'The Bible: literature and sacred text', is one of six optional topics in Unit Three of the syllabus (NCCA, 2003, p. 7). The Chief Examiners' Reports on Leaving Certificate Religious Education reveal that aspects of the syllabus which are Bible-centred exhibit reduced student engagement and lower levels of participation compared to other aspects of the Religious Education curriculum (SEC, 2008; 2013). Biblical sections have the lowest average mark (of 55%) and were ranked the least popular in terms of uptake. Overall, the data suggests poor student engagement and achievement in this section of the Leaving Certificate Religious Education syllabus. In 2008 Leaving Certificate HL Religious Education, Section H, 'The Bible: literature & sacred text', was ranked least popular among candidates. The Chief Examiner writes that this unit also was 'not a popular choice among candidates' in the Leaving Certificate OL examination paper (SEC, 2008, p. 12). Further, at HL, Section H proved to be 'the least popular choice of candidates' (SEC, 2008, p. 24).

The 2013 report on Leaving Certificate Religious Education from the Chief Examiner reveals that Section H, 'The Bible: literature & sacred text', was used as one of two options for coursework. Coursework or project work is a mandatory component of the Religious Education syllabus, worth 20% of the total marks. Given a choice between Section H and Section E, 'Religion and gender', here again, the Bible unit featured least (SEC, 2013). Given the cyclical, indeed occasional, nature of the publication of the Chief Examiner's Religious Education reports, unfortunately there is no longitudinal evidence which can track student engagement with curriculum units. The publication of the SEC's Chief Examiners' reports is at variance with what happens in New Zealand Aotearoa. There, assessment reports are produced annually and provide insights into enhanced performance over a unified chronological framework (New Zealand Qualifications Authority, 2019). The lack of sequential data has major implications for Catholic students, among others. Reduced engagement with the Bible has implications for their theological understanding of Church teaching. This is particularly pertinent given that examination candidates in their teenage years, a time of their lives that students' faith is challenged cognitively and psychologically by a range of societal distractions. Welbourne further contends that, 'to understand the Bible as Scripture is to understand that through the biblical texts God speaks to us' (Liddy, 2009, p. 1362).

Sacred texts, Liddy comments, are 'foundational to many religious traditions and their study indispensable to the content and process of religious education' (Liddy, 2009, p. 1361). She emphasises that Judaism and Christianity would not exist without the sacred texts that shaped, preserved and transformed their identities (2009). Several key Catholic Church documents frame the importance of the Bible and biblical methodologies which help unlock its meaning as a tool for critical engagement. Identified in *Dei Verbum* (Vatican II, 1965) as 'the soul of theology', the Bible is central to Christian life and worship, as well as a toolkit to unlock Ireland's cultural past and present. In terms of Irelands Catholic Christian milieu, Ó Fearghail writes that for 'nearly sixteen centuries the Bible has been an integral part of the religious and cultural situation of Ireland' (2012, p. 185). Its presence in the Religious Education curriculum is core for Christian students.

The challenging phenomenon of Irish students' engagement with the Bible is not geographically unique. Bowie (2018) highlights the role in which scripture has been used in proof-texting within the English Religious Studies public examination. Further afield, in Australia, Carswell (2018) observes how the Bible is used to fit pre-determined curriculum themes in Religious Education syllabuses. There, the meaning of texts is determined to fit the theme which brings with it the danger of disenfranchising the text from its original context and original meaning.

While the Chief Examiners' Reports for Religious Education serve to 'provide a review of the performance of candidates in the examinations and detailed analysis of the standards of answering' (SEC, 2020), it must be observed, too, that the data represents a random sample and not the total cohort. In the case of Religious Education at Junior Certificate level, the random sample represents 10.7% of the cohort (SEC, 2008). For Leaving Certificate OL the random sample represents 24% of the cohort, and for Leaving Certificate HL it represents 33%. These reports are based on the written examination paper and the journal booklet.

Recognising a Need for Change

Curriculum assessment in Ireland has been dominated until recently by summative, terminal examinations which are sometimes viewed as a managerial tool where it is used to select appropriate levels and give information to parents and others (Black & Wiliam, 1998). The two state examinations have dominated the educational experience and assessment landscape of the individual for decades. Looney (2006) calls the Junior Certificate one of two deafening noises which characterised the educational landscape and successfully silenced any other form of assessment discourse. In 2020, responding to the Covid-19 pandemic, the Department of Education and Science established an alternative to the historic Junior Certificate and Leaving Certificate written terminal assessments. In collaboration with the SEC, it issued a series of calculated grade assessments to students. O'Leary (2020) highlights how the new process shone a critical light on the Leaving Certificate. While the Leaving Certificate examination system had many strengths, and has high status in Irish society, he argues against holding it up as a paragon of accuracy and fairness. In reality, he suggests that there is no ultimate truth in terms of assessing students in a Leaving Certificate result, just as there is no such ultimate truth in any assessment.

Over a period of years now, Ireland has been grappling with educational change and with greater emphasis on formative assessment. Central to this change is the call to shift assessment practice from external summative assessment or 'Assessment of Learning' to formative assessment or 'Assessment for Learning' (A4L). The Junior Certificate examination previously concentrated three years of learning into a two-hour examination mostly for each subject, limiting student engagement with broader dimensions of teaching and learning. The new Junior Cycle framework, on which the recently launched *Junior Cycle Religious Education Specification* (NCCA, 2019) has been developed, embodies these assessment shifts. The new Religious Education curriculum at Junior Cycle focuses on three strands – expressing belief, exploring questions, and living our values (see Byrne, Chapter 3 of this volume). The core aim of this new approach is that students should have an 'understanding of religion and its relevance to life, relationships, society and the wider world' (NCCA, 2019, p. 5). The first cohort of students began their engagement with the new Junior Cycle Religious Education Specification in September 2019 and will complete the first cycle of assessment in 2022.

Conclusion

An analysis of the first two decades of state assessment of Religious Education in Ireland shows that while Religious Education has been a popular examination subject at Junior Certificate level very few students go on to take Religious Education for the high-stakes Leaving Certificate, although most schools continue with low-status, non-examination Religious Education with varying degrees of commitment to the subject. Secondly, it is clear that there is a pattern of slightly more girls than boys sitting the Religious Education examinations, with girls outperforming boys. Thirdly, the discussion here has clarified that SEC data reveals that there are significant concerns about student engagement with units which have a Bible focus, particularly at Leaving Certificate level. For Catholic schools, among others, there is an urgent need, then, to consider their attitude toward participation in Religious Education as an examination subject, the levels of attainment that can be achieved by both girls and boys, and the need to put a variety of resources into supporting understanding of and engagement with the Bible. Given the importance of the Bible in the Christian tradition, this has implications specifically for Catholic schools as well as for Reformed Tradition schools and for the variety of schools which Catholics students attend.

As the traditional certainties of a once conservative society are challenged in Ireland, the experiences discussed in this chapter pose a social and educational challenge for the Religious Education community. Byrne encourages those committed to the values and potential of Catholic education in Ireland 'to acknowledge the new context, to recognise, to celebrate and draw on the great heritage of Catholic schools' (Byrne, 2018, p. 216). On an optimistic note, he and his co-authors observe elsewhere that recent research shows that 82% of 3,000 13- to 15-year-old students surveyed agreed that we must respect all religions (Byrne, Francis & McKenna, 2019, p. 213). They concluded that the Junior Certificate Religious Education syllabus, whether taken as an examination subject or not, also contributed a social benefit (Byrne, Francis & McKenna, 2019). As part of the thrust to maintain the ethos of Catholic education, a purposeful response to the new 2019 Religious Education Specification at Junior Cycle, building on the Catholic Religious Education tradition would be important. Equally with negotiations underway for the new framework promised at Senior Cycle (NCCA, 2018), a review within Catholic schools of their support for Religious Education at this level is overdue. Support for students in studying the Biblical sections within both the Junior and Senior Cycle syllabuses would count as a meaningful response to Byrne's clarion call that Catholic schools draw on their tradition to support student engagement with Religious Education. The provision of a revised framework at Senior Cycle, with newer modes of assessment, and a committed attitude to the subject in Catholic schools, could lead to an increase in the numbers of girls and boys taking the subject through to Leaving Certificate. Herein lies the potential for an uptick in Biblical studies within the Leaving Certificate Religious Education programme.

References

Black, P.J. & Wiliam, D., *Inside the Black Box: Raising Standards through Classroom Assessment*, London: GL Assessment, 1998.

Bowie, R.A. & Coles, R., 'We Reap What We Sew: Perpetuating Biblical Illiteracy in New English Religious Studies Exams and the Proof Text Binary Question', in *British Journal of Religious Education*, 40/3 (2018), pp. 277-287.

Byrne, G., 'Encountering and Engaging with Religion and Belief: The Contemporary Contribution of Religious Education in Schools', in G. Byrne & P. Kieran (eds), *Toward Mutual Ground: Pluralism, Religious Education and Diversity in Irish Schools*. Dublin: The Columba Press, 2013, pp. 207-224.

Byrne, G., 'Religious Education in Catholic Second-Level Schools in Ireland: Drawing on Our Heritage, Living in the Present, Anticipating New Directions', in S. Whittle (ed), *Researching Catholic Education*, Singapore: Springer, 2018, pp. 205-217.

Byrne, G., Francis, L.J. & McKenna, U., 'Exploring the social benefit of religious education in post-primary schools within the Republic of Ireland: An empirical enquiry among 13- to 15-year-old students', in G. Byrne & L.J. Francis (eds), *Religion and Education: The Voices of Young People in Ireland*, Dublin: Veritas Publications, 2019, pp. 201-221.

Carmody, B., 'Religious Education: The Irish Secondary School', in S. Whittle (ed), *Religious Education in Catholic Schools: Perspectives from Ireland and the UK*. Oxford: Peter Lang, 2018, pp. 105-126.

Carswell, M., 'Promoting Fundamentalist Belief? How Scripture is Presented in Three Religious Education Programmes in Catholic Primary Schools in Australia and England and Wales', in *British Journal of Religious Education*, 40/3 (2018), pp. 288-297.

Coolahan, J., Drudy, S., Hogan, P., Hyland, Á. & McGuinness, S., *Towards a Better Future: A Review of the Irish School System*. Glounthane, Cork: IPPN and NAPD, 2017.

Deenihan, T., 'Religious Education and Religious Instruction: An Alternative Viewpoint', in *The Furrow*, 532 (2002), pp. 75-83.

Department of Education and Science, *Junior Certificate Religious Education Syllabus*, Dublin: Stationery Office, 2000.

Department of Education and Science, *Leaving Certificate Religious Education Syllabus*, Dublin: Stationery Office, 2003.

Department of Education and Science, *Sé Sí: Gender in Irish Education*, Dublin: Department of Education and Science, 2007.

Devitt, P.M., *Willingly to School: Religious Education as an Examination Subject*, Dublin: Veritas, 2000.

Dillon, S., 'Religious Education at Second Level in Ireland: Inclusive Practice', in G. Byrne & P. Kieran (eds), *Toward Mutual Ground: Pluralism, Religious Education and Diversity in Irish Schools*. Dublin: Columba Press, 2013, pp. 71-78.

Elwood, J. & Carlisle, K., *Examining Gender: Gender and Achievement in the Junior and Leaving Certificate Examinations 2000/2001*, Dublin: National Council for Curriculum and Assessment, 2003.

Elwood, J., Hopfenbeck, T. & Baird J.-A., 'Predictability in High-stakes Examinations: Students' Perspectives on a Perennial Assessment Dilemma', in *Research Papers in Education*, 32/1 (2017), pp. 1–17.

Elwood, J., 'Gender Issues in Testing and Assessment', in B. Francis, L. Smulyan & C. Skelton (eds), *The Sage Handbook of Gender and Education*, Thousand Oaks, CA: Sage, 2006, pp. 262-278.

Engebretson, K., *Connecting: Teenage Boys, Spirituality and Religious Education*, Strathfield, NSW: St Paul's Publications, 2007.

Flinders, D.J., Noddings, N. & Thornton, S.J., 'The Null Curriculum: Its Theoretical Basis and Practical Implications', in *Curriculum Inquiry*, 16/1 (1986), pp. 33-42.

Gipps, C.V. & Murphy, P., *A Fair Test? Assessment, Achievement and Equity*. Buckingham: Open University Press, 1994.

Kellaghan, T. & Millar, D. *Grading in the Leaving Certificate Examination: A Discussion Paper*, Dublin: Educational Research Centre, St. Patrick's College, 2003.

Kieran, P. & Hession, A. (eds), *Exploring Religious Education: Catholic Religious Education in an Intercultural Europe*, Dublin: Veritas, 2008.

Liddy, S.A., 'Teaching Scripture in Religious Education', in M. de Souza, G. Durka, K. Engebretson, R. Jackson & A.M. McGrady (eds), *International Handbook of the Religious, Moral and Spiritual Dimensions in Education*.

International Handbooks of Religion and Education, Vol 1, Springer: Dordrecht, 2009.

Looney, A., 'Assessment in the Republic of Ireland', in *Assessment in Education: Principles, Policy & Practice*, 13/3 (2006), pp. 345–353.

National Council for Curriculum and Assessment (Ireland) [NCCA], *Senior Cycle Review*, NCCA, 2018. Available at: https://www.ncca.ie/media/3878/ncca_sc_single_pages_en.pdf

National Council for Curriculum and Assessment (Ireland) [NCCA], *Junior Cycle Religious Education Specification*, 2019. Available at: https://www.ncca.ie/en/junior-cycle/subjects-in-development/religious-education

New Zealand Ministry of Education Te Tāhuhu o te Mātauranga, *Ka Hikitia – Accelerating Success 2013–2017*, 2013. Available at: https://education.govt.nz/our-work/overall-strategies-and-policies/ka-hikitia-ka-hapaitia/ka-hikitia-history/ka-hikitia-accelerating-success-20132017/

New Zealand Ministry of Education Te Tāhuhu o te Mātauranga, *Statement of Intent 2018–2023*, 2018. Available at: https://education.govt.nz/assets/Documents/Ministry/Publications/Statements-of-intent/Statement-of-Intent-2018-2023-web.pdf

New Zealand Ministry of Education Te Tāhuhu o te Mātauranga, *Action Plan for Pacific Education 2020–2030*, 2020. Available at: https://conversation-space.s3-ap-southeast-2.amazonaws.com/Pacific+Education+Plan_WEB.PDF

New Zealand Qualifications Authority, *Level 3 Geography 2019*, 2019. Available at: https://www.nzqa.govt.nz/ncea/subjects/assessment-reports/geography-l3/

Ó Buachalla, S., *Education Policy in Twentieth Century Ireland*, Dublin: Wolfhound, 1988.

Ó Fearghail, F., 'The Bible in Ireland', in B. Leahy & S. Ryan (eds), *Treasures of Irish Christianity*, Dublin: Veritas Publications, 2012, pp. 185–187.

O'Dell, G., 'Gender', in P. L. Barnes (ed), *Debates in Religious Education*, London: Routledge, 2012, pp. 77–87.

O'Leary, M., 'Would Leaving Cert Students' Estimates of Their Own Grades Help Teachers?', in *The Irish Times*, 13 May 2020. Available at: https://www.irishtimes.com/news/education/would-leaving-cert-students-estimates-of-their-own-grades-help-teachers-1.4252424

Praat, A., 'Gender Differences in Student Achievement and in Rates of Participation in the School Sector, 1986–1997: A Summary Report', in *Research Bulletin*, 10 (1999), pp. 1–11.

State Examinations Commission, *State Examinations Commission: Annual Exam Statistics*, 2019. Available at: https://www.examinations.ie/statistics/

State Examinations Commission, *State Examination Commission: Chief Examiners' Report*, 2013. Available at: https://www.examinations.ie/?l=en&mc=en&sc=cr

State Examinations Commission, *State Examination Commission: Chief Examiners' Report*, 2008. Available at: https://www.examinations.ie/?l=en&mc=en&sc=cr

State Examinations Commission, *Chief Examiners' Reports*, 2020. Available at https://www.examinations.ie/?l=en&mc=en&sc=cr

STEM Education Review Group, *STEM Education in the Irish School System*. Available at: https://www.education.ie/en/publications/education-reports/stem-education-in-the-irish-school-system.pdf

Smyth, E., *Students' Experiences and Perspectives on Secondary Education: Institutions, Transitions and Policy*, London: Palgrave Macmillan, 2016.

Sweetman, B., *Godparenthood in Ireland: An Empirical Study into the Educational Intentions Influencing Parental Selections of Godparent*, EdD thesis. Dublin City University, 2016.

Vatican II, *Dei Verbum: Dogmatic Constitution on Divine Revelation*, 1964, in Abbott W. (ed), *The Documents of Vatican II*, New York: Herder and Herder, 1966.

Welbourne, L., 'Critical Biblical Literacy in the School Curriculum', in *Journal of Religious Education*, 51/4 (2003), p. 1.

Chapter 14

∿∿∿∿∿∿∿∿

'Why Are Catholic Schools Afraid to Be Catholic Schools?' Challenges to Leaders of Catholic Secondary Schools in Ireland

Aiveen Mullally

Introduction: The Current Context for Catholic Secondary Schools in Ireland

The population in the Republic of Ireland (hereafter, Ireland) has become increasingly diverse over the past two decades. New demographics in terms of culture, language and belief systems are enriching her once relatively homogeneous society and a school system which continues to reflect the country's historic relationship with the Roman Catholic Church.

During penal times in Ireland, generally, schools for Catholics were forbidden until the *Relief Acts* of the late eighteenth century when Nano Nagle, Catherine McAuley and Edmund Rice, among others, began to establish schools for Catholic children. Following Catholic emancipation in 1829, Catholics sought to assert their new-found freedom and to establish schools which reflected their empowered sense of identity. This has resulted in the Roman Catholic Church being responsible for the patronage of 90% of primary schools and approximately 50% of post-primary (second-level) schools in the Republic of Ireland today.

While the majority of the country's population still identify as Roman Catholic, there has been a rise in the number of people in Ireland declaring that they have no religion and an increase in those loosely attached to their Christian identity. The 2016 census highlights the decline in numbers of people identifying as Roman Catholic, falling from 84.2% in 2011 to 78.3% in 2016 (Central Statistics Office, 2017). While these figures are still high, religious practice rates, particularly among young people, have declined considerably. Mass attendance dropped from 91% in 1971 to 35% in 2012 according to some estimates (Ganiel, 2016).

Parents within minority faith groups and parents who wish for multi-denominational or secular schooling for their children in Ireland are now seeking to establish primary and second-level schools which reflect their own identity and ethos, for which the Irish Constitution allows. However, educational provision has not yet caught up with developments in Irish society. This has resulted in many Catholic schools welcoming a growing religiously and secularly diverse student body within their school communities, both enriching and posing challenges for the schools.

Research Informing National Guidelines

To help with a review of guidelines on the inclusion of students of different beliefs in Catholic secondary schools, research was conducted in 2018 with principals and members of trustee bodies for Catholic schools. A short online questionnaire was sent in February 2018 to all principals of Catholic voluntary secondary schools in Ireland (approximately 340 schools) and to members of the trustee bodies who own the schools. Responses were returned from 118 of these and provided rich data to inform the writing of the guidelines.

Participants were asked to identify the matters they considered it would be very important to address in the guidelines.

Table 1: Participants selection of most important areas to be addressed in guidelines

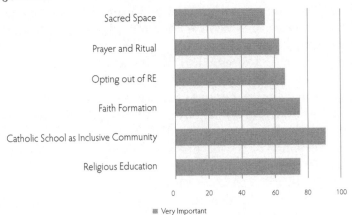

As can be seen in Table 1 the theme considered most important to be addressed in the guidelines was an understanding of the Catholic school as an inclusive community (89.6%). The next most important area highlighted by participants was the fostering of faith formation for Catholic students (75.22%). This was closely followed by the teaching of Religious Education (72.81%). This points to the change in focus within religious education in many Irish Catholic voluntary secondary schools over the last twenty years from being catechetical in nature to being focused through the State-sponsored syllabuses on learning *about* and *from* Christianity, and from different beliefs.

The challenge of parents using the 'right to withdraw' their children from religious education was highlighted by 63.25% of participants. Guidance on sacred spaces (56.9%) and leading prayer and rituals in a diverse Catholic school (62.28%) was also considered very important.

Challenges to Leaders in Catholic Schools

The participants were also asked to comment on the challenges and opportunities they face regarding religious diversity in their school context. Three main themes emerged from the data:

- The reality of nominal Catholicism and the new 'nones'
- The pressure on Religious Education (RE) as a subject
- Faith formation of Catholic students

Nominal Catholicism and the New 'Nones'

A significant number of respondents highlighted the challenge that there is '...an increasing number [of students] wanting to withdraw from RE class or not wanting to engage with the ethos of the school or participate in rituals and retreats' (Principal 38). One participant stated:

> It would appear that students of no faith and students of different faiths are now the majority in our schools. Many parents see little value in their sons studying RE. Indeed, in the staff room there are many non-Catholics. This is the context. The overwhelming majority of teachers support the school ethos but some from a humanist point of view. Prayer and ritual can be problematic especially a full school Mass which we celebrate once a year. (Principal 60)

Principal 32 also stated: 'We have a great RE programme and great teachers but students in Leaving Certificate, with permission from their Catholic parents, sign their daughters out at RE time.' Another participant highlighted handling nominal Catholicism as more challenging than accommodating different beliefs including those of no religious belief: 'For us it is the students who are nominally Catholic whose parents don't want them to attend RE class rather than the students of other or no religion who have approached us' (Principal 6).

In 2010, the Joint Managerial Body for secondary schools (JMB) along with the Association of Management of Catholic Secondary Schools (AMCSS) commissioned the first set of national guidelines for inclusion of students of different faiths in Catholic secondary schools (Mullally, 2010). The challenge for school principals, then, was mainly concerning how they could actively welcome and include different faith groups in their Catholic schools. Eight years later this reality seems to have changed as highlighted by Principal 20: 'The challenge of dealing with students with no faith is greater than dealing with a student who has a faith'. A lack of clarity as to expectations in relation to the growing need to address inclusion can, clearly, create situations in the daily running of a school that should be dealt with initially when students and their parents are applying to and being initiated into the workings of the school and its ethos.

One of the fastest growing groups in the 2016 Irish census were those identifying as having 'no religion'. In the 2016 census 10% of the Irish population indicated they had no religion, up from 6% in the 2011 census (Central Statistics Office, 2017). This is following international trends. In Britain, for example, half the population reported themselves as having no religion in 2016 (Woodhead, 2016). The 2016 census in Australia also revealed that 30% of the population state they have no religion. This category is more numerous than those identifying as Catholics in every generational age-group under the age of 70 in Australia (Bouma and Halafoff, 2017). Bullivant's *European Report on Young Adults and Religion* (2018) paints a vivid picture in terms of the proportion of young adults (16- to 29-year-olds) with no religious affiliation across Europe, with 91% in the Czech Republic and 70% in France not identifying with any religion.

Research in the US focused on people under the age of 30 who have disaffiliated from the Catholic Church and now identify as having no religion. 25% of the population, generally, in the US, which accounts for eighty million people, do not affiliate to any religious belief and 40% of people under the age of 30 identify as having no religion (McCarthy

&Vitek, 2018). The category for no religion includes people identifying as humanist, free-thinkers, atheists, sceptics or agnostics. They are diverse in their make-up but characterised by their common rejection of organised religion. This movement is wistfully being described as the new 'nones'. Woodhead (2016) argues, however, that 'nones' are not necessarily atheists. They resist religious labels but some believe in God. Many are not typically hostile to faith schools. This fluid belief among young people is suggesting a more blended, porous approach to religious belief and identity (Harmon, 2018), and it is a new landscape for leaders of Catholic schools in Ireland.

An increasingly plural society is in effect inviting Irish Catholic schools to engage with religious difference and indifference and to consider their own identity in a new way. At the heart of the Catholic tradition lies a deep respect for humanity. This is supportive of people following their conscience, and of the human right to practice freely and with dignity their chosen belief (Kieran & Mullally, 2020). The Christian vision continues to be relevant for Catholic schools, directing them in their goals and overall functioning. The schools continue to be animated by the gospel spirit of freedom and love and are inclusive spaces where every student is welcomed and belongs. The particular ethos of a Catholic school is characterised by the belief that the living presence of Jesus 'is the foundation of the whole enterprise in a Catholic School' (Congregation for Catholic Education [CCE], 1977, par. 34), and permeates every aspect of the school day. The Catholic school embraces the risen Jesus, his presence, his teaching, his command to love God and love neighbour. Pope Francis, in his recent exhortation to young people, *Christus Vivit* (2019), describes Catholic schools as seeking to nurture the personal development of every student, fostering their sense of values and encouraging robust dialogue between culture and the gospel message.

Catholic schools are also called to promote a spirit of mutual understanding between different beliefs and form good citizens within a democratic society. The Church calls Catholic schools to be at the forefront of creating spaces for dialogue between beliefs, including those with no religious interpretation of life, and to model in practice what an inclusive pedagogy is all about (CCE, 2013).

The Pressure on Religious Education as a Subject

The National Council for Curriculum and Assessment (NCCA) has recently developed a new specification for Religious Education at Junior Cycle published in 2019 (NCCA, 2019). While this work was in development, the Minister for Education, in February 2018, issued a circular letter to all state managed post-primary schools on religious instruction and worship in community and Education and Training Board (ETB) state-managed post-primary schools (Department of Education and Skills, 2018a). The majority of these schools are multi-denominational. In Ireland, religious instruction is taken to mean the kind of religious education that takes place 'in accordance with the doctrines, practices and traditions' of a particular religion such as the Catholic religion, and formation of the pupils in that faith (Catholic Primary School Management Association, 2012, p. 23). *Circular Letter 0013/2018* addressed Article 44.2.4 of the *Irish Constitution*, and Section 30 of the *Education Act, 1998*, which refer to the rights of parents to withdraw or opt their child out of religious instruction in schools under state-management, or for students to do so once they reach the age of 18. This 2018 circular stated that those who do not want to receive religious instruction should be timetabled for alternative tuition rather than supervised study during religious instruction. Parents, the circular stated, must be made aware that where religious instruction is provided for, alternative tuition is made available. Parents were to be invited, it suggested, to choose for their sons and daughters between religious instruction and the alternative subject(s) offered by the school. The letter caused confusion by moving between religious instruction and Religious Education without differentiating between the two. It went on to also state that parents should inform the school whether or not they wish their child to participate in or be present during religious worship.

The premise for this circular refers to an historical arrangement made between the Irish State and the Catholic Church in the 1930s to include religious instruction among the subjects provided for in a, then, new model of state-managed post-primary schools that were multi-denominational in nature. At the time the majority of students attending these schools were either Roman Catholic or belonging to the Church of Ireland.

Historically, in Ireland, the term 'religious instruction' has been used in the Constitution and legal documents and circulars to refer to an educating *into* a particular religious tradition. However, while the term 'religious instruction' is still championed in some quarters, the subject has been referred to as 'Religious Education' for many decades and has changed dramatically in the last twenty years. The advent of the state curricula for Religious Education (Department of Education and Science, 2000, 2003), reviewed in Chapter 13, above, and the renewed version at Junior Cycle (NCCA, 2019), explained by Byrne in Chapter

3 of this volume, has seen a move away from the direct formation of students *into* a particular faith (catechesis) and more towards a broader religious education that reflects the growing diversity of beliefs present in Ireland today. The minister's February 2018 circular was deemed misleading for schools that were already teaching an inclusive state syllabus that was written in such a way that students of all beliefs could participate from their own perspective (Byrne, 2018a). Clarification was sought and another circular, *Circular Letter 0062/2018* (Department of Education and Skills, 2018b), was issued in October 2018. This clarified that schools teaching the state Religious Education syllabi intended for examination, since they are open to all and are not religious instruction in one faith, would not necessitate a particular opt-out facility. Religious instruction and worship, in future, if they were to take place in such schools, would be opt-in, and formally so.

Importantly, the timing of the survey, taking place within the context of the publication of *Circular Letter 13/2018* which had been issued specifically to state-managed schools, meant that principals of Catholic schools were responding to the questionnaire at the height of this controversy, and before the clarifying circular was issued some months later. Many expressed concern about the effect the minister's circular would have on Catholic schools and the pressure they would receive from parents who may wish to withdraw their son or daughter from religious education. Principal 24 stated:

> The greatest concern for our Catholic schools is the downgrading of religious education in our schools ... students who wish to withdraw from RE class may do so but they should not be rewarded or encouraged by offers of extra tuition in other subjects.

Principal 9 raised a similar concern:

> There is also a growing pressure from parents and students especially at senior cycle to be able to withdraw. Given that most of what is taught at senior cycle is very important for the spiritual development of all, irrespective of faith, I think there is a need to educate our parents re the content and importance of RE at senior cycle.

Principal 41 stated: 'a clear distinction between religious education and religious instruction has to be drawn. Religious Education as an academic subject is very different to faith formation or proselytism.' Catholic schools teaching the Religious Education state curricula are not offering religious instruction as such. Religious Education, as set-out now at second level by the state in Ireland, takes a broader more dialogical approach. It seeks to open students to education *about* different beliefs in society as well as providing an opportunity to learn *from* these different religions and beliefs in order to deepen their own belief and commitment. As stated earlier, the curricula are written to encompass all beliefs, and students in Catholic schools are invited into dialogue with the Christian vision as well as with each another's beliefs. There is no reason why students of different faiths or students with no religious belief in a Catholic school should not participate fully in this curriculum. Principal 52 echoed this, stating that Religious Education in their school seeks to:

> nurture the faith of those within the school's faith; listen to those from other faith practices share their stories and beliefs. Create a climate of respectful dialogue for the whole school community where the notion of each person's faith is a gift in their lives.

It is important that students in a Catholic school learn *about* each other. The Council of Europe emphasises the importance of teaching about religions and non-religious beliefs and of fostering respect for religious differences (Keast 2007; Jackson, 2014). This is because it could be argued that this helps to develop a cohesive, harmonious society. The Council of Europe identifies Religious Education as one curricular area where students can learn *about* and *from* those whose beliefs are different to theirs while simultaneously developing their own belief perspective (Byrne, 2018b). It also promotes the social development of students and enhances their moral and spiritual development. One of the Trust Board Members in the research stated:

> We are very strongly of the view that all students who have opted to go to our schools should participate in religious education classes – and in all ethos related activities. The intellectual, spiritual and moral development of the students all relate to the holistic development of the young person. There is no question of 'indoctrination' but rather a belief that students coming from a particular faith system or none, can learn about and from the Catholic faith tradition. The respectful engagement will help deepen their own beliefs. (Trust Member 82)

Different approaches are taken to Religious Education in Catholic secondary schools in Ireland, but it is essential that, whatever Religious Education programme is offered by the school, in preparation for state examination or otherwise, the school needs to consider how it invites students of different beliefs into dialogue with the programme, and with the Catholic ethos of the school (Boeve, 2019).

Religious Education: A Pedagogy of Dialogue

Religious Education that seeks to facilitate conversations between different voices and perspectives calls for a dialogical pedagogy. In the CCE's most recent publication, *Educating to Intercultural Dialogue in Catholic Schools* (2013), schools are called to place intercultural dialogue as an overarching aim of Catholic schooling. An understanding of the growing multi-religious reality of society needs to be fostered where students learn about different beliefs and dialogue with those beliefs and with non-believers. *Share the Good News* (Irish Episcopal Conference, 2010) also provides a rationale and vision for Religious Education in Catholic secondary schools. It states:

> Religious Education offered in a Catholic school, particularly at post-primary level, as well as supporting Catholic students in their faith, may find itself facilitating discussion not only among Catholic students, but also between them and students of a variety of faiths, as well as those who may not be committed to a religious interpretation of life. Religious Education holds open the possibility of helping all people to grapple, within their own reality, with crucial questions central to life and to living, playing its part in personal faith formation if the young person is open and interested and supported in following this through in their lives. (par. 39)

Faith Formation for Catholic Students

The third theme to emerge from the data was the concern leaders in Catholic schools have for the faith formation of Catholic students. Principal 31 stated: 'Students of other religions are much stronger in their faith than Catholic students, so the emphasis must be on educating Catholic students in instruction in that faith'. Another principal suggested:

> Faith as a source of resilience, faith as a map of how we treat each other, faith as a crutch for leaning on when needs must, should not be ignored. Having a faith or not is becoming more important than what faith one belongs to. (Principal 46)

Catholic schools are called to meet their students where they are in their faith or belief journey and to provide space, not only for healthy dialogue between students, but also for reflection and opportunities for the faith development of students who are aligned, however tenuously, with the Catholic faith. This space is always invitational, and while Religious Education may open the Catholic student to their own faith development it is often outside the classroom that this conversation will take place. Students from other faith backgrounds are also encouraged to grow in knowledge of their own tradition and religious practice in a Catholic school (Mullally, 2019).

Opportunities for prayer and ritual are crucial components of what Catholic schools offer to Catholic students and to others if they wish to participate (Byrne, 2017). A great many of the Catholic students in Catholic schools have less and less experience of ritual and prayer outside that which they are offered in their school. Prayer and sacramental experience are a central feature of a Catholic school. Principal 76 stated:

> Accommodation of other faiths or none in an inclusive setting is critical but so is celebration of our own Catholic faith tradition in our schools. Living with that tension between accommodation and celebration is key.

Some respondents highlighted the challenge of engaging students with rituals and the liturgical year, for example: 'How do we cater for students who refuse to attend RE classes, Masses, the Sacrament of reconciliation, carol services, etc.?' (Principal 33), and another principal who asked: 'Why are Catholic schools afraid to be Catholic schools...?' (Principal 26).

Catholic schools recognise the religious freedom of their students and their families and do not seek to coerce or indoctrinate students of different beliefs into the Catholic faith. Rather, the Catholic school 'offers itself to all, non-Christians included, with all its distinctive aims and means, acknowledging, preserving and promoting the spiritual and moral qualities, the social and cultural values, which characterise different civilisations.' (CCE, 1977, par 85). At the same time, the Catholic school holds the right and duty to offer faith formation based on the values of the gospel to Catholic students (CCE, 1988, par. 6).

Whilst uncertainty was expressed by some principals about how best to honour this challenge, this moment, it seems, offers an opportunity to involve all partners of the school community in a review of what it means to be a Catholic school in a contemporary context. Boeve (2019) argues that Catholic education can reimagine its identity in the context of difference and plurality. Catholic schools do not have to choose between being either Catholic or being open to difference. It is precisely through the process of dialogue between people of differing beliefs that one's own identity is deepened. Crucially, dialogue 'opens up the room to introduce once again the Christian voice within the conversation' (Boeve, 2019, p. 37).

Conclusion

The research which took place, and the process of writing the JMB national guidelines for inclusion of students of differing beliefs, reflect the challenges faced by school leaders in Catholic schools in Ireland today. Catholic schools need not fear the credibility of their identity or their voice in a landscape of unbelief and religious diversity. The Catholic voice has as valid a position in the public square as any other voice. Inter-religious and inter-belief dialogue is at the heart of the Catholic school enterprise as one of the means to imitate and live the vision and mission of Jesus (Congregation for Catholic Education, 2013).

Catholic schools in Ireland, as part of the Catholic community and providing for the education of Catholic students, have recently embraced more clearly the variety of students attending these schools. Leaders in Catholic schools, as the majority tradition in the Republic of Ireland, therefore, seek to be hospitable to people of different beliefs and dedicated to their inclusion in the school community. The school, of course, holds the right and duty to contribute to the faith formation of Catholic students based on the values of the gospel. At the same time the Catholic school invites everyone in the school community into dialogue with the vision and mission of the school. This process is always invitational and respectful. It encourages all the partners in the Catholic school to reflect, to listen, to discuss and to be open to deepening their own spiritual lives.

References

Boeve, L., 'Faith in Dialogue: the Christian Voice in the Catholic Dialogue School', in *International Studies in Catholic Education*, 11/1, (2019), pp. 37-50.

Bouma, G. & Halafoff, A., 'Australia's Changing Religious Profile - Rising Nones and Pentecostals, Declining British Protestants in Superdiversity: Views from the 2016 Census', in *Journal of the Academic Study of Religion*, 30/2, (2017), pp. 129-143.

Bullivant, S., *Europe's Young Adults and Religion: Findings from the European Social Survey (2014-16) to inform the 2018 Synod of Bishops*, St Mary's College, Twickenham: Benedict XVI Centre for Religion and Society, 2018.

Byrne, G. 'Religious Education in Catholic Second-level Schools in Ireland Today: An Invitation to Love, Understanding, Commitment, Hospitality and Dialogue', in M. Shanahan (ed) *Does Religious Education Matter?* London/New York: Routledge, 2017, pp. 114-129.

Byrne, G. 'Religion and Education in Ireland: A Changing and Challenging Relationship', in B. Mooney (ed), *Ireland's Yearbook of Education 2018-2019*. Dublin: Education Matters: 2018a, pp. 32-37. Available online at: https://issuu.com/educationmattersie/docs/irelands_yearbook_of_education_2018_fd142f04af68b3?e=36219384/66963017

Byrne, G., 'The Place of Religious Education in the Changing Landscape That Is Ireland Today', in S. Whittle (ed), *Religious Education in Catholic Schools: Perspectives from Ireland and the UK*, Oxford: Peter Lang, 2018b, pp. 33-50.

Catholic Primary School Management Association, *Board of Management Handbook*, revised version, Maynooth: CPSMA, 2012. Available at: https://www.cpsma.ie/wpcontent/ uploads/files/_Secure/Handbook/CPSMA_Handbook_2012.pdf

Central Statistics Office, *Census 2016 Summary Results – Part 1*, Dublin: The Stationery Office, 2017. Available at: https://www.cso.ie/en/media/csoie/newsevents/documents/census2016summaryresultspart1/Census2016SummaryPart1.pdf

Congregation for Catholic Education, *The Catholic School*, Vatican City: Vatican Polyglot Press, 1977. Available at: http://www.vatican.va

Congregation for Catholic Education, *The Religious Dimension of Education in a Catholic School*, Vatican City, 1988. Available at: http://www.vatican.va

Congregation for Catholic Education, *Educating to Intercultural Dialogue in Catholic Schools: Living in Harmony for a Civilization of Love*, Vatican City, 2013.

Department of Education and Science, *Junior Certificate Religious Education Syllabus*, Dublin: The Stationery Office, 2000.

Department of Education and Science, *Leaving Certificate Religious Education Syllabus*, Dublin: The Stationery Office, 2003.

Department of Education and Skills, *Circular Letter 0013/2018*, 2018a. Available at: www.education.ie/en/Circulars-and-Forms/Active-Circulars/cl0013_2018.pdf

Department of Education and Skills, *Circular Letter 0062/2018*, 2018b. Available at: https://www.education.ie/en/Circulars-and-Forms/Active-Circulars/cl0062_2018.pdf

Harmon, M. *"I am a Catholic Buddhist": The Voice of Children on Religion and Religious Education in an Irish Catholic Primary School*, Doctor of Education thesis, Dublin City University, 2018.

Ganiel, G., *Transforming Post-Catholic Ireland: Religious Practice in Late Modernity*, Oxford: Oxford University Press, 2016.

Irish Episcopal Conference, *Share the Good News: National Directory for Catechesis in Ireland*, Dublin: Veritas, 2010.

Jackson, R., *Signposts: Policy and Practice for Teaching about Religions and Non-Religious Worldviews in Intercultural Education*, Strasbourg: Council of Europe, 2014.

Keast, J., *Religious Diversity and Intercultural Education: A Reference Book for Schools*, Strasbourg: Council of Europe, 2007.

Kieran, P. and Mullally, A., 'The New "Nones": Implications of Ticking the "No Religion" Census Box for Educators in Ireland', in *The Furrow: A Journal for the Contemporary Church*, 71/7-8 (2020), pp. 387–395.

McCarthy, R.J, and Vitek, J.M., *Going Going Gone: The Dynamics of Disaffiliation in Young Catholics*, Winona, MN: St Mary's Press, 2018.

Mullally, A., *Guidelines on the Inclusion of Students of Different Faiths in Catholic Secondary Schools*, Dublin: JMB/AMCSS, 2010.

Mullally, A., *Guidelines on the Inclusion of Students of Different Beliefs in Catholic Secondary Schools*, Dublin: JMB/AMCSS, 2019.

National Council for Curriculum and Assessment, *Junior Cycle Religious Education Specification*, 2019. Available at: https://ncca.ie/media/3785/junior-cycle-religious-education-specification.pdf

Pope Francis, *Christus Vivit, Christ is Alive: Apostolic Exhortation to Young People and to the Entire People of God*, Dublin: Veritas, 2019.

Woodhead, L., 'The Rise of "No Religion" in Britain: The Emergence of a New Cultural Majority' in *Journal of the British Academy*, 4, (2016), pp. 245-61.

Chapter 15

~~~~~~~~~~~~~~~~

Multidimensional Competence and the Space between Faith Formation and Scripture Study

Robert Bowie

Introduction

This chapter identifies aspects of the relationship between the formal education of religion in English state-funded schools, which we might generally frame as a secular study of religion, including the study of mainly a single-faith tradition in English state-funded Christian schools, and the community formation (informal or non-formal) learning that is associated with the passing on of religious faith that happens in homes, parish church groups and retreat contexts. This chapter reviews two strands of research. One strand is a series of studies exploring the teaching of scripture in English Religious Education school contexts. The other strand contains projects that explored aspects of faith formation and spiritual development. This chapter draws on insights from these two strands.

The development of faith involves intellectual and affective dimensions: these include curiosity, pursuit, questioning, clarification and understanding on the one hand; and assent, commitment, trust and surrender on the other. Given what is widely understood about the relationship between early childhood experience in life and early education in life, including, most basically, the experience of love and the learning of a first language, there is no tidy divide between formal intellectual learning and spiritual or faith development. How the capacity to think develops likely influences conceivability and the imaginability of things, and the possibility of committing to, or trusting in, ideals, ideas, beliefs and narrative traditions. The mind needs a well-resourced imaginal landscape of metaphors, associations, symbols and experiences to provide material to support what might then be imaginable. The intentions of our actions and practice in education may be according to aims defined by an intellectual frame or a faith formation frame. Still, there is an overlapping space between those frames that should be acknowledged, recognised and considered to understand the aspects of education that impact the development of faith.

Research on Teaching Scripture in Publicly Funded Schools and Faith Development

Research on the teaching of sacred texts in English school classrooms has identified a range of critical issues linked to the organisation of the curriculum, the design of questions, and the place (or absence) of sacred text scholarship in schools (Bowie, 2020a; Bowie & Coles, 2018). These can generally be described in terms of widening gaps. One gap is between what happens in the classroom and the scholarly study of sacred texts; the methods used by sacred text scholars are not modelled and practiced in classrooms. In secondary classrooms, texts are commonly used as proofs for arguments in binary debates and this is a strong feature of secondary school examinations; quotes are arranged by themes; the processes of interpretation are not foregrounded in the study. I have argued elsewhere through literature reviews and research studies that this is an embedded problem (Bowie, 2017, 2018). Another gap is with the religious reading of texts practiced by faith communities. Methods of religious reading are not the kinds that are part of the study of texts that exams recognise and affirm. In English school Religious Education there are examples of experiential approaches that have some parallels with religious reading but these are not thought to be widespread.

This is not simply a matter of secular examination requirements. Carswell (2018) identifies a deviation between the Catholic Church's teaching on the study of scripture and the ways scripture is presented in programs of study authorised or recommended by Catholic education authorities in England and Wales. It could be argued that approved Catholic curricula in schools have departed from the recommended approaches to scripture by the Church. Instead of the Religious Education classroom being a site for scholarly study of sacred texts, it has become an arena for conflict and disagreement.

The 'Texts and Teachers' research project has shown that the study of sacred texts in schools is something that can be improved, made more scholarly, more intellectually demanding and also more important for the faith development process (Bowie, Panjwani & Clemmey, 2020). This was a qualitative study focused on ten teachers in seven secondary schools of different kinds who applied good sacred text scholarship practices to their teaching. Though not a generalisable finding or an aim of the project, it found examples of where that kind of study contributed to student personal faith conversations. These crossed faith and worldview boundaries for young people with examples of challenge to deepen faith and challenge to learn from the scholars. There are also signs that taking a more disciplined and knowledge-rich approach to the teaching of Christianity, through a theological approach as exemplified by the Church of England's 'Understanding Christianity' curriculum project (Pett & Cooling, 2018), has positively impacted on faith-talk in the home (Casson, Hulbert, Woolley & Bowie, 2020.).

Separate research about the passing on of faith in the home and community environments has revealed that Christian parents are unclear about their own responsibility in that process. Given this, they are reluctant to be directive about faith development with their children and unsure how to manage issues of autonomy around matters of identity (Mark, 2016). They have also been found to be unsure how to support children when they ask tricky existential questions at home and unclear how to support their spiritual development in the home more generally (Casson, Hulbert, Woolley & Bowie, 2020). This is particularly the case around issues of death and the science and religion debate. It is reasonable to surmise that engaging scripture on or around these issues plays a part in that uncertainty.

The space between what happens in formal schooling and informal and non-formal faith formation is an important one that we need to better understand. Intellectual and spiritual development both play a part in shaping a person's worldview. In what follows, I want to draw on my own experience and insight into this space.

Autobiographical Reflections on the Shaping of Worldview

When it comes to my faith, my mother has been one of my most important teachers. During my teenage years, we engaged in many long conversations in the kitchen, after school, about her journey and understanding of Catholic Christianity. She had been a teenage convert from a typical rural English Anglicanism to Roman Catholicism just before Vatican II (1962–5). These kitchen conversations were deep, and comparable with the kinds of conversations I was later to have on retreats and with priests, ministers and religious in many settings. One notable difference was that in the kitchen she did most of the talking and I the listening. These conversations contrast starkly, moreover, with most of what I experienced in formal education settings.

A characterising difference between the non-formal faith formation and the formal study of theology at university was that the theological and spiritual content at home tended to be wrapped into personal experiences, memory and feeling. My postgraduate theological work did not include personal reflective components. 'Academic study' meant impersonal, formal language as far as my university writing was concerned. This approach is something Trevor Cooling has recently questioned, arguing it is as an ongoing fallacious assumption that educators make (Cooling, Bowie & Panjwani, 2020).

The kitchen conversations were of a different, more personally reflective character. One kitchen conversation was about Adam and Eve. 'Of course, they did not exist – these events did not happen,' she said. My mother was a leader (a catechist) of the RCIA (Rite of Christian Initiation of Adults) for our home parish in Westminster Diocese. Launched under Cardinal Hume, the RCIA process saw lay people (catechists, or teachers of faith) take a leading role in preparing adults who were becoming Catholic. This meant my mother had a great deal of experience as a result; skilled at conversing with adults as they prepared to join the Church. She explained to me that her Adam and Eve pronouncement was grounded in her conversations with formally Protestant Christians on the RCIA programme. She was helping them to explore the nuanced differences in Catholic teaching on and approaches to scripture, and here specifically about science and religion. Their catechesis was about understanding the centrality of *tradition*, and this involves an appreciation of the different conceptualisation of scripture interpretation.

Being confronted with my devout mother's clarity around her faith, and her pronouncement of Adam and Eve and the Garden of Eden story not happening in that way brought me face to face with a multidimensional way in which scripture is understood to have meaning. I use the word 'meaning' here not because of any relativistic underpinning, but simply that, whilst something may hold truth or be true, the connection between the thing and a person is what it means for and/or to them. It is within the nature of this connection that how they conceive and perceive things is also found. This, in turn, might impact on what they commit to – how they approach life. The things I find deeply meaningful are more likely to motivate a response than what I regard as true but hold little meaning to me.

I had to ponder for years the matter of how to regard and read scripture. In that pondering, the experience that a devout person could have reading scripture, but not in an exclusively literal manner, became significant for me. It led me to make connections with the kind of learning that had previously gone on in my English classes and other formal study, the retreat activities that involved the use of the imagination in encountering texts. This pathway of thought was opened by an understanding that a spiritual reality in texts could sustain a very deep faith, as the experience of my mother demonstrated.

It meant I never had that difficulty, that some seem to have today, of reconciling a passion for astronomy and the sciences in general, with a deep sense of a spiritual and sacramental reality in faith. Catholic teaching or doctrine remains nuanced about the historicity of the Garden of Eden, in fact more nuanced than my mother in that conversation. Still, her statement was *interruptive*, a kind of critical incident, and it shaped my pondering. It acted to shove or guide my thinking about scripture, such that when I discovered historical-critical hermeneutics on the St Mary's University, then College, course for the Catholic Certificate in Religious Studies (see Chapter 1 of this volume). I gained the intellectual tools to articulate this aspect of my family faith formation. As I later learnt about Augustine and Origen's understandings of the 'Quadriga', the senses of scripture, and, for instance, Ezra's work around the Moses narrative, I came to see that multidimensionality was both normative and directing within the Christian tradition's approach to sacred text scholarship. Scripture contains multiple layers of personal engagement, including that of the writers, early interpreting communities and the present interpreting Christian community. In Catholic approaches to hermeneutics, a historical dimension in scripture is not entirely abandoned (and sometimes it is more vividly present), but this is not the only dimension that matters because scripture was formed by the (already) believing community. It has within it, a trans-generational coil that spirals to the present and is still spiralling.

A second memory is my mother's account of the role of dreams in her faith journey and one dream in particular, which she understood to bring her to confront death. This too led me to see my 'imaginal landscape' in a different way. It was something, however, that took time to integrate into an intellectual understanding of how I could meaningfully make sense of that dimension. Through ongoing study, I have understood (through esoteric, psychological, cognitive-linguistic and hermeneutical kinds of literature) how the imaginal landscape of the mind interrelates language, experience and the collective consciousness. I now see the deep importance of these layers and features for conception and consciousness and realise these are extensively developed fields of study with associated academic disciplines.

The Interplay between Personal Faith and Formal Education

In retrospect, I now look back at these two memories as key nudges in my thinking, critical marker points that led to a course of progression. They were not the only influencing factors. The significance of Ignatian spiritual exercises and the Taizé community were parts of my spiritual formation, changing how I engaged with scripture. Ignatian spiritual exercises involve considerable focus on the affective dimensions, with attention to emotions, processes that immerse the person in the narrative of the text, engaging with it in the imagination and drawing on those experiences to aid in discernment around decision-making (Bowie, 2017; Cooling, Bowie & Panjwani, 2020). The spirituality of the ecumenical and international Taizé community is framed through the practice of silence, contemplative singing and community living, features of many practices of religious communities.

Nevertheless, in my own experience, the key critical domestic moments in those kitchen conversations influenced the course my senses of understanding took. In themselves, they are inadequate accounts, mere subjective anecdotes of conversations between a mother and son. Yet their animation in making the direction of thought possible is impossible for me to easily discount. That I continue to hold them in memory is testimony to their significance. More striking is the observation that the multidimensional nature of my developing understanding of reality later helped me comprehend the senses of meaning that deeply impacted on that perception of reality. The way was opened up to a variety of accounts of the nature of reality, in particular from psychology and quantum physics. I had been required to develop a multidimensional understanding of meaning to reconcile what might otherwise have been irreconcilable. The development of a multidimensional character to the kinds of meaning entertained within my imaginal landscape became a general framing for a reflective Christian worldview.

It is worth briefly noting that this combination of the personal with reasoning processes is significant for many other areas of human life. Such as with the perception of pain, and in many aspects of mental health and well-being, as well as in art and the performing arts.

How thinking happens impacts intellectual and perceptive aspects of faith, aiding in the development of a conceptual worldview that integrates and inter-relates different strands of meaning. These are not the only dimensions of faith as there are of course dimensions that are about trusting, holding to and aligning towards, that relate to temperament, character and affective dimensions of human development, but these are not my concern here for the moment. The concern here is that a system of thinking which can be established early on in a human being's development plays a part in the possibility, the conceivability of conceptualisations of faith. If a young person establishes a multidimensional account of reality, then many things become possible: a sense of rightness and wrongness that might transcend preference or utility; the possibility of a spiritual understanding; and, beyond faith, the possibility of quantum physics; a multiverse; the possibility of multiple layers of consciousness within the self and so on. This is also a requirement of many arts, performing arts and humanities in a broader sense.

From Binary to Multidimensional

If a binary notion of religion and science is established, along with an exclusively literal magical conceptualisation of faith, then one of two extremes becomes possible and perhaps more likely. On the one hand, a rejection of faith entirely as incompatible with the modern rational world, perhaps also including faith in truth, goodness, universal human rights, etc., with the danger of nihilism or utter relativism. On the other, a rejection of reason entirely, endangering the powerful civilizational benefits of modern sciences and reason.

Through the secularisation of the school curriculum, such as in England, there is the removal of spiritual domains of meaning from multiple subject fields and identity, with the remnant relegated to something called Religious Education. This is the ultimate consequence of a process that began with the rise of the social sciences, in part a rejection of scholastic development within a faith frame (Gearon, 2013). However, this rise also seems to have had an unduly reductive impact on the dimensionality of thought. The multidimensionality that is part and parcel of many intellectual explorations (understandings of negative and unreal numbers in mathematics, the potency of metaphor in literacy, quantum physics in science, and so on) can be occluded in the study of religion by a narrowly materialistic and individualistic account of reality.

Learning in multidimensional modes of meaning continues to be fruitfully animating in many disciplines, rich in the arts but also present in the social sciences as well as the natural sciences. Many studies, however, signal that within Religious Education in England a strikingly binary mode of thinking is preeminent (Bowie, 2020a; 2020b). Once the universe of meaning is divided into sacred and profane, then the gravity of argumentation pushes each into oppositional corners. Either there are miracles, or there are not. Either Jesus rose from the dead, or he didn't. Either the wine becomes the blood of Christ, or it doesn't. This binary argumentation frames much of the curriculum as a kind of scholastic disputation exercise in which each side is battling for victory. In the English Religious Education curriculum, it is writ large across content domains (under the mantle of diversity within and between religion) and in the value attached to sorts of answers preferred or triggered by examinations. It can be argued that curricula, correct reasoning and valued evaluation are controlled and framed by this approach.

This is not only a problem of the secular business of education. Rather than learn the lessons of Ezra, Jesus, Augustine, Origen and even Calvin when it comes to a multidimensional reading of Genesis, for instance, there are trends in religion that have been lured away from the pursuit of knowledge and the development of multidimensional modes of meaning, preferring what could be characterised as a 'Yeah–Booh' binary alternative. This retains a distinctive boundary, but at some intellectual cost. This is most vividly seen in the 'culture wars' present in politics and society in, for instance, Western liberal democracies as they struggle to manage competing pressures of welcoming diversity and plurality and different views on the legislation of moral frameworks. Theological exclusivism and religious fundamentalism may also be seen as holding a vested interest in framing things as a binary battle.

For some the concern around indoctrination and the desire to promote reason might be necessary protection to wrap around progress and enlightenment and reasoned thinking. However, such protection might inadvertently limit the novel imaginability that human thought needs to make breakthrough insights, in the study of sciences, and also in the discernment of revelation, in the spiritual dimension of life.

Conceivability, Creativity, New Possibilities

It is in the moment that something inconceivable is encountered (inconceivable in so far as present norms are accepted) that the enquiring mind concludes that an adjustment of norms is required. A bigger picture is needed. This is the moment that creativity opens possibilities for new development and deeper insights. This is illustrated by John Moffat, where he critiques the traditional framing of miracles as breaking the rules of nature (Moffatt, 2013). This framing, commonplace in classrooms and literature today, fails to recognise that, in the process of scientific discovery, it is in the moment that something breaks the rules of nature that the need for a modification of the rules emerges and the pursuit of a revision of the rules begins. The definition of a miracle as 'breaking the rules of nature' is inadequate, even for the practice of science. Moffatt refers to this example of miracles as part of a general critique that the translation and integration of faith into mainstream Western culture is very difficult. This, he argues, is because this Western frame has already shaped our thought-world such that any loose bundle of assumptions about evidence is already part of the language that we use.

There is no assurance, however, that this bigger understanding of the rules will actually be found. The significance of the possibility of the unknowability of the universe came home to me when listening to quantum physicists and cosmologists working at Durham University (experimenting with different formulations of the rules of nature using computer-generated models of the universe). They observed that at present what they know about *that which is unknown* in the universe may well be forever unknowable. From this, it might reasonably be the case that as time progresses our understanding of the proportion of the universe that we *think we understand*, might shrink rather than grow. Put another way, the unknowability of the universe might grow as we become more confident about the limits of possible knowledge and understanding. Education is often thought of as the process of explaining things so that they may be better understood, but part of education could just as well be learning to live well with the limits of knowledge, with mystery, and that which we do not, perhaps cannot understand (see Whittle 2014).

Robert Bowie

Reduction without Limiting Future Conceivability

A prerequisite of education must be to ensure the conceivability of other things beyond the immediate horizon of the pupil to avoid leaving young people with a narrow conception of the possible, such that creative leaps of the imagination, necessary for scientific discovery as well as the kind of thinking that is required in the development of faith, are ruled out. David Lewin has explored this theme (Lewin, 2020) using the metaphor of a balance bike to explain the significance of how reduction can still allow for progress without becoming reductionistic. The curriculum entails a necessary reduction, but there are dangers. The balance bike is a good example of reduction as, though it has neither brakes nor gears, it is a more effective tool for learning to ride a bike as it helps a child establish balance and steering first. Once these are established, the child will more quickly learn about braking and gears. A poor curriculum decision is to put stabilisers on the bike, which makes balance more difficult to learn and makes steering more difficult. A poor curriculum slows progression or even closes down opportunities for future exploration and development by not enabling later steps to be built on earlier ones. From this, we may ask, what should we seek to do when designing a curriculum? How can we avoid slowing progression in understanding? At the very least we should try wherever possible to not limit the future conceivability of greater complexity, even if we have to reduce. We must not close down the possibility of future intellectual development through reductions that unduly narrow the lens of possibility.

The Metaphorical Imagination

Teaching children that Bible stories are to only be read as simple historical truths, rather than mythic or etic texts rich in multidimensionality, is surely closer to adding stabilisers to the bike. To begin with the story is one thing, but this is a starting point for possibilities of understanding that go beyond the words of the story themselves. Many children's stories are filled with rich and deep meanings that operate at multiple levels, so it is entirely reasonable to suppose that scripture can be likewise introduced to children in ways that reflect these levels. As Margaret Carswell cogently argues, with the children's story for young children called *Penguin and Pinecone* (Yoon, 2012; discussed by Bowie & Carswell, 2020), children know it is a story about friendship, growth and change. They know it has layers beyond the (in this case fictional) account of a penguin befriending a pinecone. The metaphorical sophistication of narratives is not something reserved for fiction but is rather a feature of many types of texts and much of the language we use, some cognitive linguists argue (Lakoff & Johnson, 1980). These metaphors are not the exclusive preserve of authors but the product of far greater cultural forces and also the experiences of human interaction with life, such that this might well have impacted the evolutionary biological development of the brain (McGilchrist, 2019).

What is unjustifiable is the exclusive study of texts in fragments, as props for dogmas or arguments for use in debates. Yet this is the mainstay of much of the teaching of scripture, as far as research in the UK has shown, as well as research in Australia. The curriculum plans and associated resources of approved and authorised Catholic education programmes used in the UK and Australia utilise texts for thematic arguments, with imposed meanings, to serve in the delivery of truth claims. Similarly, secular qualifications choose themes to be debated and sustained by different texts in the service of debate. These fragmentary encounters offer little or no space for the processes of contextualisation that can open up depths of meanings: the author(s), the linguistic factors, historical dimensions, the first audience, the contemporary audiences in their different settings, the intended and unintended meanings carried through the words, the dimension of interpretation and so on. In the Christian tradition, scripture carries 'Good News', not 'good olds'. The educational opportunity of learning to read and interpret sacred texts, stepping into the forms of meaning that nourish people's faith life is not prioritised, recommended or even advanced in the plans and resources mentioned. Propositional truth claim debate, or a narrow form of apologetics dominate approved curricula. These approaches implicitly, or explicitly, prioritise the literal treatment of texts and also binary approaches to making sense of things. In the English exam system, these approaches are directed by the question frames and curriculum organisers which have little or no space for scriptural hermeneutics. In the religiously approved curricula in England, a particular approach to catechetics decides how meaning is afforded to texts, essentially to uphold Church teachings. The texts are not encountered as gateways into revelation, into encounters with the Word which stand up in a more educated and intellectual age.

Conclusion

The development of hermeneutical expertise would nourish the metaphorical and symbolic imagination, and the absence of this is sorely felt in the development of young minds. It leaves children with few tools to deal with encounters between spiritual meanings in faith and modern intellectual advances. While this is doubtless a binary generalisation that should have more nuance, there is a sense that young people must either develop a myopic approach separating 'faith and reason', or they must abandon one or the other. The possibility of an integrative approach is diminished without an animating hermeneutical reservoir to resource the senses of meaning that are possible and which, if encouraged, would furnish a richer metaphorical and symbolic imagination.

My own experience as a young person of the interplay between a particular combination of informal and non-formal education, alongside classroom learning, nurtured a multidimensional approach to meaning that left open the possibility of faith understanding. It provided gateways into the philosophy of science and the insights of social sciences, psychology and cognitive linguistics. It has left me with a clear sense that the formation of young people's worldviews is complex, related to the kind of education they receive, formally, informally and non-formally. I am convinced that for a flourishing faith life to be possible, there are weaknesses that need addressing in the organisation of the school curriculum, particularly in Religious Education.

References

Bowie, R., 'Stepping into Sacred Texts: How the Jesuits Taught Me to Read the Bible', in A. Voss & S. Wilson (eds), *Reenchanting the Academy*, Seattle, WA: Rubedo Press, 2017, pp.139-156.

Bowie, R., 'Interpreting Texts More Wisely: A Review of Research and the Case for Change in English Religious Education', in R. Stuart-Buttle, & J. Shortt (eds), *Christian Faith, Formation and Education*, Cham, Switzerland: Palgrave, 2018, pp. 211-228.

Bowie R., 'The Collective Consciousness of an RE Department During Curriculum Change: Scripture, Representation, Science, Fear and Anger', in *Journal of Religious Education* 68/3 2020a, pp. 305-313.

Bowie, R., 'The Implicit Knowledge Structure Preferred by Questions in English Religious Studies Public Exams', in G. Biesta & P. Hannam (eds), *Religion and Education: The Forgotten Dimensions of Religious Education?* Leiden: Brill, 2020b.

Bowie, R. & Carswell, M., 'A Message Wrapped in Words', YouTube, 2020. Available at: https://youtu.be/MOx_Dcnu04o

Bowie R., & Coles, R., 'We Reap What We 'Sew': Perpetuating Biblical Illiteracy in New English Religious Studies Exams and the Proof Text Binary Question', *British Journal of Religious Education* 40/3 (2018), pp. 277-287.

Bowie, R. Panjwani, F. & Clemmey, K., *Texts and Teachers: Findings Report*, Canterbury: Canterbury Christ Church University, 2020.

Carswell, M.F., 'Promoting Fundamentalist Belief? How Scripture is Presented in Three Religious Education Programmes in Catholic Primary Schools in Australia and England and Wales', *British Journal of Religious Education* 40/3 (2018), pp. 288-297.

Casson, A.E, Hulbert, S., Woolley, M. & Bowie, R., *Faith in the Nexus: Church Schools and Children's Exploration of Faith in the Home: A NICER Research Study of Twenty Church Primary Schools in England*, Canterbury: Canterbury Christ Church University, 2020.

Cooling, T., Bowie, R. & Panjwani, F., *Worldviews in Religious Education*, London: Canterbury Christ Church University and Theos, 2020.

Gearon, L., *On Holy Ground: The Theory and Practice of Religious Education*, London: Routledge, 2013.

Lakoff, G. & Johnson, M., *Metaphors We Live By*, Chicago, IL/London: University of Chicago Press, 1980.

Mark, O., *Passing on Faith*, London: Canterbury Christ Church University and Theos, 2016.

McGilchrist, I., *The Master and His Emissary: The Divided Brain and the Making of the Western World*, New Haven, CT/London: Yale University Press, 2009.

Moffat, J., *The Resurrection of the Word: A Modern Quest for Intelligent Faith*, Oxford: Way Books, 2013.

Pett, S. & Cooling, T., 'Understanding Christianity: Exploring a Hermeneutical Pedagogy for Teaching Christianity' *British Journal of Religious Education* 40/3 (2018), pp. 257–267.

Yoon, S., *Penguin and Pinecone*, London: Bloomsbury, 2013.

Part V:

~~~~~~~~~~~~

Lifelong Catholic Education:
A Personal Reflection

Chapter 16

∿∿∿∿∿∿∿∿

Fifty-five Years in Catholic Education: Formal, Informal and Lifelong

Gerry O'Connell

*All you need is love … and vision …
and ethos … and reflective space …*

Introduction

I have loved teaching Religious Education to initial teacher education students for the past fifteen years. Some years ago, while researching in the area of transformative learning, I realised that the 'extra-rational turn' in transformative learning (Mezirow & Taylor, 2009; Taylor & Cranton, 2012), with its use of aesthetic approaches, illustrated something important about the approach that I take to the work. This excerpt, from a verse that I wrote for my students, tries to capture the struggle that it can be to teach in that tentative way, as well as the faith and perseverance required:

> And there's going to be times when others help and don't help
> And there's going to be times when you listen and hear nothing
> And there's going to be times when 'try' just won't cut it
> And you'll think of Gaudi in his little room
> And you'll think of Machado in his little room
> And you'll think of Hildegard in her little room
> And you'll think of Therese in her little room
> And you'll be reminded of Thomas and 'so much straw'
> And you'll remember Joseph's warning
> that if you can see your life clearly mapped out in front of you,
> that's not your life …

All that we can ever teach another is our own story. In conversation, our story turns our listeners to reflect on their own story, and so the dialogue begins. This dialogue in turn leads to learning in the silence of the heart, a form of prayer:

I talk, you listen.
You talk, I listen,
Neither talks, both listen.
Neither talks, neither listens.
Silence.

(de Mello, 1988, p. 29)

This chapter reflects on my story of fifty-five years in Catholic education – as a child, as a student, as a teacher, as a lecturer and as a researcher. Autobiographical in nature, it aims to enable readers to reflect firstly on their own stories and secondly on the broader questions of vision and ethos in Catholic education and the place of reflective space in living those questions.

The chapter begins with my earliest experiences as a child in an infant classroom of over one hundred children, through to primary and secondary and third level education. It will then reflect on twenty-five years teaching in Catholic primary schools, in parallel with an ongoing engagement with adult Catholic education in informal settings. A return to formal education via a Master's in Religious Education, leading to a lecturing role in Religious Education in a teacher education college, will be the focus of a further stage on the journey. Finally, the findings from my doctoral thesis, examining past-students' perceptions of my practice in Religious Education in teacher education, along with my thoughts on the role of vision and ethos in Catholic education and the enormous importance of teaching in teacher education colleges, will be offered. My hope is that this reflection may contribute something of a personal perspective at the end of the engaging conversation in this volume opening up our thinking in regard to Catholic education: formal, informal and lifelong.

The Vocation That Teaching Is

I have been teaching for almost as long as I can remember. Sister Francis gave me my first teaching job when I was in Senior Infants in 1965. She sent for me to come to First Class and teach a small group of children to read. I failed. It was the first of many failures that I have experienced in over half a century of teaching. I have many memories of sleepless nights. Sometimes I think that teaching is like a high jump competition. It always ends in failure. At some point in the competition, one jumper remains who has cleared a height that nobody else has managed and that jumper continues to jump until she or he fail three times. Teachers are in constant danger of developing a sense of never quite being good enough.

I remember that first experience of teaching for another reason too, however. I saw a teaching sister, with over a hundred children in her class, improvise in an attempt to teach the weakest ones to read. I have always believed that teaching children (and adults) how to read (and read between the lines) is the primary task of any educator. Reading is the road to freedom. In their book of conversations on education and social change, Myles Horton and Paulo Freire emphasise the importance of reading, even to the point of calling it 'a loving event' (Horton & Freire, 1990).

My experience of education from that first experience in infant school, through primary and secondary school, left me heading off to teacher education college well prepared for the journey and blissfully unaware that it would become a journey towards my own diminishment. My experience in teacher education college in the late seventies was formative, but not in a good way. I left that college at nineteen years of age with my morale bruised and almost broken. Twenty-one years later, when I applied to enrol on a Master's in Education in that same college, I was turned down based on my results from my original degree. The director of the programme told me that my undergraduate results showed that I would not have the academic ability to do the degree. A couple of weeks later, however, I was accepted into a new degree associated jointly with that same college and a neighbouring college – a new Master's in Primary Religious Education. The application this time included an interview where I had an opportunity to talk about the workshops that I had done in the Mount Oliver Institute and the co-chair of this programme, the wonderful Ray Topley, indicated that the team was prepared to take a risk on my ability. On this course, I experienced outstanding teachers and students. My morale was renewed as my self-worth grew, particularly under the initial influence and inspiration of Anne Hession and Dermot Lane, and subsequently as new horizons of learning were opened up to me by outstanding teachers such as Brendan Leahy, Michael Drumm, Michael Maher, Ian Leask and Gareth Byrne.

The reason why I tell this mundane story is that it is utterly central to the reason why I do what I do in my practice in teacher education. I want my students to become the outstanding teachers and people that they are called to be, to recognise their call to teaching as a vow in the same way that Wordsworth, in his *Prelude*, saw his calling to be a poet:

> Two miles I had to walk along the fields
> Before I reach'd my home. Magnificent
> The Morning was, a memorable pomp,
> More glorious than I ever had beheld ...
> Ah! need I say, dear Friend, that to the brim
> My heart was full; I made no vows, but vows
> Were then made for me; bond unknown to me
> Was given, that I should be, else sinning greatly,
> A dedicated Spirit. On I walk'd
> In blessedness which even yet remains.

(Wordsworth, 1850)

For Wordsworth, the catalyst for him to recognise his calling to be a poet was the beauty of a Lake District morning. Nurturing that calling, to their vocation to be the teacher that the world needs, is essential to my work with teacher education students. Without the reflective space afforded them in Religious Education sessions, students would never find the time, as Parker Palmer says, to listen to their lives speaking to them. Palmer insists that without deep listening 'my life will never represent anything real in the world, no matter how earnest my intentions ... Before I can tell my life what I want to do with it, I must listen to my life telling me who I am' (Palmer, 1999, p. 4). The dialogue with teacher education students is intended to lead them to an understanding of vocation as 'the place where your deep gladness and the world's deep hunger meet' (Buechner, 1993, p. 119).

Creating a Welcome

I often tell my students the story of one of my past pupils in primary school. Lynn (not her real name) was in my First Communion class and, even though she was very bright, she could not read in any way fluently. I noticed that she was late for class most mornings. Even still, I made a point of telling her that she was most welcome to class and that we would have missed her if she wasn't there. I began to understand the reason for her delayed reading. All through the infant years at school, she had been late. That meant that she had missed most of the early morning literacy work. Books were not valued at home and so we needed to intervene and direct our resources at improving her reading levels. The intervention was a success even though she continued to be late for school. One wet morning, Lynn arrived into class later than ever, with one third of the day's classes finished. I found myself getting angry, but I just held it and told her that she was most welcome and that we thought she wasn't coming to school that day – which would have saddened us terribly. I told her she could work at her Maths with the girl beside her and come to me with questions. She did a little bit of work and then suddenly arrived at my shoulder to tell me something. She told me that her mother had been out the night before and hadn't been able to get up that morning. So Lynn got herself and her little sister dressed, prepared their breakfast and lunches and then walked two miles in the rain to school. It was only then that I noticed that she was soaked to the skin. She said that she did that because she knew that her teacher and her classmates needed her. This story always seems to resonate with students in college. It is the reason why I always welcome students to class in teacher education college, even those who are late. I have even had post-graduate students tell me how much they appreciated being welcomed when they had been delayed in a stressful commute!

Some time ago, I was out in a school supervising school placement and found myself visiting a disadvantaged Catholic school where the class teacher was one of my past students. The warmth of the relationship between the boys in her class and their teacher was tangible. I asked her how she had nurtured that atmosphere. She told me that it starts first thing in the morning when she welcomes every boy as they come in, especially those who are late, just as she had heard in the story and experienced herself in Religious Education sessions in college. It is my contention that if students learn through their experience that everyone is welcome at the table in college, then they will ensure that everyone is welcome at the table in the primary classroom, thus ensuring that their classroom will be the place where their deep gladness and the children's deep hunger do indeed meet.

Contemplation, Depth, Symbol

Classrooms like that can only be created when space is made for the kinds of approaches that lead to such classrooms being created and nurtured. I have written elsewhere about the elements that lead to making such space in primary Religious Education classrooms – contemplation, depth, symbol, (CDS; O'Connell, forthcoming). 'CDS' is a way of working that ensures that each Religious Education lesson has three elements of space – space for contemplation, space for depth of wonder or conversation, and space for symbol or story. As well as providing an opportunity for prayer or meditation or wonder, this approach affords teachers the opportunity to engage children in deep conversations about things that matter, often arising from a story for example, and from the connection that is made to the child's story. In this way, reflective space for the child (and the teacher) is integral to the work. Incorporating all three spaces attempts to ensure that a Religious Education lesson does not just pay lip service to the patron's half hour per day but rather seeks to provide the space that children require for the work. Such space is found not only in one particular lesson every day, although the Religious Education lesson has a particular role in that regard; this space can become available across the curriculum in a classroom where the teacher seeks out opportunities to make real connections with the children and where the children also have opportunities to make connections with one another. Making a connection with a child or student is possibly the single most important thing that any teacher can do. It is something that lives on after the class, after school is finished and perhaps even after the teacher's lifetime.

I have also outlined elsewhere (O'Connell 2015, forthcoming) seven elements of my practice in Religious Education in teacher education designed to create a reflective and learning space for teacher education students: a 'waiting and wondering' time around a centrepiece; a threshold crossing experience of meditation and verse; a space for 'asking the question' (following Rilke, 1934); a 'gathering around the subject' space, for experiential learning; time for journaling; a 'pushing back the horizon' moment, that attempts to expand students' experience or knowledge and open up new territories; and a concluding ritual that gives expression to the work of the day.

Coming to Wisdom

Working in teacher education I became convinced that I should proceed to doctoral-level research. In some ways, the findings of my doctoral research in which I interviewed past students about their experience of my practice, were a great disappointment to me. I had spent a number of years sourcing materials, developing engaging ideas and resources, researching journal articles, designing centrepieces, writing verses, learning poems and songs by heart, improving my abilities to lead students in meditation and dance, and other time consuming elements of preparation. I was all in. I invested myself utterly in the work. So when the research showed that what I didn't do may have been more significant than what I did do, I experienced the pain that is often necessary in order to come to wisdom.

There is an ancient Irish tale from a collection of stories known as the '*Fiannaíocht*', which tells how Fionn Mac Cumhaill, the leader of the *Fianna* became wise. The story goes that as a young boy, he was sent to learn from a wise man who spent his days on the banks of the River Boyne, fishing for the *Bradán Feasa*, the Salmon of Knowledge. At long last he caught the salmon and gave it to Fionn to cook it for him. As Fionn was cooking the salmon, a blister appeared on the fish. Fionn burst it with his thumb and immediately put his thumb into his mouth to soothe the burning. In this way, he inadvertently gained the wisdom that the fish bestowed on the one who caught it. When unfolding the story in school, we used to tell the children that whenever Fionn needed wisdom from that day on, he just had to suck his thumb – a classic thinking pose. There is an underground version of this story however that says that whenever he needed wisdom Fionn had to bite his thumb right down to the bone because great wisdom only comes with great pain.

When my past students told me that the space that Religious Education afforded them, along with my ability as a lecturer to be present to them, was the most important element of my practice, I realised that wisdom may come quietly but not necessarily without pain. That pain, however, is as nothing compared to the pain I experience seeing the needs of teacher education students (not to speak of the needs of the thousands of pupils in their classrooms into the future) being neglected due to the current trend which sees publishing as much more important than teaching (Lynch, Ivancheva, O'Flynn, Keating, & O'Connor, 2020). While Lynch et al. express their dismay at the increasing lack of care for students at third level generally, it is my conviction that those of us engaged in teacher education should understand that our students learn more from what we are than what we say as we bring ourselves into the classroom and lecture theatre (Palmer, 1998).

The Inner Life of the Religious Educator

In my doctoral research study, the research question was: 'In what ways, personally and professionally, have teacher education students experienced a pre-service Religious Education course, which recognises the importance of a focus on their inner lives?' In the thesis, three research themes emerged and these are discussed under the umbrella theme of 'the inner life', reflecting the centrality of the theme of 'inner-ness'. One participant described it in this way:

> The thing that's forefront in my mind still is ... the time – a time for meditation, stillness, a time for ourselves, you would go in and have a time for your thoughts ... you just thought about things the whole way home. And I think that was the key thing ... it didn't finish ... when you left ...

The first of the three themes was 'Particularity', where the journey of participants and their experience of particular elements of the course, was discussed in terms of 'inner life as curriculum content'. A participant described it like this:

> ... our lecture about death ... about the clowning ... about giving back ... are 'stand out moments' – 'wow' moments that even at the time you knew – that this was something special – whereas it's very hard to say that about any other subject ... Religious Education is probably the only subject in which you're not being taught how to teach it and instead you learn from your own experiences and you build a way and teach it in a way that's for you ...

The second and central theme was 'Inner-ness', where how participants may have experienced the space for 'inner' work provided by the Religious Education course was discussed in terms of 'inner life for professional identity'. A participant elaborated on that in this way:

> I think the biggest thing I learned ... is to be really present in the moment... to be present for children while you're there I think is a huge, huge thing I've learned... because a lot of people don't listen to children ... I think the RE course – of all the courses offered in Marino ... for me was probably the biggest part of my professional development – and ... personally as well ... and I'm surprised that something college-wise – had that power to do that for me – personally ...

The final theme was 'Ongoing-ness', where the ongoing Religious Education journey of participants from primary and secondary school to college and into their teaching lives was discussed in terms of the 'inner life as personal story'. One participant described it thus:

I think that my spirituality has grown and not just the religious side of me ... but my spirituality of where I am and who I am and my place in the world – that definitely was helped and blossomed ... RE played a central role and a vital role in actually preparing us for our careers and life and not just for the children and for the children's benefit ...

Meeting Deep Needs

Reflecting on my research data, I wondered if the elements of the process that contributed to the positive experience of research participants in the study might be worthy of consideration by others teaching at third level. Would they, in their discipline, value a process that recognises the importance of a focus on the inner life? I wondered if the inner lives of students might be seen as an essential aspect of their professional development. Could space be created within which their inner lives might be nourished? Finally, I wondered if students' lives might be considered as part of a continuum of learning that is lifelong but that is focused on the present moment. Could the person who is the student be seen as real and important, with a history that matters and a future full of possibilities, and with present needs that are worth attending to?

It was clear that the space provided by the course for inner-life work was valued by participants. Furthermore, they signalled that it met a deep need in their lives as students. Perhaps it might meet a need in the lives of students in other places and at other stages of their education.

As I have already pointed out, it was the space created for inner-life work, much more than the lecture content, that seemed to make a difference to participants. I heard Maura Hyland, a lifelong catechist and at that time Director of Veritas Publications, speak at the Religious Education Congress in Anaheim in 2005 about the danger of alienating four-year-olds by teaching them what we think they will need to know in twenty years' time. This brought me to an understanding of the truth about teaching. We do not teach programmes or content but rather students, and that we must teach them what they need now in the present moment. That rings as true for me for students in teacher education as it does for four-year-olds in the primary classroom. We may hope of course that what they are learning, that is of significance for them at a particular moment, will have transference at some level into the whole of their lives.

The Importance of Scripture

I come from a Catholic education context and for the past fifty-five years I have been marinated in that space. It has fired my religious imagination and underpinned my convictions in regard to what should happen in Catholic schools. That religious imagination began to be encouraged in 1967 when an aunt of mine, who was a teaching sister in New York, sent me a hardback book called *Heroes of the Bible* (Komroff, 1966), a book of stories and illustrations from the Hebrew scriptures, as a gift to celebrate my First Holy Communion. I still have it. I learned the stories. I had it in my class library for twenty-five years as a primary teacher and I still have it in teacher education college so that I can pass it around the class when we are wondering about scripture. In 1977, as I was heading off to teacher education college, a grand-aunt, also a teaching sister but this time in California, gave me a copy of the New American Bible. I had referred to it for assignments in college at the time but later on, when I had started teaching, I read it so often that the cover fell off. Over the next thirty years, my eyes were opened to the hidden worlds of scripture, and particularly to the historical Jesus by great teachers like Tom Hamill and Dermot Lane. This led me to read everything I could about the historical Jesus as my journey in Catholic education, informal and formal, formed my conviction about the need for education to be an utterly ethical enterprise, where, following Levinas, the other (the student) has priority over me (the teacher).

The Liberating, Healing and Subversive Memory of Jesus

I have written elsewhere about my critique of school mottoes. I have seen schools adopt a motto such as, 'That every child would be the best that they can be'. For a Catholic school, that motto should read, 'That every child would be the best that they can be – for others!' I have watched the Irish media laud one particular school type over others because it aspires to be 'equality-based'. For a Catholic school, the aspiration should not be towards equality but rather utterly biased towards the needs of the poor and most vulnerable, where teachers don't hesitate to leave the ninety-nine in the wilderness and go after the lost one! It's now forty years since I began to teach in primary school and I still don't understand why teachers spend so much time listening to children, who can already read, reading! To change the norms that exist will require teachers to be subversive. In doing this they could usefully draw insight from Dermot Lane; particularly relating to a crisis of imagination in

Catholic education. He argues for the need to keep alive the 'liberating, healing and subversive memory of Jesus' and for that memory of Jesus to 'become imaginatively inserted into our understanding of the world (and education) today' (Lane, 2006, p. 137). In addition, Lane challenges those of us who work in teacher education to bring Jesus as good news to the poor, and not just in name but in compassion for all, in opening our students' eyes, in freedom from whatever it is that oppresses or imprisons them, and in the hope that they in turn will do the same in school classrooms.

Concluding Reflection

I am saddened by the current trend towards the emphasis on publishing rather than care of students and good teaching. It is clear, for example, that promotional posts at third level are decided not by the quality of your teaching but by the length of your publications list and that care for students is not always valued in the academy (Lynch et al., 2020). I understand why that may be so as third-level institutes compete for public profile. The downside in a college of education however is that the diminishment of the quality of teaching in college will ultimately lead to a diminishment in the quality of teaching in the primary or second-level classroom. My doctoral research made it clear to me that students drew from what they found meaningful in college to inform their practice in the classroom. I will leave the final word with one of my research participants:

> I really realised where you could go ... what you could really do with RE – how you could change – or not even change – but how you could awaken these things in children so they could see it as something outside a building or a church ... they could really feel that this is about being with other people – this is about something more than – 'You have to do this' ... we had these experiences that were so different than anything we'd ever experienced – probably in life, never mind college ...

My life has been nourished in the sanctuary of Catholic education for over fifty-five years now. In turn, I have tried to respond to the needs of those I teach, and on the days when I find myself in my element, there is nothing quite like it for a teacher. When I experience failure, I am energised by the search to connect in a more meaningful way in the next class. I have great memories of students finding meaning in the work. I believe that the future of Catholic education – formal, informal and lifelong – is utterly dependent on the quality of teaching that students experience in whatever setting they find themselves, and also on the care-*filled* approach of their teachers. If the quality becomes diminished and we are not care-*full*, our future research will simply illustrate our failures.

References

Buechner, F., *Wishful Thinking: A Seeker's ABC*, San Francisco: HarperSanFrancisco, 1993.

de Mello, A., *Taking Flight: A Book of Story Meditations*, New York: Doubleday, 1988.

Horton, M. and Freire, P., *We Make the Road by Walking: Conversations on Education and Social Change*, Philadelphia: Temple University Press, 1990.

Komroff, M., *Heroes of the Bible*, New York: Golden Press, 1966.

Lane, D.A., 'Challenges Facing Catholic Education in Ireland', in E. Woulfe & J. Cassin (eds), *From Present to Future: Catholic Education in Ireland for the New Century*, Dublin: Veritas, 2006.

'Levinas and the Other in Psychotherapy and Counselling', editorial, in *European Journal of Psychotherapy & Counselling*, 7/1-2 (2005), pp. 1-5, 2005, DOI: 10.1080/13642530500134765

Lynch, K, Ivancheva, M., O'Flynn, M., Keating, K., and O'Connor, M., 'The Care Ceiling in Higher Education', in *Irish Educational Studies*, 39/2, (2020), pp. 157-174, https://doi.org/10.1080/03323315.2020.1734044.

Mezirow, J., Taylor, E.W., et al. (eds), *Transformative Learning in Practice: Insights from Community, Workplace, and Higher Education*, San Francisco: Jossey-Bass, 2009.

O'Connell, G., *The Significance of a Pre-service RE Course, which Recognizes the Importance of a Focus on the Inner Life: Exploring the Experience of Primary Teacher Education Students in a Small Teacher Education College in Dublin*, doctoral thesis, Exeter University, 2015. Available at: http://hdl.handle.net/10871/16567

O'Connell, G., 'Putting Space in Place: Reflective Space and Ethos', in D. Robinson (ed), *Living Ethos: Promoting Human Flourishing in an Educational Environment*, Dublin: Veritas [forthcoming].

Palmer, P.J., *Let Your Life Speak: Listening for the Voice of Vocation*, San Francisco: Jossey-Bass, 1999.

Palmer, P.J., *The Courage to Teach: Exploring the Inner Landscape of a Teacher's Life*, San Francisco: Jossey-Bass, 1998.

Rilke, R.M., *Letters to a Young Poet*, trans M.D.H. Norton, New York: Norton, 1934.

Taylor, E.W. & Cranton, P. (eds), *The Handbook of Transformative Learning: Theory, Research and Practice*, San Francisco: Jossey-Bass, 2012.

Wordsworth, W. *The Prelude or, Growth of a Poet's Mind: An Autobiographical Poem*, London: Edward Moxon, 1850.

Contributors

~~~~~~~~~~~~~~~

Robert Bowie

Professor Robert Bowie is Director of the National Institute of Christian Education, a research centre at Canterbury Christ Church University which investigates all aspects of Christian education including schooling, Christian universities, Religious Education and faith development. He was chair of the Association of University Lecturers in Religion and Education until 2018. He is on the boards of several journals including the *British Journal of Religious Education* and the *Journal of Beliefs and Values*, and is an editor for the *International Journal of Christianity and Education*. His own research areas are around religious and human rights education, with a current specific focus on teaching texts in Religious Education classrooms. He has also written recently on tolerance of religions and morality in values education policy. Professor Bowie researches worldviews and hermeneutics in education specialising in the Catholic and Church of England sectors.

James G. Briody

James G. Briody joined the Salesians of Don Bosco in 1985 and was ordained priest in 1995, having studied at the University of Durham-Heythrop College, University of London, and All Hallows College, Dublin. Following ordination Fr Briody served in Salesian schools in Chertsey, Surrey, and Farnborough, Hampshire, in which he held a number of leadership roles before being appointed Headteacher of Savio Salesian College, Liverpool. He was appointed Provincial of the UK Province of the Salesians of Don Bosco in August 2016 and is currently engaged in research on the maintenance of the Salesian education vision in a contemporary context.

Gareth Byrne

Doctor Gareth Byrne is Associate Professor of Religious Education and Director of the Mater Dei Centre for Catholic Education, Dublin City University. His primary areas of teaching, research and engagement are religious education and Catholic education. He is a member of the Irish Episcopal Conference's Council for Catechetics, Council for Pastoral Renewal and Adult Faith Development, and National Faith Development Team. He is a member of the steering committee of the Network for Researchers in Catholic Education and was the convenor of their 2019 conference at DCU. He was editor with Leslie J. Francis of *Religion and Education: The Voices of Young People in Ireland*, (Veritas, 2019), and with Patricia Kieran of *Toward Mutual Ground: Pluralism, Religious Education and Diversity in Irish Schools* (Columba Press, 2013). Recent contributions also include, with Leslie J. Francis, Christopher Alan Lewis and Bernadette Sweetman, 'Religious Affect and Personal Happiness: Are There Significant Differences between Catholic Adolescents in the Republic of Ireland and in Northern Ireland?', in *Journal of Religious Education* (April, 2020), and chapters in two volumes edited by Sean Whittle, *Religious Education in Catholic Schools: Perspectives from Ireland and the UK* (Peter Lang, 2018), and *Researching Catholic Education* (Springer, 2018).

Ann Casson

Doctor Ann Casson is currently Senior Research Fellow at the National Institute for Christian Education Research at Canterbury Christ Church University. Her research interests include faith schools in a plural society, and students' spiritual development in schools with a Christian foundation. Prior to becoming a full time researcher, Ann taught Religious Education in Church of England, Catholic and community secondary schools across the north east of England. Ann was the lead researcher on the Ten Leading Schools project (2014–17), which investigated the features that contribute to students' spiritual development in secondary schools with a Christian foundation. The findings are now written up as ten case studies in *Lessons in Spiritual Development: Learning from Leading Christian-ethos Secondary Schools*, available from Church House Publishing.

Philomena Clare

Philomena Clare is a native of Co. Meath, Ireland. For over two decades she has been a secondary teacher of Religious Education in Ireland, and internationally, in New Zealand/Aotearoa. She is passionate about the discipline of Religious Education and how it is animated in the public domain. Philomena is also interested in the use of the Bible within the classroom and in Religious Education curriculum. She has a first class Master's of Theology from the University of Auckland, New Zealand, and is currently a doctoral student at the Institute of Education, Dublin City University.

Raymond Friel

Raymond Friel has worked in Catholic secondary education in England for thirty years, as a teacher, head of faculty and, between 2002 and 2016, a headteacher of two schools. From 2016 to 2018 he was the General Secretary of the Catholic Independent Schools' Conference. From 2018 and 2020 he was the CEO of Plymouth CAST, a multi academy trust of thirty-six Catholic schools in Plymouth Diocese. From 2020 to 2021 he was Interim CEO of the Diocese of Westminster Academy Trust. He is the author of a number of books, including *How to Survive in Leadership in a Catholic School* (Redemptorist Publishing, 2014), and *Gospel Values for Catholic Schools* (Redemptorist Publishing, 2017). His collections of poetry include *Stations of the Heart*, Salt, 2008. You can find him on Twitter @friel_raymond.

Thomas G. Grenham

Doctor Thomas G. Grenham is currently Assistant Professor of Chaplaincy Studies and Pastoral Work in the School of Human Development, Institute of Education, DCU. He was formally the Director of Undergraduate Programmes and Head of Theology at All Hallows College, a then college of Dublin City University. He has lectured in Religious Education at Mary Immaculate College, University of Limerick, and was formerly the Associate Dean for Student Affairs and Head of the Department of Pastoral Theology at the Milltown Institute of Philosophy and Theology, Dublin. He served as a missionary for many years among the Turkana of Kenya (1985–95). His publications include *The Unknown God: Religious and Theological Interculturation* (Peter Lang, 2005). He was editor of *Pastoral Ministry for Today: 'Who Do You Say That I Am?'* (Veritas, 2009), and of *Transformative Education in Contemporary Ireland: Leadership, Justice, Service* (Peter Lang, 2018). He also co-edited, with Patricia Kieran, *New Educational Horizons in Contemporary Ireland: Trends and Challenges Rethinking Education Series*, Volume 9, Peter Lang, 2012.

Anne Hession

Anne Hession is Assistant Professor in Spirituality and Religious Education at the Institute of Education, Dublin City University. A graduate of Boston College, she has taught Religious Education at both primary and third levels. She was the writer for the Irish Episcopal Conference of *The Catholic Preschool and Primary School Religious Education Curriculum for Ireland* (2015) and a member of their Council for Catechetics for many years. She is the author of *Catholic Primary Religious Education in a Pluralist Environment* (Veritas, 2015) and, with Patricia Kieran, of two companion volumes also from Veritas, *Exploring Theology: Making Sense of the Catholic Tradition* (2007), and *Exploring Religious Education: Catholic Religious Education in an Intercultural Europe* (2008).

David Kennedy

David Kennedy is Assistant Professor in Religious Education at the Institute of Education, Dublin City University. From 2013 to 2015, he was a departmental assistant at Mary Immaculate College, University of Limerick, were he lectured in Biblical and Systematic Theology. From 2015 to 2019, he worked as a researcher for numerous national bodies in Catholic education such as the Catholic Schools Partnership (CSP), the Association of Trustees of Catholic Schools (ATCS), the Catholic Primary School Management Association (CPSMA) as well as the Irish Episcopal Conference. He is currently associated with the Mater Dei Centre for Catholic Education, and is a member of the Network for Researchers in Catholic Education, Global Researchers Advancing Catholic Education (GRACE) and the European Society for Catholic Theology.

John J. Lydon

Alongside being the Director of the MA in Catholic School Leadership programme at St Mary's University, London, Associate Professor John J. Lydon is Associate Director of the Centre for Research and Development in Catholic Education and Associate Editor of the leading journal, *International Studies in Catholic Education*. He is also Associate Professor at the University of Notre Dame, Indiana. Lydon is Facilitator of the education group of the Catholic-Inspired NGO Forum working in partnership with the Vatican Secretariat of State. He is a founding member of the International Catholic Education Alliance with universities in Australia, America, Ireland and Scotland. His work combines the disciplines of theology and education and has had a long-standing focus on applying teaching as a vocation in practice by Catholic educators and leaders. Significant areas of Lydon's scholarship and research focus on building spiritual capital, Catholic school leadership and maintaining distinctive religious charisms. Some notable publications include *Transmission of a Charism* (2009) *The Contemporary Catholic Teacher* (2011) and the edited volume *Contemporary Perspectives on Catholic Education* (2018).

Aiveen Mullally

Doctor Aiveen Mullally is Senior Lecturer in Religious Education at Marino Institute of Education, Dublin. She is Acting Head of the Department of Inclusion, Religious Education and Student Life and coordinator of the Master of Education Studies in Christian Leadership in Education. She holds a Doctorate in Education specialising in Religious Education. Her research interests are in religious diversity in education. She is the author of national guidelines, *Inclusion of Students of Different Beliefs in Catholic Secondary Schools*, in Ireland (JMB/AMCSS, 2010, 2019). She is a member of the Council for Catechetics and the Interreligious Dialogue Advisory Group of the Irish Catholic Bishops' Conference.

Gerry O'Connell

Doctor Gerry O'Connell has been teaching Religious Education to primary teacher education students in Marino Institute of Education since 2005, following twenty-five years teaching at all class levels of the primary school. Gerry's Master's in Religious Education (Primary) thesis involved exploring Jesus the Parabler and a chapter derived from that thesis was published in Raymond Topley and Gareth Byrne (eds), *Nurturing Children's Religious Imagination: The Challenge of Primary Religious Education Today* (Veritas, 2004). His doctoral thesis concerned students' experience of the pre-service Religious Education course that he teaches in Marino Institute of Education, which has a strong focus on the inner life.

Paul F. Perry

Paul F. Perry is a lecturer at the Irish Bible Institute, Dublin. He has worked in second-level education and diverse adult education settings, including over thirty years involvement in teaching and development work within Church contexts. In his work, Paul draws upon his wide life experience and is passionate about engendering creative and holistic educative experiences for students within educational and Church settings. He is a postgraduate researcher on the Doctor of Education programme at Dublin City University taking the Religious Education pathway. He lives in Dublin with his wife and daughter.

Ros Stuart-Buttle

Doctor Ros Stuart-Buttle was Director of the Centre for Christian Education and Pastoral Theology at Liverpool Hope University for many years. She has taught across school, diocese, seminary and higher education sectors. She gained an MA in Catholic Religious Studies in New York, USA, and completed a PhD with the University of Liverpool, UK. Her professional and research interests explore the relationship between theology and education and include books, chapters and peer-reviewed journal publications on adult learning and theological formation, teacher professional development for Church schools, religious education, and online learning. Ros is a longstanding member of the Board of Religious Studies, working with the Catholic Bishops Conference of England and Wales, and was principal investigator and main author for the national research project, *CCRS Twenty Five Years On: One Size Fits All?* She is married with three adult children and five grandchildren.

John Sullivan

John Sullivan is Emeritus Professor of Christian Education at Liverpool Hope University and Visiting Professor in Theology and Education at

Newman University, Birmingham. For the first half of his career he taught in Catholic secondary schools, from classroom teacher (head of Religious Education for eight years) to headteacher, as well as serving as Deputy Chief Inspector (and then Acting Chief Inspector) in a local education authority in London for four years. For seven and a half years he taught at (what is now) St Mary's University, Twickenham; for five of these he developed and directed the MA programme in Catholic School Leadership. Author and editor of eight books, the latest being *The Christian Academic in Higher Education: The Consecration of Learning* (Palgrave Macmillan, 2018), and more than ninety chapters and articles in the field of religion and education, he continues to be invited to provide professional development for university and school staff, for chaplains, heads and governors, as well as talks for parishes and Church groups. His long-term interests include the mutual bearing on each other of theology and education, mission into practice, the communication of Christian faith and the vitality of the Christian intellectual tradition.

Bernadette Sweetman

Doctor Bernadette Sweetman is a post-doctoral researcher in Adult Religious Education and Faith Development at the Mater Dei Centre for Catholic Education at Dublin City University. A qualified primary school teacher, Dr Sweetman completed her doctoral studies in Religious Education in 2016. She is the author of the *Our Family Mass: Resources for Family Sunday Liturgy* series, published by Veritas, and was part of the writing team for the *Credo* series of high school Catholic education textbooks in the USA. She has been a researcher at third level since 2013 and has lectured across a range of undergraduate and postgraduate programmes at DCU. She was a contributing author to 'Religious Affect and Personal Happiness: Are There Significant Differences between Catholic Adolescents in the Republic of Ireland and in Northern Ireland?', in *Journal of Religious Education* (April, 2020), to a number of chapters in *Religion and Education: The Voices of Young People in Ireland*, edited by Gareth Byrne & Leslie J. Francis (Veritas, 2019) and to *Religious Education in Catholic Schools: Perspectives from Irelands and the UK*, edited by Sean Whittle (Peter Lang, 2018).

Sean Whittle

Doctor Sean Whittle is a Visiting Research Fellow at St Mary's University, London, and a Research Associate with the Centre for Research and Development in Catholic Education, with Professor Gerald Grace. He also held a fellowship at Heythrop College, University of London, for four years. Alongside these academic roles he works part-time as a secondary school Religious Education teacher at Gumley House FCJ Catholic School in West London. His book, *A Theory of Catholic Education* (Bloomsbury 2014), presents a robust philosophy of Catholic education that draws heavily on insights from Karl Rahner. He has edited three books on Catholic education (*Vatican II and New Thinking about Catholic Education*, 2016; *Researching Catholic Education* 2018; *Religious Education in Catholic schools in the UK and Ireland*, 2018), with two further edited books to be published in 2021. In recent years he has been collaborating with other academics working in the field of Catholic education in order to create the Network for Researchers in Catholic Education. Recently he has been working as a post-doctoral research fellow at Brunel University on a religious literacy project and as a visiting lecturer at Newman University. He is secretary for the NfRCE and also serves as vice-chair of the academic association AULRE.

Select Bibliography

~~~~~~~~~~~~~~~~

Alison, J., *Jesus the Forgiving Victim*, Book I, Glenview, Il: Doers Publishing, 2013.

Anderson, B., Byrne, G. & Cullen, S., 'Religious Pluralism, Education, and Citizenship in Ireland', in E. Aslan, R. Ebrahim &. M Hermansen (eds), *Islam, Religions, and Pluralism in Europe*, Dordecht: Springer, 2016, pp. 161–172.

Arnold, J., *The Big Book on Small Groups*, rev. edition, Downers Grove, IL: InterVarsity Press, 2004.

Arweck, E. & Nesbitt. E., 'Young People's Identity Formation in Mixed-Faith Families: Continuity or Discontinuity of Religious Traditions?', in *Journal of Contemporary Religion* 25/1, (2010), pp. 67–87.

Astley, J., 'The Psychology of Faith Development', in M. De Souza, L.J. Francis, J. O'Higgins-Norman, D.G. Scott, (eds), *International Handbook of Education for Spirituality, Care and Wellbeing*, Dordrecht: Springer, 2009.

Atkinson, H.T., *The Power of Small Groups in Christian Formation*, Eugene, OR: Resource Publications, 2018.

Atkinson, J.C., 'Family as Domestic Church: Developmental Trajectory, Legitimacy, and Problems of Appropriation', in *Theological Studies* 66/3, (2005), pp. 592–604.

Attard, F. & Garcia, M. (eds) *Salesian Accompaniment*, Bolton: Don Bosco Publications, 2018.

Balswick, J., King, P. & Reimer, K., *The Reciprocating Self: Human Development in Theological Perspective*, Downers Grove, IL: InterVarsity Press, 2005.

Select Bibliography

Banks, R., *Reenvisioning Theological Education: Exploring a Missional Alternative to Current Models*, Grand Rapids, MI: Eerdmans, 1999.

Barkin. J. *Realist Constructivism: Rethinking International Relations Theory*. Cambridge: Cambridge University Press, 2010.

Bass, D. & Dykstra, C. (eds), *For Life Abundant: Practical Theology, Theological Education, and Christian Ministry*, Grand Rapids, MI: Eerdmans, 2008.

Beckham, W.A., *The Second Reformation: Reshaping the Church for the Twenty-First Century*, Houston, TX: TOUCH Publications, 2005.

Biesta, G. & Hannam, P. (eds), *Religion and Education: The Forgotten Dimensions of Religious Education*, Leiden: Brill, 2020.

Bevans, S., *Models of Contextual Theology*, Maryknoll, N.Y: Orbis Books, 2002.

Black, P. J. & Wiliam, D., *Inside the Black Box: Raising Standards through Classroom Assessment*, London: GL Assessment, 1998.

Boeve, L., *God Interrupts History: Theology in a Time of Upheaval*, London: Continuum, 2007.

Boeve, L., 'Religious Education in a Post-Secular and Post-Christian Context', in *Journal of Beliefs & Values* 33/2, (2012), pp. 143–156.

Boeve, L., 'Faith in Dialogue: the Christian Voice in the Catholic Dialogue School', in *International Studies in Catholic Education* 11/1, (2019), pp. 37 – 50.

Boff, L. & Boff, C., *Introducing Liberation Theology*, New York: Orbis, 1987.

Bouma, G. & Halafoff, A., 'Australia's Changing Religious Profile – Rising Nones and Pentecostals, Declining British Protestants in Superdiversity: Views from the 2016 Census', in *Journal of the Academic Study of Religion* 30/2, (2017), pp. 129–143.

Bowie, R. 'Stepping into Sacred Texts: How the Jesuits Taught Me to Read the Bible', in A. Voss & S. Wilson (eds), *Reenchanting the Academy*, Seattle, WA: Rubedo Press, 2017, pp.139–156.

Bowie, R., 'Interpreting Texts More Wisely: A Review of Research and the Case for Change in English Religious Education', in R. Stuart-Buttle & J. Shortt (eds), *Christian Faith, Formation and Education*, Cham, Switzerland: Palgrave, 2018, pp. 211–228.

Bowie R., 'The Collective Consciousness of an RE Department During Curriculum Change: Scripture, Representation, Science, Fear and Anger', in *Journal of Religious Education* 68/3, (2020), pp. 305-313.

Bowie, R., 'The Implicit Knowledge Structure Preferred by Questions in English Religious Studies Public Exams', in G. Biesta & P. Hannam (eds), *Religion and Education: The Forgotten Dimensions of Religious Education?* Leiden: Brill, 2020.

Bowie, R. & Carswell, M., 'A Message Wrapped in Words', YouTube, 2020. Available at: https://youtu.be/MOx_Dcnu04o

Bowie R. & Coles, R., 'We Reap What We 'Sew': Perpetuating Biblical Illiteracy in New English Religious Studies Exams and the Proof Text Binary Question', in *British Journal of Religious Education* 40/3, (2018), pp. 277-287.

Bowie, R. Panjwani, F. & Clemmey, K., *Texts and Teachers: Findings Report*, Canterbury: Canterbury Christ Church University, 2020.

Boyatzis, C.J. & Janicki. D.L., 'Parent-child Communication about Religion: Survey and Diary Data on Unilateral Transmission and Bi-directional Reciprocity Styles', in *Review of Religious Research* 44/3, (2003), pp. 252-270.

Bradley, I., *Pilgrimage A Spiritual and Cultural History*, Oxford: Lion Hudson, 2009.

Braido, P., *Don Bosco Writings and Testimonies*, Rome: LAS, 2005.

Brondos, D.A., *Jesus' Death in New Testament Thought*, San Angel, México: Comunidad Teológica de México, 2018.

Browning, D.S. & Cooper, T. D., *Religious Thought and the Modern Psychologies*, 2nd edition, Augsburg: Fortress, 2004 [1987].

Bryce, B., 'Theology in Practice: Context for Minister Formation', in *Restoration Quarterly* 59/2, (2019), pp. 105-115.

Buber, M., *To Hallow This Life: An Anthology*, Westport, CT: Greenwood Publishing Group, 1974.

Buchanan, M.T., 'Pedagogical Drift: The Evolution of New Approaches and Paradigms in Religious Education', *Religious Education; Decatur* 100/1, (2005), pp. 20-37.

Bullivant, S., 'Catholic Disaffiliation in Britain: A Quantitative Overview', in *Journal of Contemporary Religion* 31/2, (2016), pp. 181-197.

Select Bibliography

Bullivant, S., 'Contemporary Catholicism in England and Wales: A Statistical Report Based on Recent British Social Attitudes Survey Data', St Mary's College, Twickenham: Benedict XVI Centre for Religion and Society, 2016.

Bullivant, S., *Europe's Young Adults and Religion: Findings from the European Social Survey (2014–16) to Inform the 2018 Synod of Bishops*, St Mary's College, Twickenham: Benedict XVI Centre for Religion and Society, 2018.

Burggraeve R., 'The Soul of Integral Education Orientations for a Contemporary Interpretation of "Religione"', *The Salesian Pedagogical Project*, KU Leuven: 2016.

Butler, J., Habermas, J., Taylor, C. & West, C., 'Concluding Discussion', in E. Mendieta & J. Van Antwerpen (eds), *The Power of Religion in the Public Sphere*, New York: Columbia University Press, 2011, pp. 109-117.

Byrne, G., 'Lifelong Faith Development in the Home, Parish and Other Educational Environments', in P. Kieran & A. Hession (eds), *Exploring Religious Education: Catholic Religious Education in an Intercultural Europe*, Dublin: Veritas, 2008, pp. 35-41.

Byrne, G., 'Communicating Faith in Ireland: From Commitment, through Questioning to New Beginnings', in J. Sullivan (ed), *Communicating Faith*, Washington, DC: University of America Press, 2011, pp. 261-276.

Byrne, G., 'Encountering and Engaging with Religion and Belief: The Contemporary Contribution of Religious Education in Schools', in G. Byrne & P. Kieran (eds), *Toward Mutual Ground: Pluralism, Religious Education and Diversity in Irish Schools*. Dublin: The Columba Press, 2013, pp. 207-224.

Byrne, G., 'Pluralism, Dialogue and Religious Education in *Share the Good News: National Directory for Catechesis in Ireland*', in G. Byrne & P. Kieran (eds), *Toward Mutual Ground: Pluralism, Religious Education and Diversity in Irish Schools*, Dublin: Columba, 2013, pp. 147-155.

Byrne, G., 'Religious Education in Catholic Second-level Schools in Ireland Today: An Invitation to Love, Understanding, Commitment, Hospitality and Dialogue', in M. Shanahan (ed), *Does Religious Education Matter?* London/New York: Routledge, 2017, pp. 114-129.

Byrne, G., 'Catholic Schools Engaging with Family Today: Inspiration from the World Meeting of Families 2018', in L. Franchi (ed), *Catholicism, Culture, Education*, Paris: L'Harmattan, 2018, pp. 25-33.

Byrne, G., 'Religious Education in Catholic Second-Level Schools in Ireland: Drawing on Our Heritage, Living in the Present, Anticipating New Directions', in S. Whittle (ed), *Researching Catholic Education*, Singapore: Springer, 2018, pp. 205-217.

Byrne, G., 'Religion and Education in Ireland: A Changing and Challenging Relationship', in B. Mooney (ed), *Ireland's Yearbook of Education 2018–2019*. Dublin: Education Matters: 2018, pp. 32-37. Available online at: https://issuu.com/educationmattersie/docs/irelands_yearbook_of_education_2018_fd142f04af68b3?e=36219384/66963017

Byrne, G., 'The Place of Religious Education in the Changing Landscape That Is Ireland Today', in S. Whittle (ed), *Religious Education in Catholic Schools: Perspectives from Ireland and the UK*, Oxford: Peter Lang, 2018, pp. 33-50.

Byrne, G. & Francis, L.J. (eds), *Religion and Education: The Voices of Young People in Ireland*, Dublin: Veritas, 2019.

Byrne, G., Francis, L.J. & McKenna, U., 'Exploring the Social Benefit of Religious Education in Post-primary Schools within the Republic of Ireland: An Empirical Enquiry among 13- to 15-year-olds', in G. Byrne & L.J. Francis (eds), *Religion and Education: The Voices of Young People in Ireland*, Dublin: Veritas, 2019, pp. 201-221.

Byrne, G., Francis, L.J., Sweetman, B. & McKenna, U., 'Sustaining Churchgoing Young Catholics in the Republic, in G. Byrne & L.J. Francis (eds), *Religion and Education: The Voices of Young People in Ireland*, Dublin: Veritas, 2019, pp. 223-246.

Byrne, G. & Kieran, P. (eds), *Toward Mutual Ground: Pluralism, Religious Education and Diversity in Irish Schools*, Dublin: Columba, 2013.

Byrne, G. & Sweetman, B., 'CPD and RE: What Do RE Teachers in Ireland Say They Need?', in M. Buchanan & A. Gellel (eds), *Global Perspectives on Catholic Religious Education in Schools*, Singapore: Springer, 2019, pp. 231-243.

Byrne, G. & Sweetman, B., 'Opening up adult religious education and faith development in Ireland: The AREFD project', in *British Journal of Religious Education* April (2021 online).

Byrne, R. & Devine, D., '"Catholic Schooling with a Twist?": A Study of Faith Schooling in the Republic of Ireland during a Period of Detraditionalisation', in *Cambridge Journal of Education* 48/4, (2018), pp. 461-477.

Caperon, J., 'Case Study', in C. Swift, M. Cobb & A. Todd, (eds), *A Handbook of Chaplaincy: Understanding Spiritual Care in Public Places*, London and New York, Routledge, 2016, pp. 315-325.

Caperon, J., Todd, A. & Walters, J. (eds.) *A Christian Theology of Chaplaincy*, London and Philadelphia, PA: Jessica Kingsley Publishers, 2018.

Cardijn, J., *Laypeople into Action*, Adelaide: ATF Theology, 1964.

Carmody, B., 'Religious Education: The Irish Secondary School', in S. Whittle (ed), *Religious Education in Catholic Schools: Perspectives from Ireland and the UK*. Oxford: Peter Lang, 2018, pp. 105-126.

Carmody, B., 'Ecclesial to Public Space: Religion in Irish Secondary Schools', in *Religious Education* 114/5, (2019), pp. 551-564.

Carr, D., 'Knowledge and Truth in Religious Education', in *Journal of Philosophy of Education* 28/2, (1994), pp. 221-238.

Carrette, J. & King, R., *Selling Spirituality: The Silent Takeover of Religion*, London & New York: Routledge, 2005.

Carswell, M.F., 'Promoting Fundamentalist Belief? How Scripture is Presented in Three Religious Education Programmes in Catholic Primary Schools in Australia and England and Wales', *British Journal of Religious Education* 40/3, (2018), pp. 288-297.

Carswell, M., 'Teaching Scripture: Moving Towards a Hermeneutical Model for Religious Education in Australian Catholic Schools', in *Journal of Religious Education* 66, (2018), pp. 213-223.

Casson, A.E., *Fragmented Catholicity and Social Cohesion: Faith Schools in a Plural Society*, Bern: Peter Lang, 2013.

Casson, A.E., Hulbert, S., Wooley, M. & Bowie, R., Faith in the Nexus: *Church Schools and Children's Exploration of Faith in the Home: A NICER Research Study of Twenty Church Primary Schools in England*, Canterbury: Canterbury Christ Church University, 2020.

Catechism of the Catholic Church, London: Geoffrey Chapman, 1994.

Catholic Bishops' Conference of England & Wales, Committee for Catechesis and Adult Christian Education, *The Priority of Adult Formation*, London: Catholic Media Trust, 2000.

Catholic Education Service, *Religious Education Curriculum Directory for Catholic Schools and Colleges in England and Wales*, London: Department for Catholic Education and Formation of the Catholic Bishops of England and Wales, 2012.

Catholic Education Service, *Census Digest*, 2019. Available at: https://www. catholiceducation.org.uk/images/CensusDigestEngland2019.pdf.

Catholic Primary School Management Association, *Board of Management Handbook*, revised version, Maynooth: CPSMA, 2012. Available at: https:// www.cpsma.ie/wpcontent/ uploads/files/_Secure/Handbook/CPSMA_ Handbook_2012.pdf

CEIST: Catholic Education, an Irish Schools Trust, *CEIST Strategic Plan 2017–2020: Living Out Our Founding Mission and Catholic Ethos*, 2017. Available at: https://www.ceist.ie

Central Statistics Office, *Census 2016 Results Profile 8: Irish* Travellers, Ethnicity and Religion, Dublin: The Stationery Office, 2017. Available at: https://www.cso. ie/en/releasesandpublications/ep/p-cp8iter/p8iter/

Central Statistics Office, *Census 2016 Summary Results – Part 1*, Dublin: The Stationery Office, 2017. Available at: https://www.cso.ie/en/ media/csoie/newsevents/documents/census2016summaryresultspart1/ Census2016SummaryPart1.pdf

Chandler, Q., 'Cognition or Spiritual Disposition?', in *Journal of Adult Theological Education* 13/2, (2016), pp. 90-102.

Clarke, R., *A Whisper of God: Essays on Post-Catholic Ireland and the Christian future*, Dublin: Columba, 2006.

Clegg, M.C., 'Policy and Partnership', in *Studies: An Irish Quarterly Review* 108/429, (2019), pp. 20-31.

Clements, B., 'Weekly Churchgoing amongst Roman Catholics in Britain: Long-term Trends and Contemporary Analysis', in *Journal of Beliefs & Values* 38/1, (2017), pp. 32-44.

Comiskey, J., *2000 Years of Small Groups: A History of Cell Ministry in the Church*, Moreno Valley, CA: CCS Publishing, 2014.

Comiskey, J., *Reap the Harvest: How a Small Group System Can Grow Your Church*, Moreno Valley, CA: CCS Publishing, 2015.

Select Bibliography

Congregation for Catholic Education, *The Catholic School*, London: Catholic Truth Society. 1977. Available at: http://www.vatican.va

Congregation for Catholic Education, *The Religious Dimension of Education in a Catholic School*, London: Catholic Truth Society, 1988. Available at: http://www.vatican.va

Congregation for Catholic Education, *Educating to Intercultural Dialogue in Catholic Schools: Living in Harmony for a Civilization of Love*, 2013. Available at: http://www.vatican.va

Congregation for Catholic Education, *Lay Catholics in Schools: Witnesses to Faith*, London: Catholic Truth Society, 1982. Available at: http://www.vatican.va

Congregation for Divine Worship, *Rite of Christian Initiation of Adults*, 1972. Available at: http://www.vatican.va

Congregation for the Clergy, *General Catechetical Directory*, Vatican City: Libreria Editrice Vaticana, 1971. Available at: http://www.vatican.va

Congregation for the Clergy, *General Directory for Catechesis*, Vatican City: Libreria Editrice Vaticana, 1997. Available at: http://www.vatican.va

Coolahan, J., Drudy, S., Hogan, P., Hyland, Á. & McGuinness, S., *Towards a Better Future: A Review of the Irish School System*, Glounthane, Cork: Irish Primary Principals Network and National Association of Principals and Deputy Principals, 2017.

Cooling, T., Bowie, R. & Panjwani, F., *Worldviews in Religious Education*, London: Canterbury Christ Church University and Theos, 2020.

Cottingham, J., *Western Philosophy: An Anthology*, Cambridge: Blackwell Publishing, 2008.

Council for Catechetics of the Irish Episcopal Conference, *Junior Cycle Religious Education in Catholic Schools*, Dublin: Veritas, 2019.

Cullen, S., 'Interpreting "Between Privacies": Religious Education as a Conversational Activity', in M. Shanahan (ed), *Does Religious Education Matter?* London/New York: Routledge, 2017, pp. 37-47.

Cullen, S., 'Turn Up the Volume: Hearing What the Voices of Young People are Saying to Religious Education', in G. Byrne & L.J. Francis (eds), *Religion and Education: The Voices of Young People in Ireland*, Dublin: Veritas, 2019, pp. 271-283.

Das, R., 'Relevance and Faithfulness: Challenges in Contextualizing Theological Education', in *InSights Journal for Global Theological Education* 1/2, (2016), pp. 17–29.

Deenihan, T., 'Religious Education and Religious Instruction: An Alternative Viewpoint', in *The Furrow* 532, (2002), pp. 75–83.

Department of Education and Science, *Junior Certificate Religious Education Syllabus*, Dublin: The Stationery Office, 2000.

Department of Education and Science, *Leaving Certificate Religious Education Syllabus*, Dublin: The Stationery Office, 2003.

Department of Education and Science, *Sé Sí: Gender in Irish Education*, Dublin: Department of Education and Science, 2007.

Department of Education and Skills, *Framework for Junior Cycle, 2015*, 2015. Available at: https://www.education.ie/en/Publications/Policy-Reports/Framework-for-Junior-Cycle-2015.pdf

Department of Education and Skills, *Circular Letter 0024/2016*, 2016. Available at: https://www.education.ie/en/Circulars-and-Forms/Archived-Circulars/cl0024_2016.pdf

Department of Education and Skills, *Circular Letter 0013/2018*, 2018, Available at: https://www.education.ie/en/Circulars-and-Forms/Active-Circulars/cl0013_2018.pdf

Department of Education and Skills, *Circular Letter 0062/2018*, 2018, Available at: https://www.education.ie/en/Circulars-and-Forms/Active-Circulars/cl0062_2018.pdf

Derycke, H., 'Catholic Schooling in France: Understanding La Guerre Scolaire', in G. Grace & J. O'Keefe (eds), *International Handbook of Catholic Education: Challenges for School Systems in the 21st Century*, Part 1, Dordrecht: Springer, 2007, pp. 329–345.

Devitt, P.M., *Willingly to School: Religious Education as an Examination Subject*, Dublin: Veritas, 2000.

Dillon, S., 'Religious Education at Second Level in Ireland: Inclusive Practice', in G. Byrne & P. Kieran (eds), *Toward Mutual Ground: Pluralism, Religious Education and Diversity in Irish Schools*. Dublin: Columba Press, 2013, pp. 71–78.

Donahue, B. & Gowler, C., 'Small Groups: The Same Yesterday, Today, and Forever?', in *Christian Education Journal* 11/1, (2014), pp. 118–133.

Donovan, P., 'The Imbalance of Religious Pluralism', in *Religious Studies* 29, (1993), pp. 218-221.

D'Orsa, J. & D'Orsa, T., *Leading for Mission: Integrating Life, Culture and Faith in Catholic Education*, Mulgrave: Garratt Publishing, 2013.

D'Orsa, J. & D'Orsa, T., *Pedagogy and the Catholic Educator: Nurturing Hearts and Transforming Possibilities*, Mulgrave: Garratt Publishing, 2020.

Drumm, M., 'The Extremely Important Issue of Education', in D.A. Lane (ed), *Vatican II in Ireland, Fifty Years On: Essays in Honour of Pádraic Conway*, Frankfurt am Main: Peter Lang, 2015, pp. 285-303.

Easley, R., 'Taking Stock of Our Work as Theological Educators: An Essay on the Context, Meaning and Future of Theological Education', 2010. Available at: https://www.academia.edu/9897901/Taking_Stock_of_Our_Work_as_Theological_Educators

Elias, J., *The Foundations and Practice of Adult Religious Education*, Florida: Krieger Publishing Company, 1993.

Elwood, J., 'Gender Issues in Testing and Assessment', in B. Francis, L. Smulyan & C. Skelton (eds), *The Sage Handbook of Gender and Education*, Thousand Oaks, CA: Sage, 2006, pp. 262-278.

Elwood, J. & Carlisle, K., *Examining Gender: Gender and Achievement in the Junior and Leaving Certificate Examinations 2000/2001*, Dublin: National Council for Curriculum and Assessment, 2003.

Elwood, J., Hopfenbeck, T. & Baird J-A., 'Predictability in High-stakes Examinations: Students' Perspectives on a Perennial Assessment Dilemma', in *Research Papers in Education* 32/1, (2017), pp. 1-17.

Engebretson, K., *Connecting: Teenage Boys, Spirituality and Religious Education*, Strathfield, NSW: St Paul's Publications, 2007.

Edwards, N., 'The Archaeology of Early Medieval Ireland, c.400-1169', in Dáibhí Ó Cróinín (ed), *A New History of Ireland 1: Prehistoric and Early Ireland*, Oxford: Oxford University Press, 2008.

Fallers Sullivan, W., *A Ministry of Presence: Chaplaincy, Spiritual Care and the Law*, reprint edition, Chicago: The University of Chicago Press, 2019.

Finnegan, J., 'Spiritual Accompaniment: The Challenge of the Postmodern and the Postsecular in the Contemporary West', in F. Attard & M. Garcia (eds), *Salesian Accompaniment*, Part 3, Bolton: Don Bosco Publications, 2018, pp, 131-152.

Fisher, M.F., *The Foundations of Karl Rahner: A Paraphrase of the Foundations of Christian Faith, with Introduction and Indices*, New York: Crossroad Publishing, 2005.

Flinders, D.J., Noddings, N. & Thornton, S. J., 'The Null Curriculum: Its Theoretical Basis and Practical Implications', in *Curriculum Inquiry* 16/1, (1986), pp. 33-42.

Ford-Grabowsky, M., 'Flaws in Faith Development Theory', in *Religious Education* 82/1, (1987), pp. 80-93.

Fowler, J.W., *Becoming Adult, Becoming Christian: Adult Development and Christian Faith*, 1st edition, San Francisco: Harper & Row, 1984.

Frabutt, J.M., Holter, A.C., Nuzzi, R.J., Rocha, H. & Cassel, L., 'Pastors' Views of Parents and the Parental Role in Catholic Schools', in *Journal of Catholic Education* 14/1 (2010), pp. 24-46.

Francis, L.J., Ap Siôn, T., Lankshear, D.W. & Eccles, E.L., 'Factors Shaping Prayer Frequency among 9- to 11-Year-Olds', in *Greek Journal of Religious Education* 2/1, (2019), pp. 39-52.

Francis, L.J. & Casson, A., 'Retaining Young Catholics in the Church: Assessing the Importance of Parental Example', in *Journal of Religious Education* 67/1, (2019), pp. 1-16.

Freire, P., *Pedagogy of Hope: Reliving Pedagogy of the Oppressed*, New York: Continuum, 1997.

Freire, P., *Pedagogy of the Oppressed*, trans. M. Bergman Ramos, London: Continuum, 2005.

Friedman, H., Krippner, S., Riebel, L. & Johnson, C., 'Models of Spiritual Development', in L.J. Miller (ed), *The Oxford Handbook of Psychology and Spirituality*, New York: Oxford University Press, 2012.

Friel, R., 'Renewing Spiritual Capital: The National Retreat for Catholic Head Teachers and the National School of Formation: The Impact on Catholic Head Teachers in the UK', in *International Studies in Catholic Education* 10/1, (2018), pp. 81-96.

Fuller, L., *Irish Catholicism since 1950: The Undoing of a Culture*, Dublin: Gill & Macmillan, 2004.

Gadamer, H.G. *Truth and Method*, trans. J. Weinsheimer & G.G. Marshall, original edition in German, 1960, London: Bloomsbury Academic, 2013.

Gallagher, S.K. & Newton, C., 'Defining Spiritual Growth: Congregations, Community, and Connectedness', in *Sociology of Religion* 70/3, (2009), pp. 232-261.

Ganiel, G., *Transforming Post-Catholic Ireland: Religious Practice in Late Modernity*, Oxford: Oxford University Press, 2016.

Gearon, L., *On Holy Ground: The Theory and Practice of Religious Education*, London: Routledge, 2013.

General Synod of the Church of England, Children and Youth Ministry GS2161, 2019. Available at: https://www.churchofengland.org

Gilliat-Ray, S. & Arshad, M., 'Multifaith Working', in C. Swift, M. Cobb & A. Todd, (eds), *A Handbook of Chaplaincy Studies: Understanding Spiritual Care in Public Places*, London and New York: Routledge, 2016, p. 109-122.

Goodbourn, D., 'Overcoming Barriers to Adult Christian Education', in *Ministry Today* 7, (1996). Available at https:/www.ministrytoday.org.uk/magazines/issues/7/28/

Government of Ireland, *Education Act, 1998*, Dublin: The Irish Statute Book, 1998.

Government of Ireland, *Education (Admission to Schools) Act, 2018*, Dublin: The Irish Statute Book, 2018.

Grace, G., *Catholic Schools: Mission, Markets, and Morality*, London: Routledge, 2002.

Grace, G., 'Renewing Spiritual Capital: An Urgent Priority for the Future of Catholic Education Internationally', in *International Studies in Catholic Education* 2/2, (2010), pp. 117-128.

Grech, L., *Accompanying Youth in a Quest for Meaning*, Bolton: Don Bosco Publications, 2019.

Grenham, T.G. (ed), *Pastoral Ministry for Today: 'Who Do You Say That I Am?' Conference Papers 2008*, Dublin: Veritas, 2009.

Groome, T.H., *Christian Religious Education*, San Francisco: Jossey-Bass, 1980.

Groome, T.H., *Sharing Faith: A Comprehensive Approach to Religious Education and Pastoral Ministry*, San Francisco: Harper, 1991.

Groome, T.H., *Christian Ministry: An Overview*, San Francisco: Wipft & Stock, 1998.

Gula, R.M., *Just Ministry: Professional Ethics for Pastoral Ministers*, New York/ Mahwah, NJ: Paulist Press, 2010.

Habermas, J., 'An Awareness of What is Missing', in J. Habermas et al. (ed), *An Awareness of What is Missing: Faith and Reason in a Post-Secular Age*, Cambridge: Polity Press, 2010, pp. 15–23.

Hand, M., *Is Religious Education Possible? A Philosophical Investigation*, London: Bloomsbury Academic, 2004.

Hannam, P., *Religious Education and the Public Sphere*, London: Routledge, 2019.

Harmon, M. *"I am a Catholic Buddhist": the Voice of Children on Religion and Religious Education in an Irish Catholic Primary School*, Doctor of Education thesis, Dublin City University, 2018.

Harrington, B., *Discipleship That Fits: The Five Kinds of Relationships God Uses to Help Us Grow*, Grand Rapids, MI: Zondervan, 2016.

Harris, M., *Fashion Me a People: Curriculum in the Church*, 1st edition, Louisville, KY: Westminster/John Knox Press, 1989.

Hauerwas, S., *The Peaceable Kingdom*, Note Dame; University of Notre Dame Press, 1983.

Henderson, M.D., *John Wesley's Class Meeting: A Model for Making Disciples*, Wilmore KY: Rafiki Books, 2016.

Hervieu-Léger, D., 'The Transmission and Formation of Socio-religious Identities in Modernity: An Analytical Essay on the Trajectories of Identification', in *International Sociology* 13/2, (1998), pp. 213–228.

Hervieu-Léger, D., *Religion as a Chain of Memory*, New Brunswick, NJ: Rutgers University Press, 2000.

Hession, A., *Catholic Primary Religious Education in a Pluralist Environment*, Dublin: Veritas Publications, 2015.

Hogan, L. & Biggar, N. (eds), *Religious Voices in Public Places*, Oxford: Oxford University Press, 2009.

Hood, R.W., 'The History and Current State of Research on Psychology of Religion', in L.J. Miller (ed), *The Oxford Handbook of Psychology and Spirituality*, New York: Oxford University Press, 2012.

Horton, M. and Freire, P., *We Make the Road by Walking: Conversations on Education and Social Change*, Philadelphia: Temple University Press, 1990.

Huebner, D.E., 'Christian Growth in Faith', in *Religious Education* 81/4, (1986), pp. 511-521.

Huebner, D.E., *The Lure of the Transcendent: Collected Essays by Dwayne E. Huebner*, in V. Hillis (ed), Mahwah, NJ: Lawrence Erlbaum Associates, 1999.

Inglis, T., *Moral Monopoly: The Rise and Fall of the Catholic Church in Modern Ireland*, 2nd edition, Dublin: University College Dublin Press, 1998.

Irish Catholic Bishops' Conference, *Religious Education and the Framework for Junior Cycle*, Dublin: Veritas, 2017.

Irish Episcopal Conference, *Share the Good News: National Directory for Catechesis in Ireland* [SGN], Dublin: Veritas, 2010.

Iselin, D. & Meteyard, J., 'The "Beyond in the Midst": An Incarnational Response to the Dynamic Dance of Christian Worldview, Faith and Learning', in *Journal of Education and Christian Belief* 14/1, (2010), pp. 33-46.

Jackson, R., 'Why Education about Religions and Beliefs? European Policy Recommendations and Research', in G. Byrne and P. Kieran (ed), *Towards Mutual Ground: Pluralism, Religious Education and Diversity in Irish Schools*, Dublin: Columba Press, 2013, pp. 43-56.

Jackson, R., *Signposts: Policy and Practice for Teaching about Religions and Non-Religious Worldviews in Intercultural Education*, Strasbourg: Council of Europe, 2014.

James, W., 'Pragmatism's Conception of Truth', in D. Edwards (ed), *Truth: A Contemporary Reader*, London: Bloomsbury Academic, 2019, pp. 114-125.

Keast, J., *Religious Diversity and Intercultural Education: A Reference Book for Schools*, Strasbourg: Council of Europe, 2007.

Kellaghan, T. & Millar, D. *Grading in the Leaving Certificate Examination: A Discussion Paper*, Dublin: Educational Research Centre, St. Patrick's College, 2003.

Kieran, P. & Hession, A. (eds), *Exploring Religious Education: Catholic Religious Education in an Intercultural Europe*, Dublin: Veritas, 2008.

Kieran, P. & Mullally, A., 'The New Nones': Implications of Ticking the 'No Religion' Census Box for Educators in Ireland', in *The Furrow: A Journal for the Contemporary Church* 71/7-8, (2020), pp. 387-395.

Kleissler, T.A., LeBert, M.A. & McGuinness, M.C., *Small Christian Communities: A Vision of Hope for the 21st Century*, revised and updated edition, New York: Paulist Press, 2003.

Klingenberg, M. & Sofia, S., 'Theorizing Religious Socialization: A Critical Assessment', in *Religion* 49/2, (2019), pp. 163–178.

Knabb, J.J. & Pelletier, J., '"A Cord of Three Strands Is Not Easily Broken": An Empirical Investigation of Attachment-based Small Group Functioning in the Christian Church', in *Journal of Psychology & Theology* 42/4, (2014), pp. 343–358.

Knowles, M.S., *The Adult Learner: A Neglected Species*, Houston, TX: Gulf, 1973.

Knowles, M.S., *The Modern Practice of Adult Education: From Pedagogy to Andragogy*, Wilton, CT: Association Press, 1980.

Knowles, M.S., Holton III, E.F. & Swanson, R.A., *The Adult Learne: The Definitive Classic in Adult Education and Human Resource Development*, Burlington, VT: Routledge, 2005.

Küng, H., *On Being a Christian*, trans. E. Quinn, London: Collings, 1977.

Lakoff, G. & Johnson, M., *Metaphors We Live By*, Chicago, IL/London: University of Chicago Press, 1980.

Lane, D.A., 'Challenges Facing Catholic Education in Ireland', in E. Woulfe & J. Cassin (eds), *From Present to Future: Catholic Education in Ireland for the New Century*, Dublin: Veritas, 2006.

Lane, D.A, *Stepping Stones To Other Religions: A Christian Theology of Inter-religious Dialogue*, Dublin: Veritas Publications, 2011.

Lane, D.A., *Religion and Education: Re-Imagining the Relationship*, Dublin: Veritas Publications. 2013.

Le Chéile: A Catholic Schools Trust, *Living Our Le Chéile Charter*, 2019. Available at: https://lecheiletrust.ie

Lee, B.J., D'Antonio, W.V. & Elizondo, V.P., *The Catholic Experience of Small Christian Communities*, New York: Paulist Press, 2000.

Lemoyne, J. (ed), *Memorie Biografiche di don Giovanni Bosco* [MB], trans. from Italian, *The Biographical Memoirs of St John Bosco*, Volumes 1-XVIIII, New Rochelle, NY: Salesian Publications, 1989.

Lenti A., *Don Bosco's Educational Method*, New Rochell, NY: Salesian Publications, 1989.

'Levinas and the Other in Psychotherapy and Counselling', editorial, in *European Journal of Psychotherapy & Counselling* 7/1-2, (2005), pp. 1-5.

Liddy, S.A., 'Teaching Scripture in Religious Education', in M. de Souza, G. Durka, K. Engebretson, R. Jackson & A.M. McGrady (eds), *International Handbook of the Religious, Moral and Spiritual Dimensions in Education. International Handbooks of Religion and Education*, Vol 1, Springer: Dordrecht, 2009.

Lynch, K. Ivancheva, M., O'Flynn, M., Keating, K., and O'Connor, M., 'The Care Ceiling in Higher Education', in *Irish Educational Studies* 39/2, (2020), pp. 157-174.

Looney, A., 'Assessment in the Republic of Ireland', in *Assessment in Education: Principles, Policy & Practice* 13/3, (2006), pp. 345-353.

Mac Donald, S., 'Irish Parishes Involved in Milan Parish Cells Seminar', *Catholicireland.net*, 2014. Available at: https://www.catholicireland.net/international-seminar-parish-cells-milan/

Mallon, J., *Divine Renovation: Bringing Your Parish from Maintenance to Mission*, New London, CT: Twenty-Third Publications, 2014.

Marion, J.-M., *Le Monde*, 11 Sept 2008, quoted by Stephen England, 'How Catholic is France?', *Commonweal* 135/19, (2008), pp. 12-18.

Mark, O., *Passing on Faith*, London: Canterbury Christ Church University and Theos, 2016.

McCarthy, R.J. & Vitek, J.M., *Going Going Gone: The Dynamics of Disaffiliation in Young Catholics*, Winona, MN: St Mary's Press, 2018.

McDonough, G.P., 'Pluralizing Catholic Identity', in *Religious Education* 114/2, (2019), pp. 168-180.

McGilchrist, I., *The Master and His Emissary: The Divided Brain and the Making of the Western World*, New Haven, CT/ London: Yale University Press, 2009.

McGrath, A., 'Navigating Towards Renewal: Lay Pastoral Ministry in the Church', *Studies: An Irish Quarterly Review* 101/404, (2012), pp. 449-458.

McGrath, A., *Mere Discipleship: Growing in Wisdom and Hope*, Grand Rapids, MI: Baker Books, 2019.

McLaughlin, T, O'Keefe, J. & O'Keeffe, B. (eds), *The Contemporary Catholic School: Context, Identity, and Diversity*, Hove, East Sussex: Psychology Press, 1996.

McNeal, R., *Missional Renaissance: Changing the Scorecard for the Church*, San Francisco: Jossey-Bass, 2009.

Meehan, A., 'Wellbeing in the Irish Junior Cycle: The Potential of Religious Education', in *Irish Educational Studies* 38/4, (2019), pp. 501-518.

Mendieta E. & Van Antwerpen, J. (eds). *The Power of Relgion in the Public Sphere*, New York: Columbia University Press, 2011.

Merrigan, T., 'Religion, Education and the Appeal to Plurality: Theological Considerations on the Contemporary European Context', in G. Byrne and P. Kieran (ed), *Towards Mutual Ground: Pluralism, Religious Education and Diversity in Irish Schools*, Dublin: Columba Press, 2013, pp. 57-70.

Mezirow, J., *Transformative Dimensions of Adult Learning*, San Francisco: Jossey-Bass, 1991.

Mezirow, J., Taylor E.W. et al. (eds), *Transformative Learning in Practice: Insights from Community, Workplace, and Higher Education*, San Francisco: Jossey-Bass, 2009.

Migliore, D., *Faith Seeking Understanding: An Introduction to Christian Theology*, Grand Rapids, MI: Eerdmans, 2004.

Moffat, J., *The Resurrection of the Word: A Modern Quest for Intelligent Faith*, Oxford: Way Books, 2013.

Moore, T., *The Care of the Soul: A Guide for Cultivating Depth and Sacredness in Everyday Life*, New York: Walker, 1992.

Morcuende, M., 'Personal Accompaniment in the Salesian Educative-Pastoral Plan', in F. Attard & M. Garcia (eds), *Salesian Accompaniment*, Part 3, Bolton: Don Bosco Publications, 2018, pp. 187-200.

Mullally, A., *Guidelines on the Inclusion of Students of Different Faiths in Catholic Secondary Schools*, Dublin: JMB/AMCSS, 2010.

Mullally, A., *Guidelines on the Inclusion of Students of Different Beliefs in Catholic Secondary Schools*, Dublin: JMB/AMCSS, 2019.

Murray, D.B., *In a Landscape Redrawn*, Dublin: Veritas, 2017.

National Council for Curriculum and Assessment, *Education about Religions and Beliefs (ERB) and Ethics: Consultation Paper*, 2015. Available at: https://ncca.ie/media/1897/consultation_erbe.pdf

National Council for Curriculum and Assessment, *Background Paper and Brief for the Review of Junior Cycle Religious Education*, 2017. Available at: https://www.ncca.ie/media/3432/re-background-paper-for-website.pdf

National Council for Curriculum and Assessment, *Primary Developments: Consultation on Structure and Time Final Report*, 2018. Available at: https://ncca.ie/media/3242/primary-developments_consultaion-on-curriculum-structure-and-time_final-report.pdf

National Council for Curriculum and Assessment, *Senior Cycle Review*, NCCA, 2018. Available at: https://www.ncca.ie/media/3878/ncca_sc_single_pages_en.pdf

National Council for Curriculum and Assessment, *Junior Cycle Religious Education Specification*, 2019. Available at: https://ncca.ie/media/3785/junior-cycle-religious-education-specification.pdf
Nelson, J.M., *Psychology, Religion and Spirituality*, New York: Springer, 2009.

Nelson, J.M. & Slife, B.D., 'Theoretical and Epistemological Foundations', in L.J. Miller (ed), *The Oxford Handbook of Psychology and Spirituality*, New York: Oxford University Press, 2012.

Newberg, A. & d'Aquili, E., *Why God Won't Go Away: Brain Science and the Biology of Belief*, New York: Ballantine, 2001.

New Zealand Ministry of Education Te Tāhuhu o te Mātauranga, *Ka Hikitia – Accelerating Success 2013–2017*, 2013. Available at: https://education.govt.nz/our-work/overall-strategies-and-policies/ka-hikitia-ka-hapaitia/ka-hikitia-history/ka-hikitia-accelerating-success-20132017/

New Zealand Ministry of Education Te Tāhuhu o te Mātauranga, *Statement of Intent 2018–2023*, 2018. Available at: https://education.govt.nz/assets/Documents/Ministry/Publications/Statements-of-intent/Statement-of-Intent-2018-2023-web.pdf

New Zealand Ministry of Education Te Tāhuhu o te Mātauranga, *Action Plan for Pacific Education 2020–2030*, 2020. Available at: https://conversation-space.s3-ap-southeast-2.amazonaws.com/Pacific+Education+Plan_WEB.PDF

Nietzsche, F., *The Will to Power*, New York: Vintage Books, 1968.

O'Brien, H., 'What Does the Rise of Digital Religion during Covid-19 Tell Us about Religion's Capacity to Adapt?', in *Irish Journal of Sociology* 28/2, (2020), pp. 242–246.

O' Callaghan, P., *Children of God in the World: An Introduction to Theological Anthropology*, Washington, DC: The Catholic University of America Press, 2016.

O'Connell, G., *The Significance of a Pre-service RE Course, which Recognizes the Importance of a Focus on the Inner Life: Exploring the Experience of Primary Teacher Education Students in a Small Teacher Education College in Dublin*, doctoral thesis, Exeter University, 2015. Available at: http://hdl.handle.net/10871/16567

O'Connell, G., 'Putting Space in Place: Reflective Space and Ethos', in D. Robinson (ed), *Living Ethos: Promoting Human Flourishing in an Educational Environment*, Dublin: Veritas [forthcoming].

O'Dell, G., 'Gender', in P.L. Barnes (ed), *Debates in Religious Education*, London: Routledge, 2012, pp. 77–87.

O'Donohue, J., *Eternal Echoes: Exploring Our Hunger to Belong*, New York: Harper Perennial, 2000.

Ó Murchú, D., *Reclaiming Spirituality: A New Spiritual Framework for Today's World*. New York: Crossroad, 1998.

Ogden, G., *Discipleship Essentials: A Guide to Building Your Life in Christ*, revised and expanded edition, Downers Grove, Il: InterVarsity Press, 2018.

Ogden, G., *Transforming Discipleship: Making Disciples a Few at a Time*, revised and expanded edition, Downers Grove, Il: InterVarsity Press, 2016.

O'Halloran, J., *Small Christian Communities: Vision and Practicalities*, Dublin: Columba, 2002.

O'Leary, M., 'Would Leaving Cert Students' Estimates of Their Own Grades Help Teachers?', in *The Irish Times*, 13 May, 2020. Available at: https://www.irishtimes.com/news/education/would-leaving-cert-students-estimates-of-their-own-grades-help-teachers-1.4252424

O'Malley, D., 'The Origins of Chaplaincy', 2015. Available at: http://catholicyouthwork.com/the-origins-of-chaplaincy-from-fr-david-omalley-sdb/#

Oman, D. & Thoresen, C.E., 'Spiritual Modeling: A Key to Spiritual and Religious Growth?', in *The International Journal for the Psychology of Religion* 13/3, (2003), pp. 149–165.

Select Bibliography

Otero, L.M. & Cottrell, M.J., 'Pioneering New Paths for Adult Religious Education in the Roman Catholic Community: The Promise of Communities of Practice', in *Journal of Adult Theological Education* 10/1, (2013), pp. 50-63.

Palmer, P.J., *The Courage to Teach: Exploring the Inner Landscape of a Teacher's Life*, San Francisco: Jossey-Bass, 1998.

Palmer, P.J., *Let Your Life Speak: Listening for the Voice of Vocation*, San Francisco: Jossey-Bass, 1999.

Patton, J., *Pastoral Care: An Essential Guide*, Nashville, TN: Abingdon Press, 2005.

Pedersen, M.H., 'Becoming Muslim in a Danish Provincial Town', in *The Bloomsbury Reader in Religion and Childhood*, London: Bloomsbury, 2017, pp. 131-138.

Pett, S. & Cooling, T., 'Understanding Christianity: Exploring a Hermeneutical Pedagogy for Teaching Christianity', in *British Journal of Religious Education* 40/3, (2018), pp. 257-267.

Pontifical Council for Promoting New Evangelisation, *Directory for Catechesis*, London: Catholic Truth Society, 2020.

Pope Francis, *Evangelii Gaudium: Apostolic Exhortation on the Proclamation of the Gospel in Today's World*, 2013. Available at: http://www.vatican.va

Pope Francis, 'General Audience, September 9, 2015: The Family – 26, Community'. Available at: http://www.vatican.va/content/francesco/en/audiences/2015/documents/papa-francesco_20150909_udienza-generale.html

Pope Francis, *Laudato Si': On Care for Our Common Home*, 2015. Available at: https://www.vatican.va

Pope Francis, *Amoris Laetitia: On Love in the Family*, 2016. Available online at http://www.vatican.va

Pope Francis, *Christus Vivit, Christ is Alive: Apostolic Exhortation to Young People and to the Entire People of God*, Dublin: Veritas, 2019. Available at: https://www.vatican.va

Pope Francis, *Fratelli Tutti: On Fraternity and Social Friendship*, 2020. Available at http://www.vatican.va

Pope John XXIII, *Mater et Magistra*, 1961. Available at http://www.vatican.va

Pope John Paul II, *Catechesi Tradendae*, 1979. Available at: http://www.vatican.va

Pope John Paul II, *Christifideles Laici*, 1987. Available at: http://www.vatican.va

Pope John Paul II, *Iuvenum Patris: Father of Youth: Apostolic Letter written on the first Centenary of the Death of Don Bosco*, Rome: Libreria Editrice Vaticana, 1988.

Pope John Paul II, *Redemptoris Missio: On the Permanent Validity of the Church's Missionary Mandate*, 1990. Available at: https://www.vatican.va

Pope Paul VI, *Evangelii Nuntiandi*, 1975. Available at: http://www.vatican.va

Praat, A., 'Gender Differences in Student Achievement and in Rates of Participation in the School Sector, 1986-1997: A Summary Report', in *Research Bulletin* 10, (1999), pp. 1-11.

Pring, R., *The Future of Publicly Funded Faith Schools: A Critical Perspective*, London/New York: Routledge, 2018.

Radcliffe, T., *I Call You Friends*, New York: Continuum, 2001.

Radcliffe, T., *Why Go to Church? The Drama of the Eucharist*, London/New York: Continuum, 2008.

Rahner, K., *Theological Investigations II*, London: Darton, Longman & Todd. 1963.

Rahner, K., 'The Concept of Mystery in Catholic Theology', in *Theological Investigations Volume IV*, New York: Crossroads, 1969, pp. 36-73.

Rahner, K., *Foundations of Christian Faith: An Introduction to the Idea of Christianity*, trans W. Dych, New York: Crossroads Publishing, 1976.

Ratzinger, J., 'Faith, Philosophy and Theology', in *Communio: International Catholic Review* 11 /4, (1984), pp. 350-363.

RENEW International History, 2019. Available at: http://www.renewintl.org/ RENEW/index.nsf/GO/History?OpenDocument

Ridgely, S., 'Children and Religion', in *Religion Compass* 6/4, (2012), pp. 236-248.

Ridgely, S., 'Faith Co-creation in US Catholic Churches: How First Communicants and Faith Formation Teachers Shape Catholic Identity', in A.

Strhan, S.G. Parker & S. Ridgely, (eds), *The Bloomsbury Reader in Religion and Childhood*, London: Bloomsbury Publishing, 2017, pp. 139-146.

Rieff, P., *The Triumph of the Therapeutic: Uses of Faith after Freud*, Chicago: University of Chicago Press, 1987.

Riley, D. & McBride, J., *Best Practices in Adult Faith Formation: A National Study*, Washington, DC: NCCL, 2006.

Rossiter, G., *Life to the Full: The Changing Landscape of Contemporary Spirituality: Implications for Catholic School Religious Education*, Kensington, NSW: ASMRE, 2018.

Rothberg, D., 'The Crisis of Modernity and the Emergence of Socially Engaged Spirituality', in *REVision* 15, (1993), pp. 105-14.

Ryan, A., *Pastoral Ministry in Changing Times: The Past, Present and Future of the Catholic Church in Ireland*, Dublin: Messenger Publications, 2019.

Rymarz, R., 'Permeation of Catholic Identity: Some Challenges for Canadian Catholic Schools, Part 1', in *Journal of Religious Education* 61/1, (2013), pp. 14-22.

Schaeffler, J., 'Motivation for Adult Faith Formation', in *Lifelong Faith* 8/2, (2015), pp. 34-39.

Schweitzer, F., 'The Religious Dimension of the Self', in R.R. Osmer & F. Schweitzer, *Religious Education between Modernization and Globalization*, Grand Rapids, MI/ Cambridge, UK: William B. Eerdmans Publishing Company, 2003.

Shaw, P., *Transforming Theological Education: A Practical Handbook for Integrative Learning*, Carlisle: Langham Global Library, 2014.

Sheldrake, P., *Living between Worlds: Place and Journey in Celtic Spirituality*, London: Darton, Longman & Todd, 1995.

Simojoki, H., 'Researching Confirmation Work in Europe: An Example of Research on Non-formal Education', in F. Schweitzer, W. Ilg & P. Schreiner (eds), *Researching Non-formal Religious Education in Europe*, Münster: Waxmann, 2019, pp. 235-250.

Smith, J., *Desiring the Kingdom: Worship, Worldview and Cultural Formation*, Grand Rapids, MI: Baker Academic, 2009.

Smith, J., *Imagining the Kingdom: How Worship Works*, Grand Rapids, MI: Baker Academic, 2013.

Smyth, E., *Students' Experiences and Perspectives on Secondary Education: Institutions, Transitions and Policy*, London: Palgrave Macmillan, 2016.

Stache, K., 'Formation for the Whole Church: A New/Old Vision of Theological Education in the 21st Century', in *Dialog: A Journal of Theology* 53/4, (2014), pp. 286-292.

State Examinations Commission, *State Examination Commission: Chief Examiners' Report*, 2008. Available at: https://www.examinations.ie/?l=en&mc=en&sc=cr

State Examinations Commission, *State Examination Commission: Chief Examiners' Report* 2013. Available at: https://www.examinations.ie/?l=en&mc=en&sc=cr

State Examinations Commission, *State Examinations Commission: Annual Exam Statistics*, 2019. Available at: https://www.examinations.ie/statistics/

State Examinations Commission, *Chief Examiners' Reports*, 2020. Available at https://www.examinations.ie/?l=en&mc=en&sc=cr

Stern, J. & Shillitoe, R., *Evaluation of Prayer Spaces in Schools: The Contribution of Prayer Spaces to Spiritual Development*, 2018.

Stuart-Buttle, R., 'Communicating Faith and Online Learning', in J. Sullivan (ed) *Communicating Faith*, Washington, DC: The Catholic University of America Press, 2010, pp. 328-343.

Stuart-Buttle, R., *Virtual Theology, Faith and Adult Education: An Interruptive Pedagogy*, Newcastle upon Tyne: Cambridge Scholars, 2013.

Stuart-Buttle, R., 'Interrupting Adult Learning through Online Pedagogy', in *Journal of Christian Education and Belief* 18/1, (2014), pp. 61-75.

Stuart-Buttle, R., *CCRS Twenty Five Years On: One Size Fits All?* Stockport, UK: Rejoice Publications, Matthew James, 2019.

Sullivan, J., 'Promoting the Mission: Principles and Practice', in *International Studies in Catholic Education* 3/1, (2011), pp. 91-102.

Sweetman, B., *Godparenthood in Ireland: An Empirical Study into the Educational Intentions Influencing Parental Selections of Godparent*, EdD thesis. Dublin City University, 2016.

Sweetman, B., 'Dominant Public View of Religious Persons as Less Intelligent is Lamentable', in *Irish Times*, 25 June 2019. Available at: https://www.irishtimes.com/opinion/ dominant-public-view-of-religious-persons-as-less-intelligent-is-lamentable-1.3935842

Select Bibliography

Sweetman, B. & Byrne, G., 'What Does a Religious or Spiritual Irish Adult Look Like?', *RTÉ Brainstorm*, 2 Sept 2019. Available at: https://www.rte.ie/brainstorm/2019/0830/1071822-what-does-a-religious-or-spiritual-irish-adult-look-like/

Swift, C., Cobb, M. & Todd, A. (eds), 'Introduction to Chaplaincy Studies' in *A Handbook of Chaplaincy Studies: Understanding Spiritual Care in Public Places*, London and New York: Routledge, 2016, pp. 1-9.

Synod of Bishops, *Final Document of the Synod of Bishops on Young People, Faith and Vocational Discernment*, Rome: Libreria Editrice Vaticana, 2018.

Taylor, E.W. & Cranton, P., *The Handbook of Transformative Learning: Theory, Research and Practice*, San Francisco: Jossey-Bass, 2012.

Thagard, P., 'Coherence, Truth, and the Development of Scientific Knowledge', in D. Edwards (ed), *Truth: A Contemporary Reader*, London: Bloomsbury Academic, 2019, pp. 86-101.

Thibodeaux, M., *Reimagining the Ignatian Examen*, Chicago: Loyola Press, 2015.

Todd, S., *Learning from the Other: Levinas, Psychoanalysis, and Ethical Possibilities in Education*, in D. P. Britzman (ed), New York: State University of New York Press, 2003.

Tuohy, D., *Denominational Education and Politics: Ireland in a European Context*, Dublin: Veritas Publications, 2013.

Vandenakker, J.P., *Small Christian Communities and the Parish: An Ecclesiological Analysis of the North American Experience*, Kansas City, MO: Sheed & Ward, 1994.

Vanhoozer, K., *First Theology: God, Scripture and Hermeneutics*, Downers Grove, IL: InterVarsity Press, 2002.

Vatican II, *Lumen Gentium: Dogmatic Constitution of the Church*, 1964, in Abbott W. (ed), *The Documents of Vatican II*, New York: Herder and Herder, 1966.

Vatican II, *Ad Gentes: Decree on Missionary Activity*, 1965, in Abbott W. (ed), *The Documents of Vatican II*, New York: Herder and Herder, 1966.

Vatican II, *Apostolicam Actuositatem: Decree on the Apostolate of Laity*, 1965, in Abbott W. (ed), *The Documents of Vatican II*, New York: Herder and Herder, 1966.

Vatican II, *Christus Dominus: Decree on the Pastoral Office of Bishops*, 1965, in Abbott W. (ed), *The Documents of Vatican II*, New York: Herder and Herder, 1966.

Vatican II, *Dei Verbum: Dogmatic Constitution on Divine Revelation*, 1965, in Abbott W. (ed), *The Documents of Vatican II*, New York: Herder and Herder, 1966.

Vatican II, *Dignitatis Humanae: Declaration on Religious Freedom*, 1965, in Abbott W. (ed), *The Documents of Vatican II*, New York: Herder and Herder, 1966.

Vatican II, *Gaudium et Spes: Pastoral Constitution on the Church in the Modern World*, 1965, in Abbott W. (ed), *The Documents of Vatican II*, New York: Herder and Herder, 1966.

Vatican II, *Gravissimum Educationis*, 1965,in Abbott W. (ed), *The Documents of Vatican II*, New York: Herder and Herder, 1966.

Vatican II, *Presbyterorum Ordinis: Decree on the Ministry and Life of Priests*, 1965, in Abbott W. (ed), *The Documents of Vatican II*, New York: Herder and Herder, 1966.

Walters, J., 'Twenty-First Century Chaplaincy: Finding the Church in the Post-Secular', in J. Caperon, A. Todd & J. Walters (eds), *A Christian Theology of Chaplaincy*, London and Philadelphia: Kingsley Publishers, 2018, p. 43-58.

Walton, R., 'Disciples Together: The Small Group as a Vehicle for Discipleship Formation', in *Journal of Adult Theological Education* 8/2, (2011), pp. 99-114.

Watts, F., *Psychology, Religion and Spirituality*, New York: Cambridge University Press, 2017.

Whittle, S., 'Contemporary Perspectives on Religious Education in English Catholic Schools', in J. Lydon (ed), *Contemporary Perspectives on Catholic Education*, Gracewing: Leominster, 2018.

Whittle, S., *Religious Education in Catholic Schools: Perspectives from Britain and Ireland*, Bern: Peter Lang, 2018.

Whittle, S., *Researching Catholic Education*, Singapore: Springer, 2018.

Whittle, S., 'An Evaluation of the Catholic Response to the Final Report from the Commission on Religious Education', in *Journal of Religious Education* 68, (2020), pp. 359-369.

Whittle, S., 'On the Precarious Role of Theology in Religious Education', in G. Beista & P. Hannam (eds), *Religion and Education: The Forgotten Dimensions of Religious Education*, Leiden: Brill, 2020.

Select Bibliography

Whittle, S., *Irish and British Reflections on Catholic Education*, Singapore: Springer, 2021.

Wickett, R., 'Adult Learning Theories and Theological Education', in *Journal of Adult Theological Education* 2/2, (2005), pp. 153-161.

Wilber, K., *The Religion of Tomorrow*, Boulder, CO: Shambhala Publications, 2017.

Wilkinson, L., 'Going Deeper: Books on Celtic Christian Spirituality', in *Christianity Today* 44/5, (2000), p. 82.

Williams, J., 'Experiential Learning in Local Ministry Training: Insights from a "Four Villages" Framework', in *Journal of Adult Theological Education* 4/1, (2007), pp. 63-73.

Winstanley, M.T., *Walking with Luke*, Bolton: Don Bosco Publications, 2017.

Woodhead, L., "The Rise of 'No Religion' in Britain: The Emergence of a New Cultural Majority" in *Journal of the British Academy* 4, (2016), pp. 245-61.

Wright, A., *Post-Modernity, Education and Religion*, London: Routledge, 2004.

Wright, A., 'Book Review: Michael Hand Is Religious Education Possible? A Philosophical Investigation', in *Theory and Research in Education* 8/1, (2010), pp. 112-113.

Wright, J.E., *Erikson, Identity and Religion*, New York: Seabury, 1982.

Zeph, C., 'The Spiritual Dimensions of Lay Ministry Programs', in *New Directions for Adult and Continuing Education* 85/Spring, (2000), pp. 77-84.

Zock, H., *A Psychology of Ultimate Concern: Erik H Erikson's Contribution to the Psychology of Religion*, Amsterdam: Rodopi, 1990.